SPIDER GEDDON

COVERT OPS

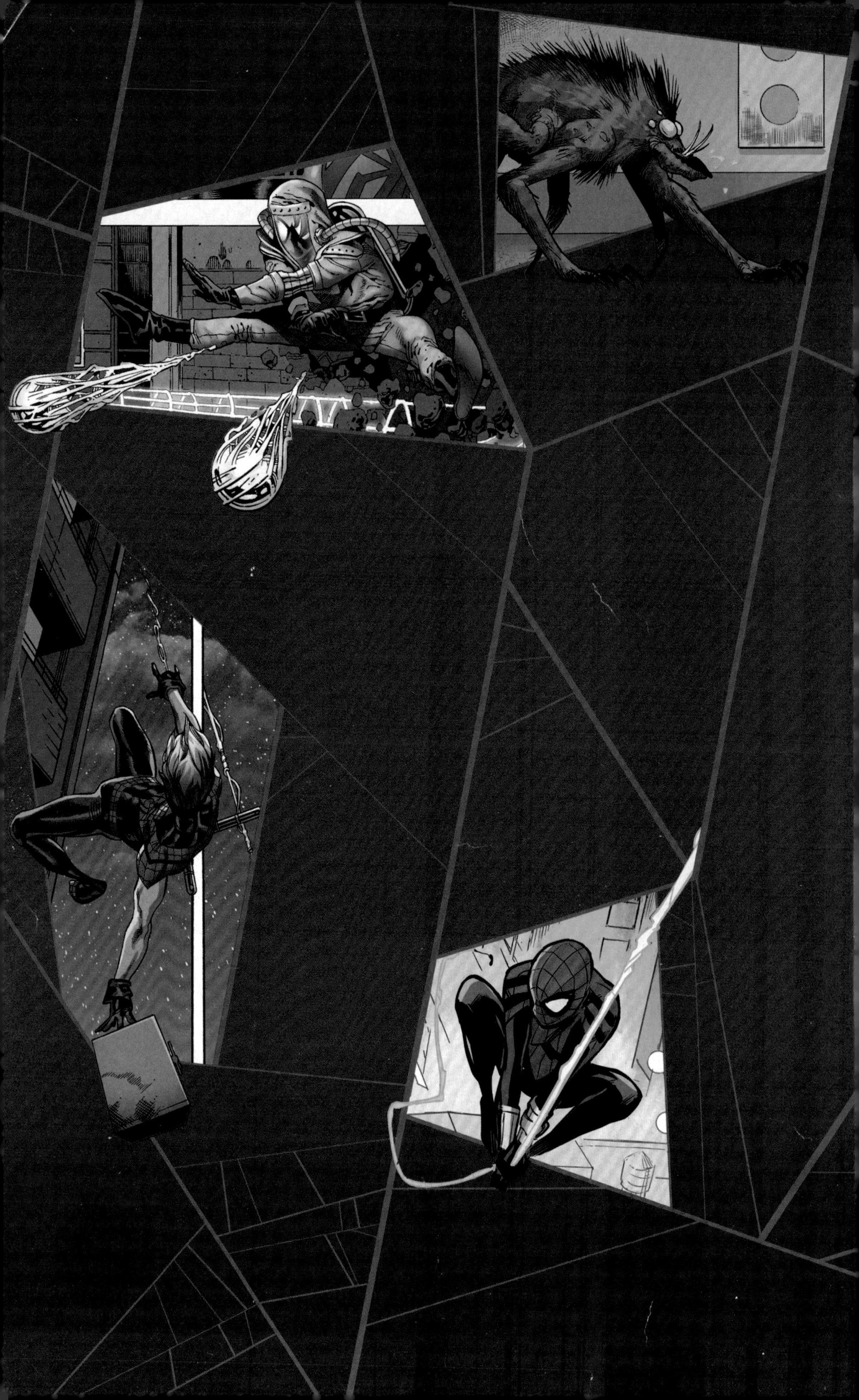

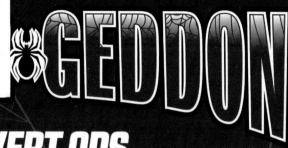

SPIDER-GEDDON

COVERT OPS

SPIDER-FORCE #1-3

WRITER PRIEST
PENCILERS PAULO SIQUEIRA (#1-3), MARCELO FERREIRA (#2-3), SZYMON KUDRANSKI (#2) & IBRAIM ROBERSON (#3)
INKERS OREN JUNIOR (#1-2), CRAIG YEUNG (#1, #3), ROBERTO POGGI (#2-3), SZYMON KUDRANSKI (#2) & IBRAIM ROBERSON (#3)
COLOR ARTIST GURU-eFX
LETTERER VC's JOE SABINO
COVER ART SHANE DAVIS, MICHELLE DELECKI & MORRY HOLLOWELL

SPIDER-GIRLS #1-3

WRITER JODY HOUSER
ARTIST ANDRÉS GENOLET
COLOR ARTISTS TRÍONA FARRELL (#1-2), JIM CHARALAMPIDIS (#2), CRIS PETER & JIM CAMPBELL (#3)
LETTERER VC's JOE CARAMAGNA
COVER ART YASMINE PUTRI (#1-2) & IVAN SHAVRIN (#3)

ASSISTANT EDITOR KATHLEEN WISNESKI
EDITOR NICK LOWE

COLLECTION EDITOR **KATERI WOODY** ASSISTANT EDITOR **CAITLIN O'CONNELL** EDITOR, SPECIAL PROJECTS **MARK D. BEAZLEY**
SENIOR EDITOR **JENNIFER GRÜNWALD** VP PRODUCTION & SPECIAL PROJECTS **JEFF YOUNGQUIST**
SVP PRINT, SALES & MARKETING **DAVID GABRIEL** BOOK DESIGNER **JAY BOWEN**

EDITOR IN CHIEF **C.B. CEBULSKI** CHIEF CREATIVE OFFICER **JOE QUESADA**
PRESIDENT **DAN BUCKLEY** EXECUTIVE PRODUCER **ALAN FINE**

SPIDER-GEDDON: COVERT OPS. Contains material originally published in magazine form as SPIDER-FORCE #1-3 and SPIDER-GIRLS #1-3. First printing 2019. ISBN 978-1-302-91497-4. Published by MARVEL WORLDWIDE, INC., a subsidiary of MARVEL ENTERTAINMENT, LLC. OFFICE OF PUBLICATION: 135 West 50th Street, New York, NY 10020. Printed in Canada. DAN BUCKLEY, President, Marvel Entertainment; JOHN NEE, Publisher; JOE QUESADA, Chief Creative Officer; TOM BREVOORT, SVP of Publishing; DAVID BOGART, SVP of Business Affairs & Operations, Publishing & Partnership; DAVID GABRIEL, SVP of Sales & Marketing, Publishing; JEFF YOUNGQUIST, VP of Production & Special Projects; DAN CARR, Executive Director of Publishing Technology; ALEX MORALES, Director of Publishing Operations; DAN EDINGTON, Managing Editor; SUSAN CRESPI, Production Manager; STAN LEE, Chairman Emeritus. For information regarding advertising in Marvel Comics or on Marvel.com, please contact Vit DeBellis, Custom Solutions & Integrated Advertising Manager, at vdebellis@marvel.com. For Marvel subscription inquiries, please call 888-511-5480. **Manufactured between 1/4/2019 and 2/5/2019 by SOLISCO PRINTERS, SCOTT, QC, CANADA.**

10 9 8 7 6 5 4 3 2 1

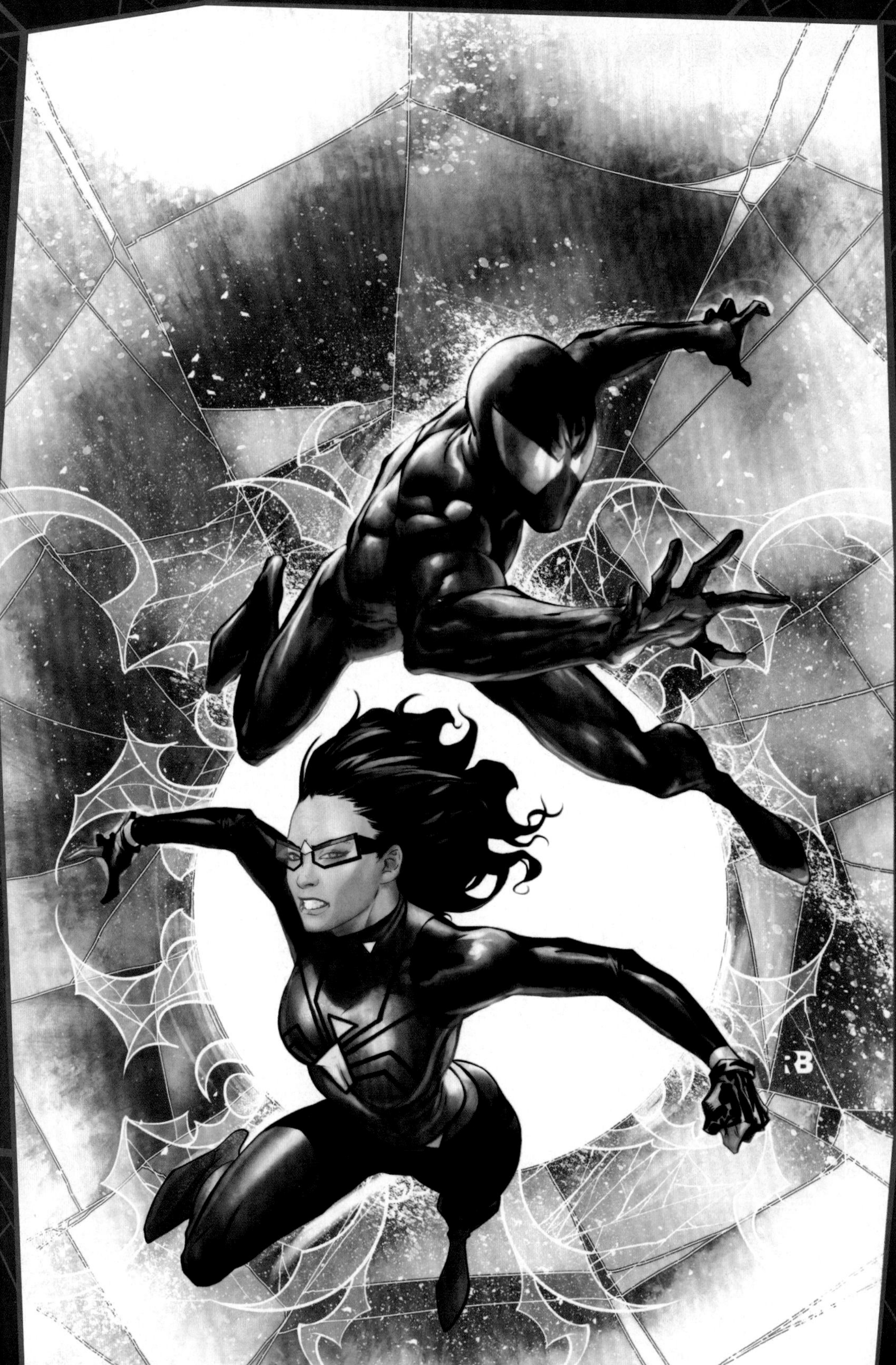

SPIDER-FORCE #1 VARIANT BY **RYAN BENJAMIN**

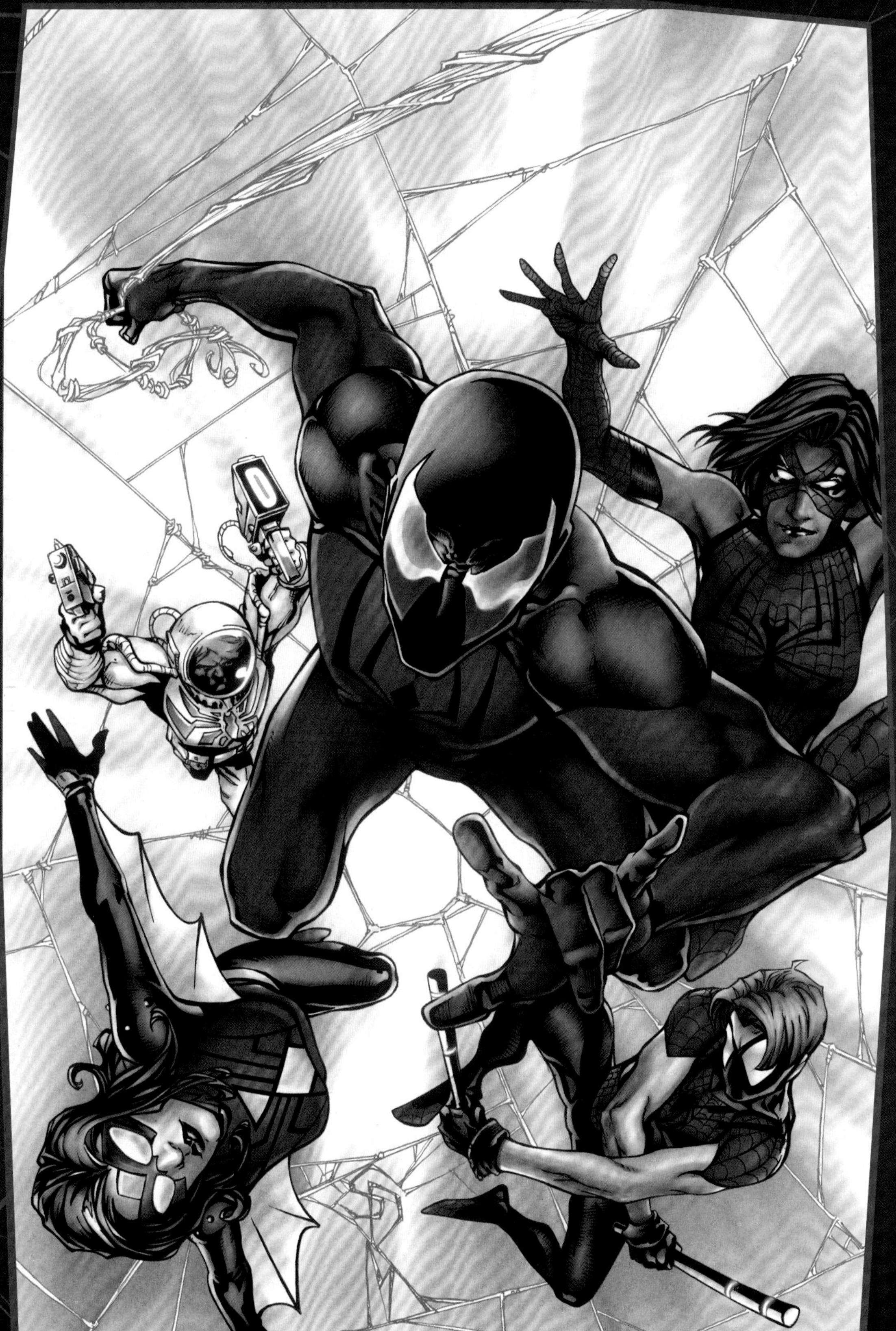

SPIDER-FORCE #1

SOME TIME AGO, THE SPIDER-POWERED HEROES OF MANY UNIVERSES UNITED IN BATTLE TO DEFEAT THE INHERITORS, A FAMILY OF SUPERHUMAN BEINGS WHO FED ON THE LIFE ESSENCE OF SPIDERS. THE SPIDER-ARMY TRIUMPHED, STRANDING THEIR ENEMY ON A RADIOACTIVE PLANET, AND RETURNED TO THEIR LIVES. THE INHERITORS WAITED.

THEN OTTO OCTAVIUS, ASPIRING TO BECOME THE PREDOMINANT HERO OF SAN FRANCISCO, USED THE INHERITORS' CLONING TECHNOLOGY AND OPENED A DOOR FOR THEIR RETURN. VETERANS OF THE FIRST WAR FOR THE SPIDER-VERSE CAME TO WARN HIM--TOO LATE. THREE INHERITORS EMERGED FROM THE CLONING TANKS AND KILLED SPIDER-MAN NOIR AND SPIDER-UK. AS OTTO'S PRIMARY LAB EXPLODED, SPIDER-GWEN FOUGHT THE INHERITORS SO THE SURVIVORS COULD ESCAPE.

OTTO IMMEDIATELY BEGAN PLANNING A COUNTEROFFENSIVE, LEAVING NO OPTION OFF THE TABLE. A CRYSTAL CONTAINING THE DATA NEEDED TO REVIVE THE INHERITORS' FATHER, SOLUS, REMAINED ON THE RADIOACTIVE PLANET FROM WHICH THEY HAD ESCAPED. IT MUST BE DESTROYED. THIS MISSION REQUIRES A TEAM THAT'S WILLING TO DO WHATEVER IT TAKES. A TEAM THAT'S NOT AFRAID TO DIE.

FORCE

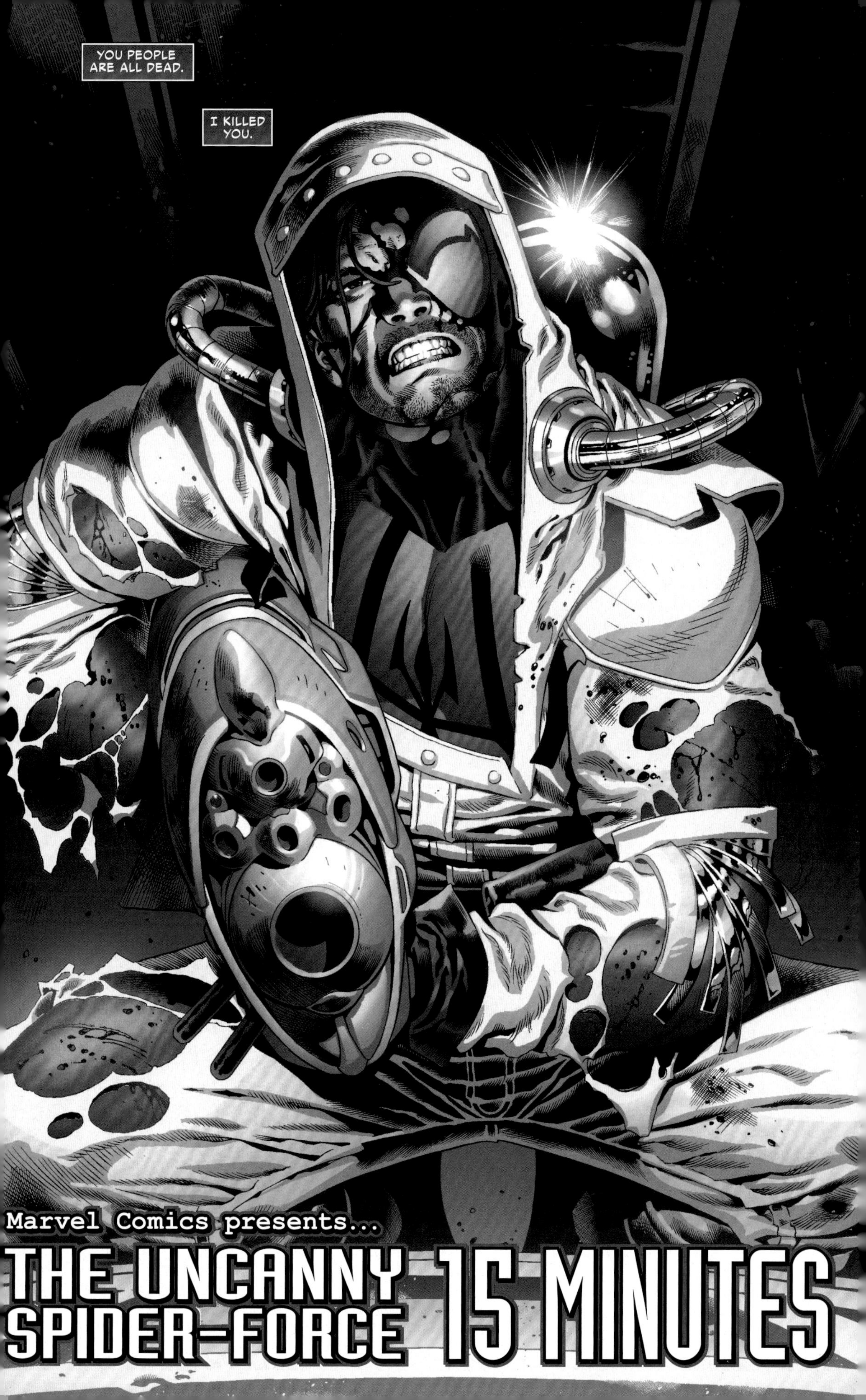
YOU PEOPLE ARE ALL DEAD.
I KILLED YOU.
Marvel Comics presents...
THE UNCANNY SPIDER-FORCE
15 MINUTES

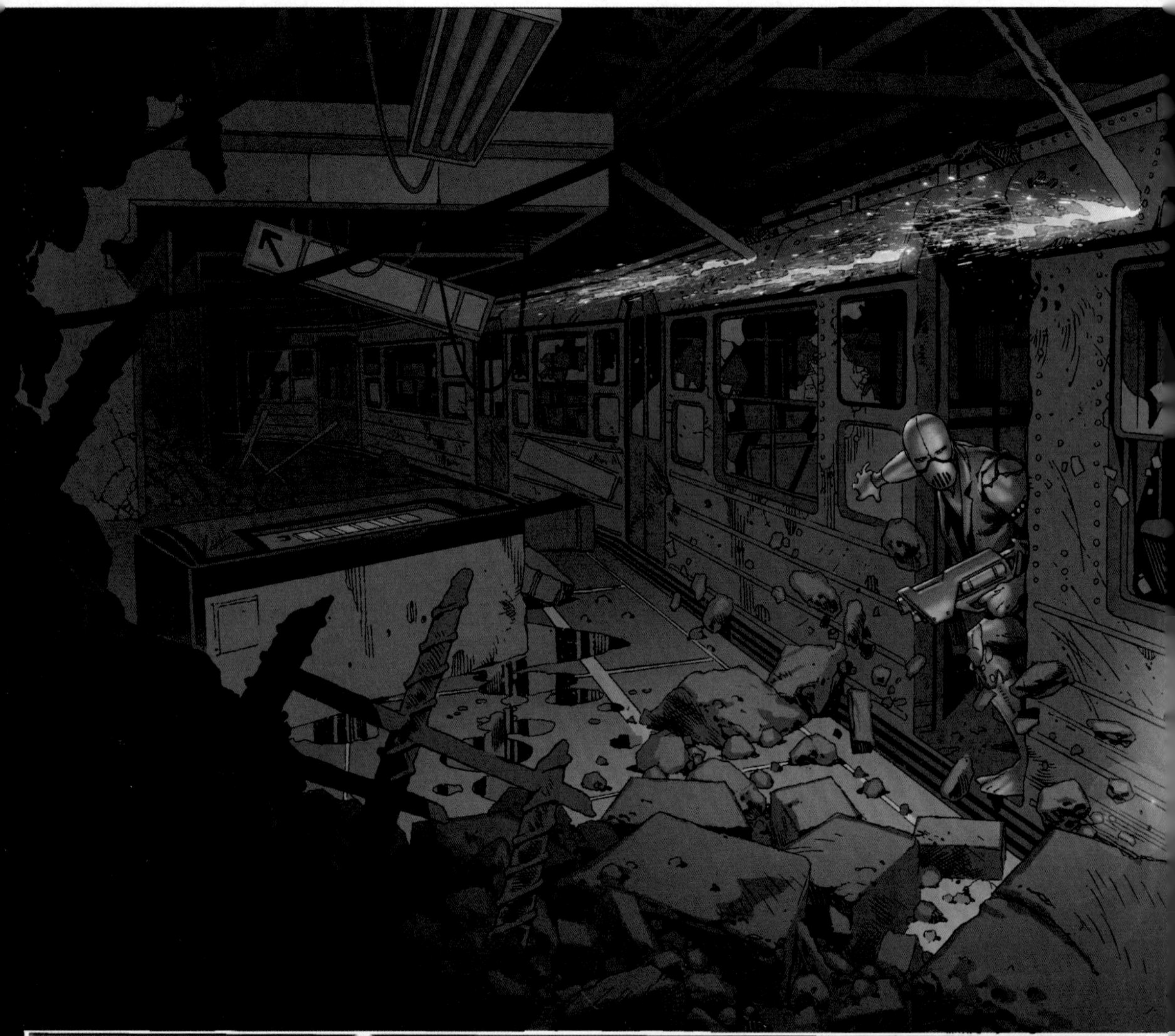

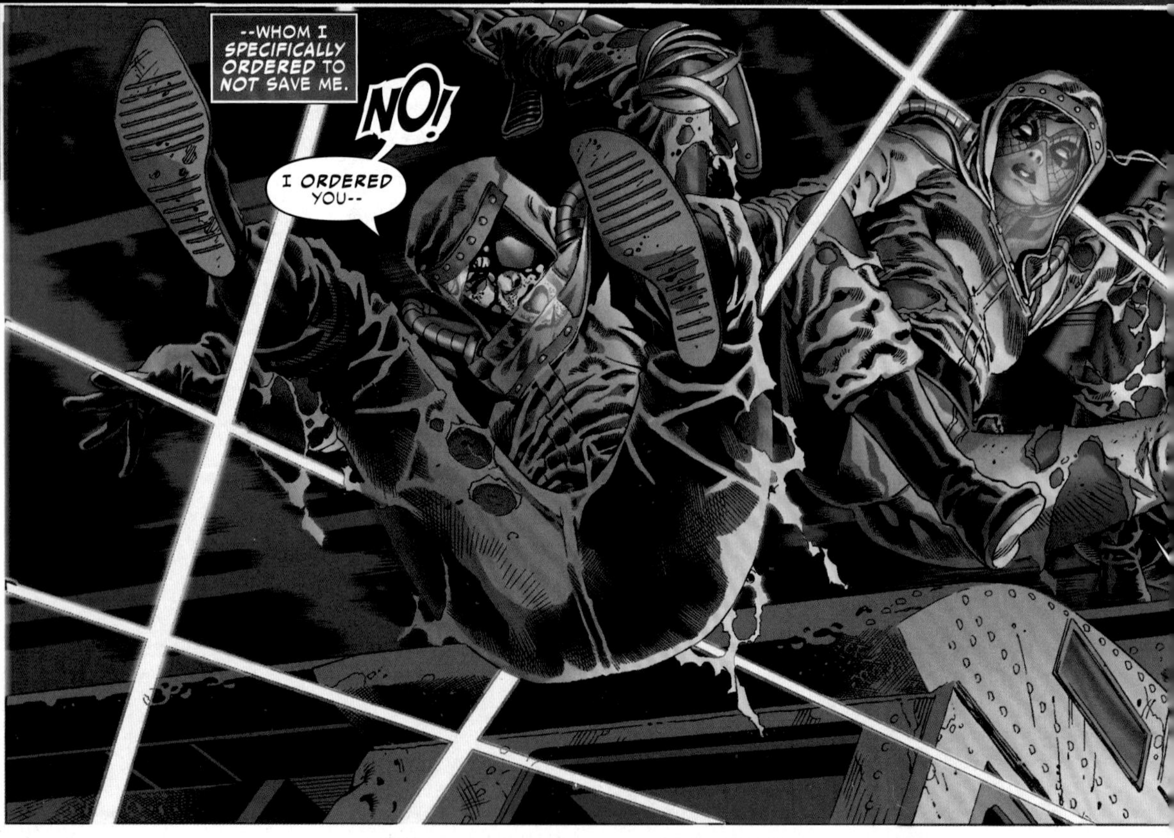
--WHOM I SPECIFICALLY ORDERED TO NOT SAVE ME.
NO!
I ORDERED YOU--

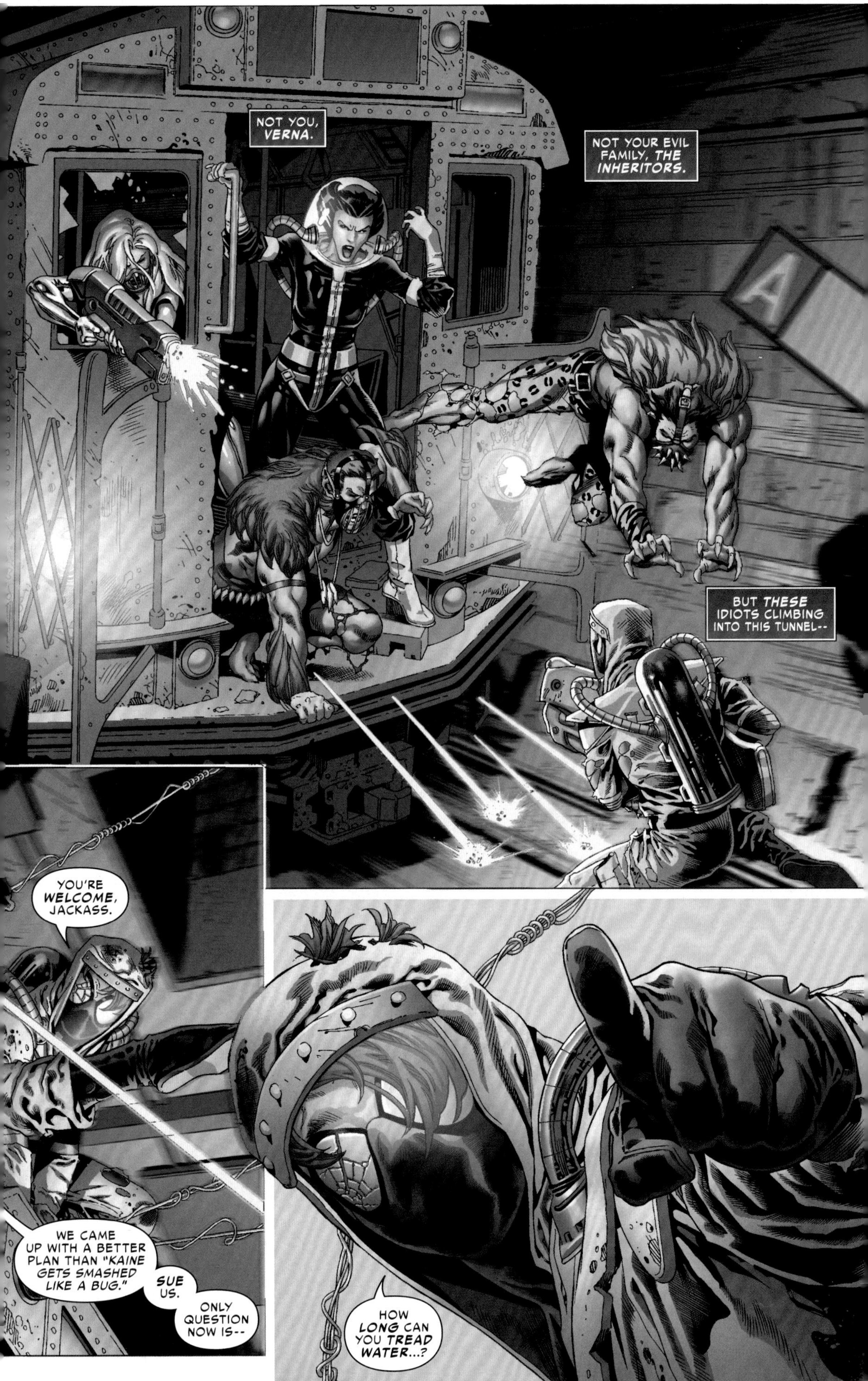
NOT YOU, VERNA.
NOT YOUR EVIL FAMILY, THE INHERITORS.
BUT THESE IDIOTS CLIMBING INTO THIS TUNNEL--
YOU'RE WELCOME, JACKASS.
WE CAME UP WITH A BETTER PLAN THAN "KAINE GETS SMASHED LIKE A BUG."
SUE US.
ONLY QUESTION NOW IS--
HOW LONG CAN YOU TREAD WATER...?

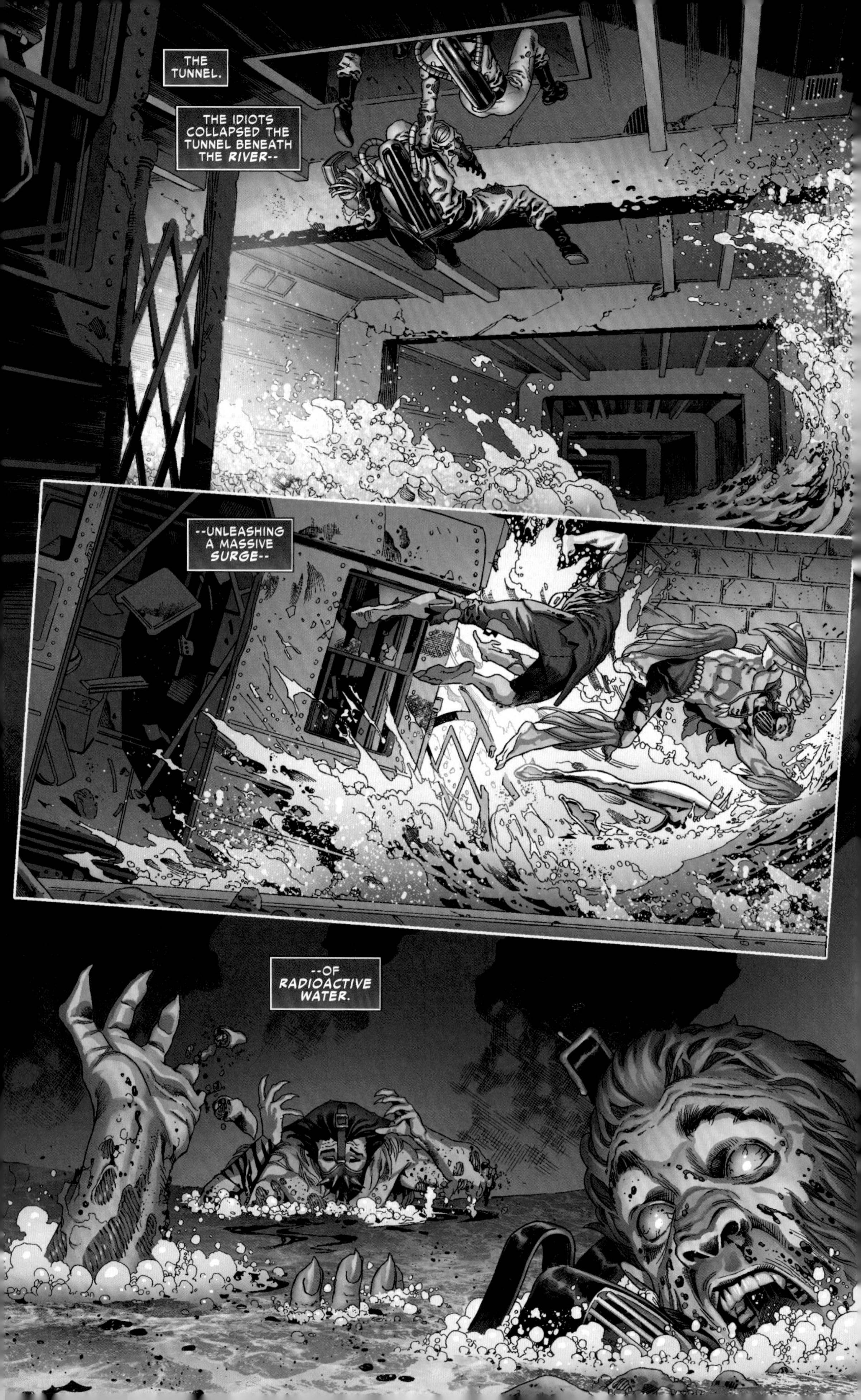
THE TUNNEL.
THE IDIOTS COLLAPSED THE TUNNEL BENEATH THE *RIVER*--
--UNLEASHING A MASSIVE *SURGE*--
--OF *RADIOACTIVE* WATER.

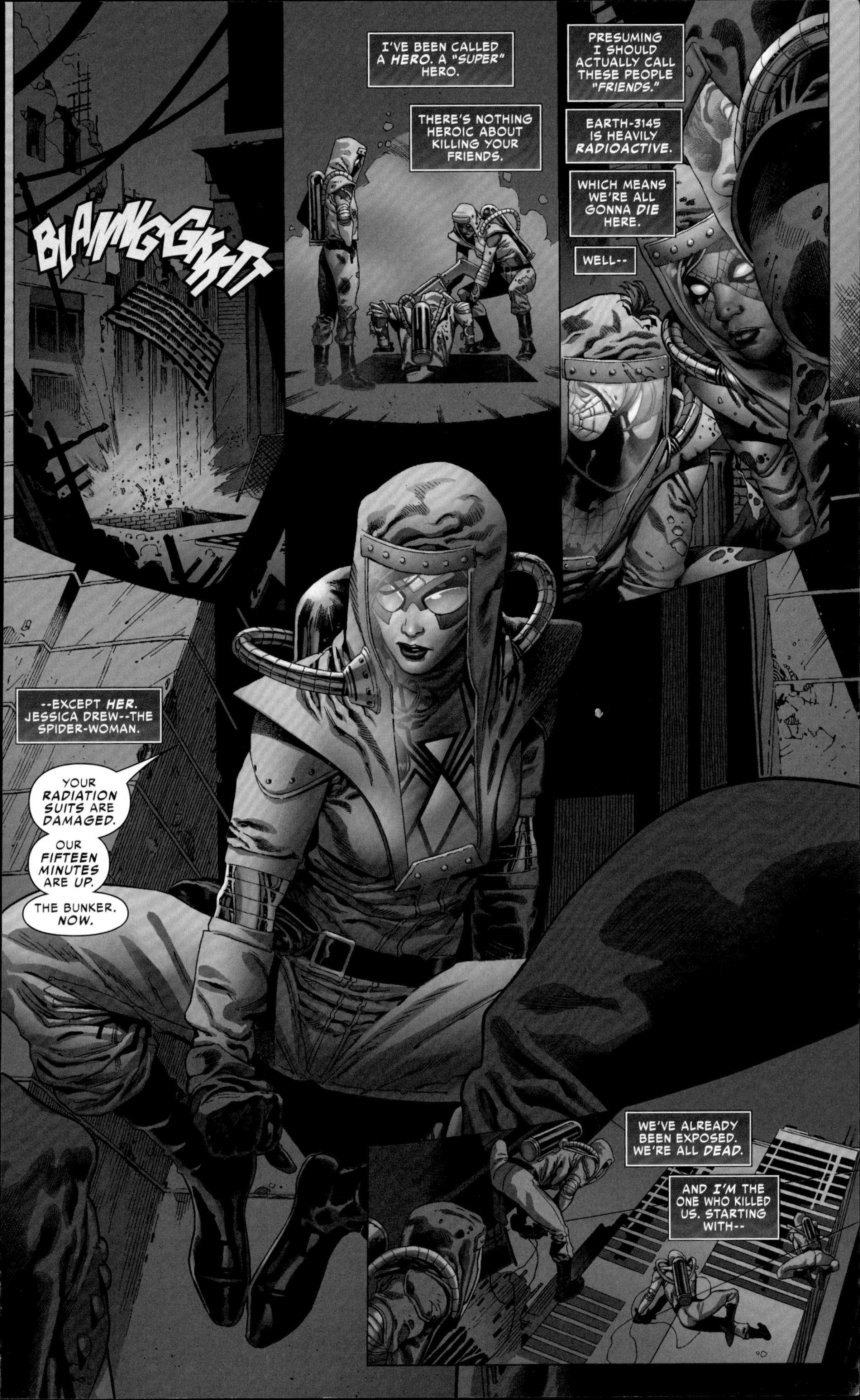
BLAMMGKKT
I'VE BEEN CALLED A HERO. A "SUPER" HERO.
THERE'S NOTHING HEROIC ABOUT KILLING YOUR FRIENDS.
PRESUMING I SHOULD ACTUALLY CALL THESE PEOPLE "FRIENDS."
EARTH-3145 IS HEAVILY RADIOACTIVE.
WHICH MEANS WE'RE ALL GONNA DIE HERE.
WELL--
--EXCEPT HER. JESSICA DREW--THE SPIDER-WOMAN.
YOUR RADIATION SUITS ARE DAMAGED.
OUR FIFTEEN MINUTES ARE UP.
THE BUNKER. NOW.
WE'VE ALREADY BEEN EXPOSED. WE'RE ALL DEAD.
AND I'M THE ONE WHO KILLED US. STARTING WITH--

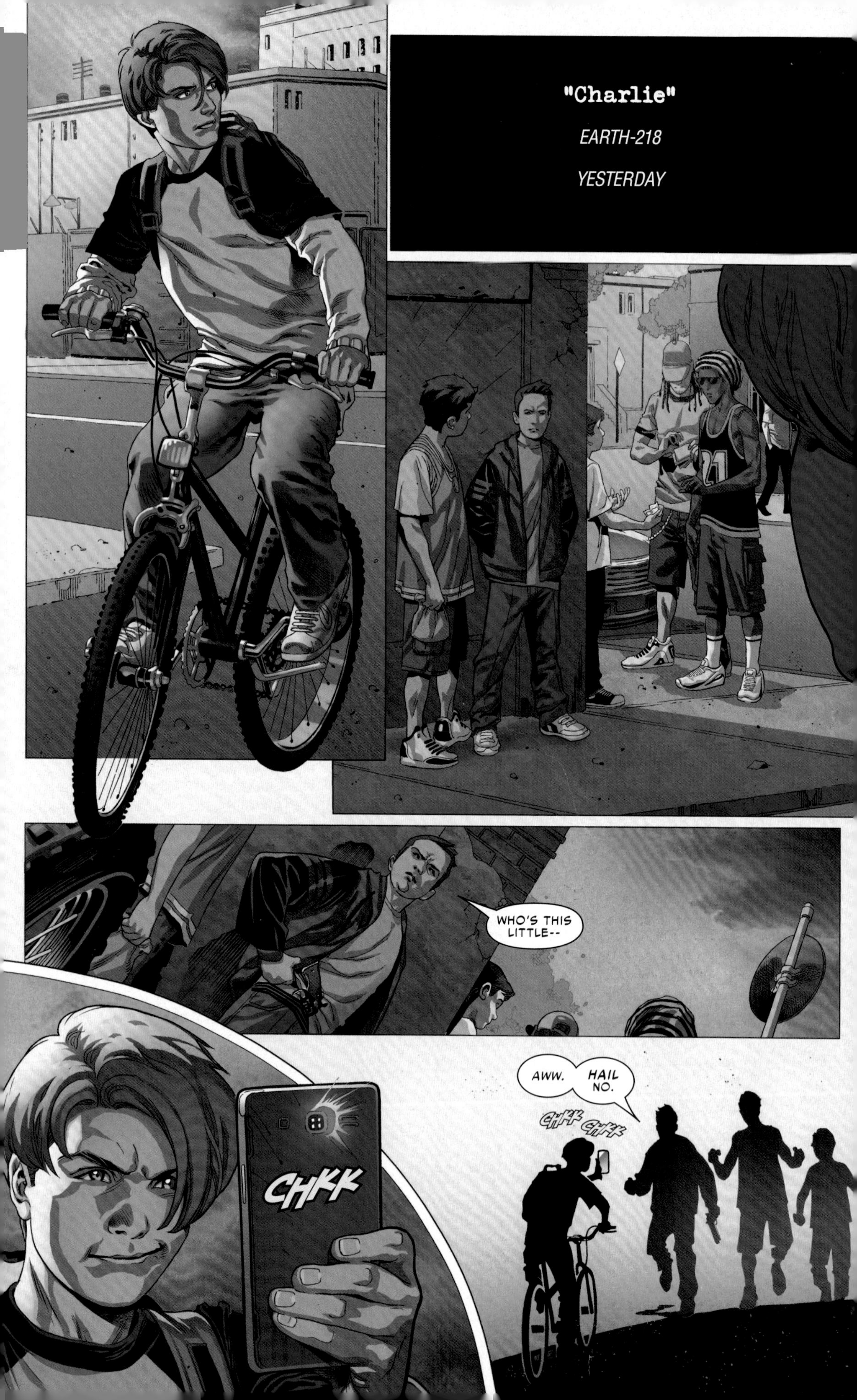
"Charlie"
EARTH-218
YESTERDAY
WHO'S THIS LITTLE--
CHKK
AWW.
HAIL NO.
CHKK CHKK

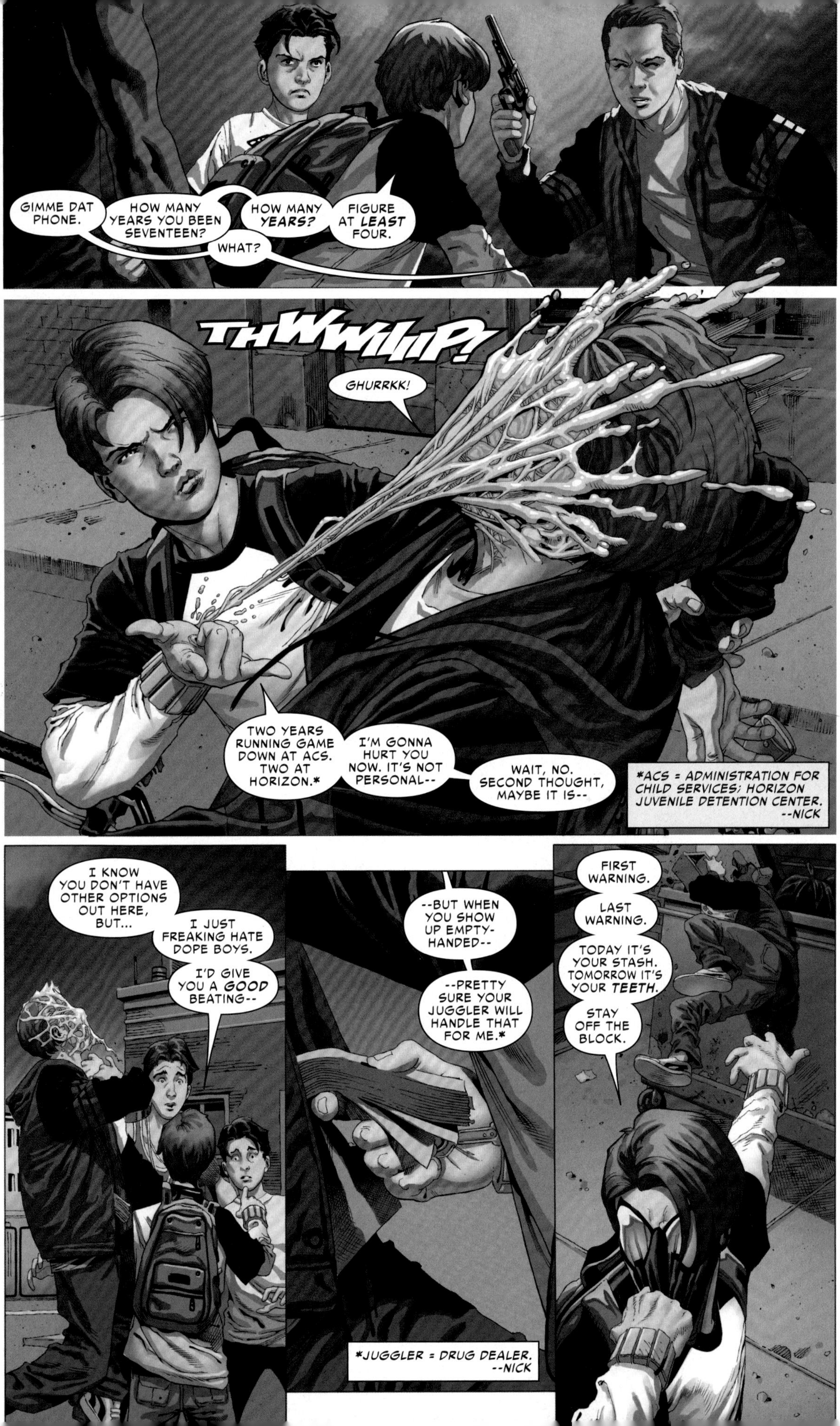
GIMME DAT PHONE.
HOW MANY YEARS YOU BEEN SEVENTEEN?
WHAT?
HOW MANY YEARS?
FIGURE AT LEAST FOUR.
THWWIIIP!
GHURRKK!
TWO YEARS RUNNING GAME DOWN AT ACS. TWO AT HORIZON.*
I'M GONNA HURT YOU NOW. IT'S NOT PERSONAL--
WAIT, NO. SECOND THOUGHT, MAYBE IT IS--
*ACS = ADMINISTRATION FOR CHILD SERVICES; HORIZON JUVENILE DETENTION CENTER. --NICK
I KNOW YOU DON'T HAVE OTHER OPTIONS OUT HERE, BUT...
I JUST FREAKING HATE DOPE BOYS.
I'D GIVE YOU A GOOD BEATING--
--BUT WHEN YOU SHOW UP EMPTY-HANDED--
--PRETTY SURE YOUR JUGGLER WILL HANDLE THAT FOR ME.*
*JUGGLER = DRUG DEALER. --NICK
FIRST WARNING.
LAST WARNING.
TODAY IT'S YOUR STASH. TOMORROW IT'S YOUR TEETH.
STAY OFF THE BLOCK.

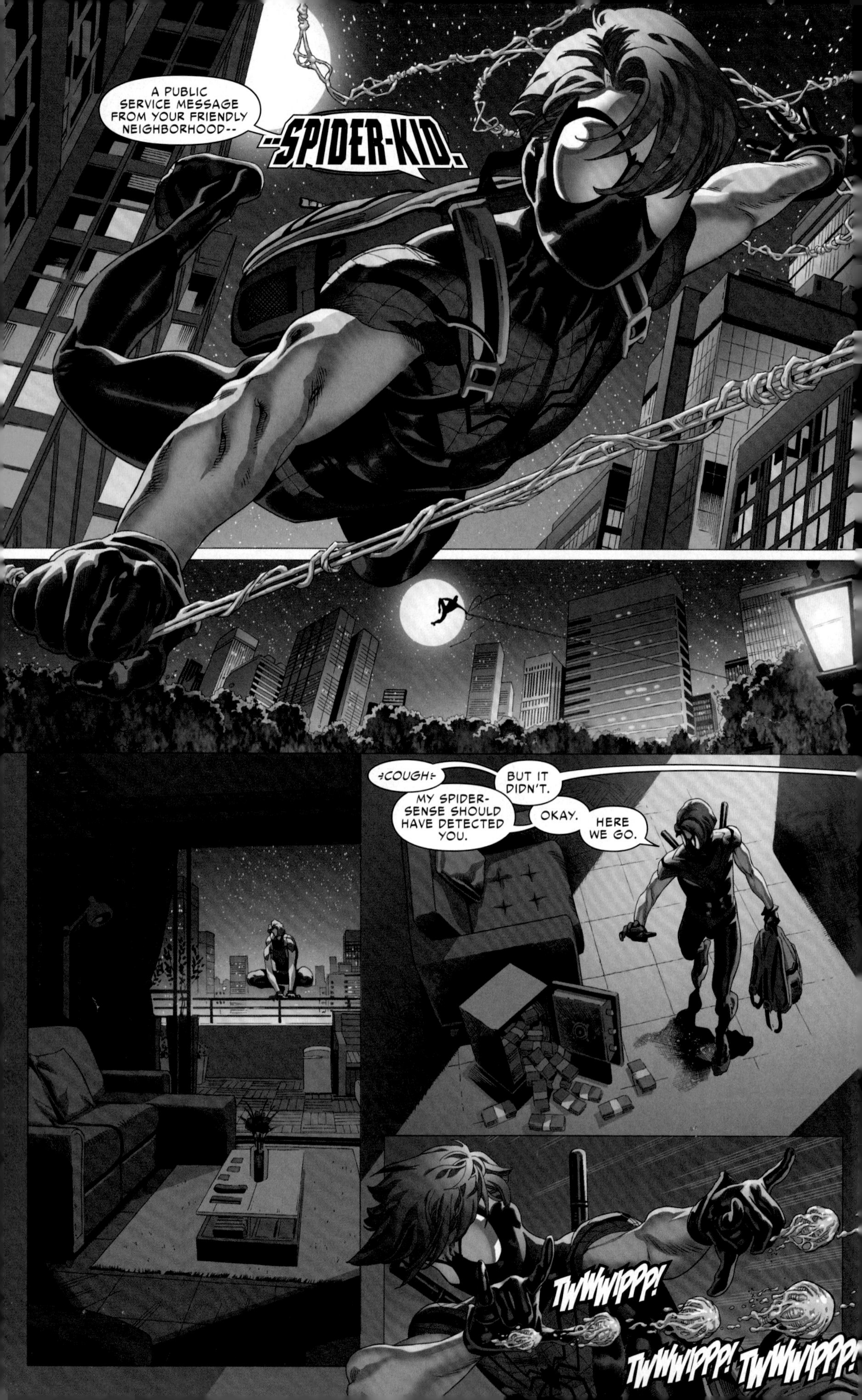
A PUBLIC SERVICE MESSAGE FROM YOUR FRIENDLY NEIGHBORHOOD--
--SPIDER-KID.
=COUGH=
MY SPIDER-SENSE SHOULD HAVE DETECTED YOU.
BUT IT DIDN'T.
OKAY.
HERE WE GO.
TWWWIPPP!
TWWWIPPP! TWWWIPPP!

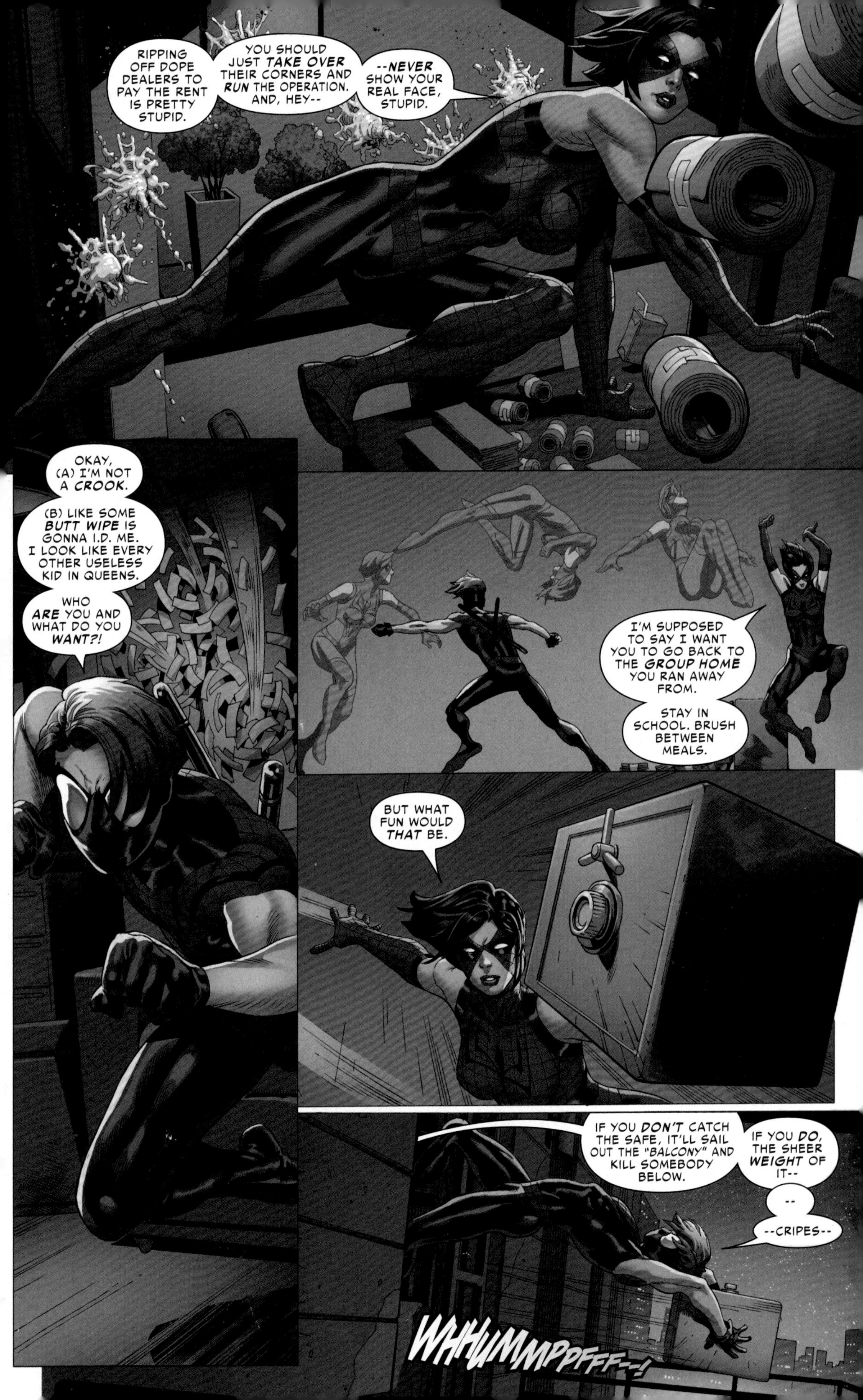
RIPPING OFF DOPE DEALERS TO PAY THE RENT IS PRETTY STUPID.
YOU SHOULD JUST TAKE OVER THEIR CORNERS AND RUN THE OPERATION. AND, HEY--
--NEVER SHOW YOUR REAL FACE, STUPID.
OKAY, (A) I'M NOT A CROOK.
(B) LIKE SOME BUTT WIPE IS GONNA I.D. ME. I LOOK LIKE EVERY OTHER USELESS KID IN QUEENS.
WHO ARE YOU AND WHAT DO YOU WANT?!
I'M SUPPOSED TO SAY I WANT YOU TO GO BACK TO THE GROUP HOME YOU RAN AWAY FROM.
STAY IN SCHOOL. BRUSH BETWEEN MEALS.
BUT WHAT FUN WOULD THAT BE.
IF YOU DON'T CATCH THE SAFE, IT'LL SAIL OUT THE "BALCONY" AND KILL SOMEBODY BELOW.
IF YOU DO, THE SHEER WEIGHT OF IT--
--
--CRIPES--
WHHUMMPPFFF--!

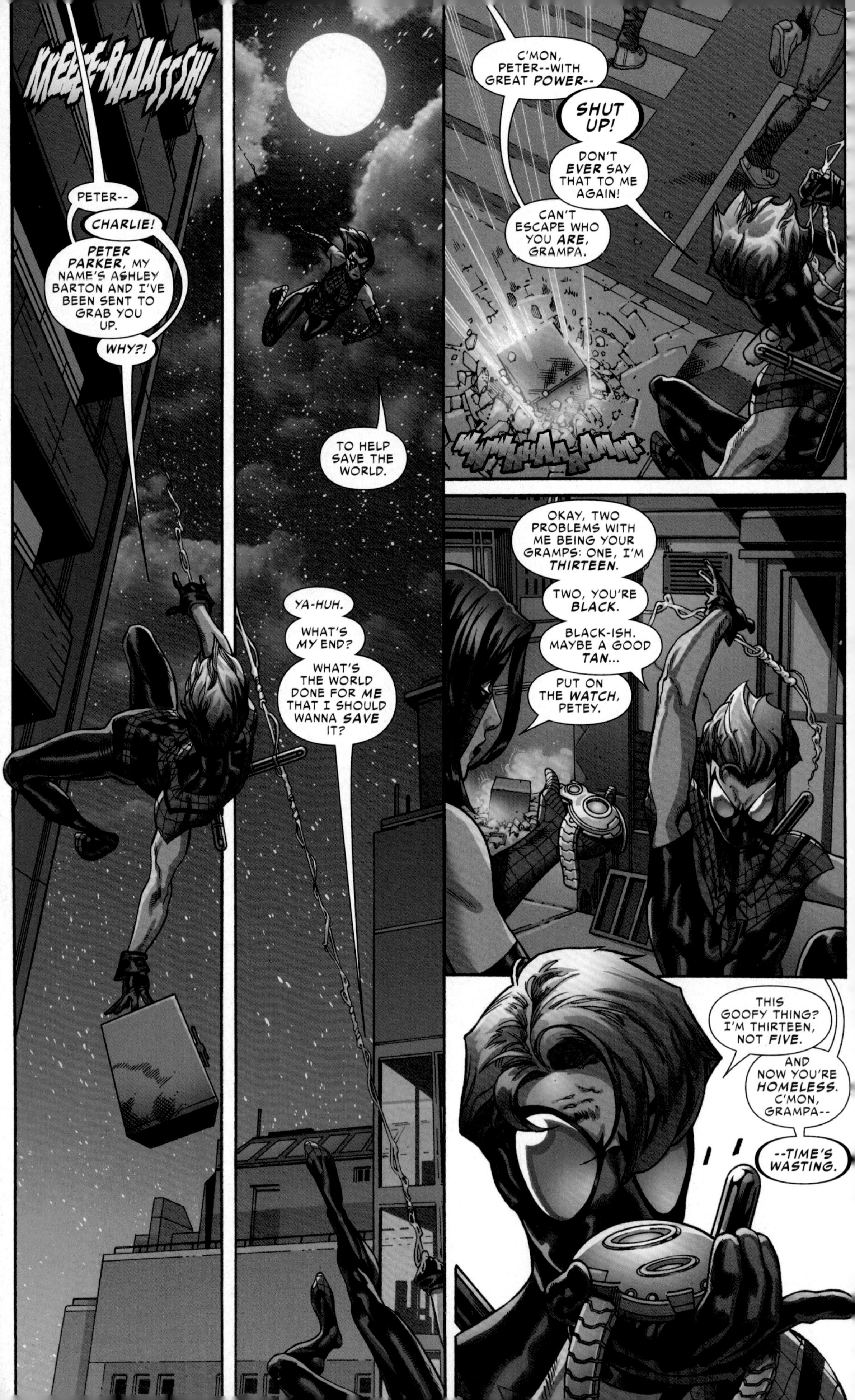
PETER--
CHARLIE!
PETER PARKER, MY NAME'S ASHLEY BARTON AND I'VE BEEN SENT TO GRAB YOU UP.
WHY?!
TO HELP SAVE THE WORLD.
YA-HUH.
WHAT'S MY END?
WHAT'S THE WORLD DONE FOR ME THAT I SHOULD WANNA SAVE IT?
C'MON, PETER--WITH GREAT POWER--
SHUT UP!
DON'T EVER SAY THAT TO ME AGAIN!
CAN'T ESCAPE WHO YOU ARE, GRAMPA.
OKAY, TWO PROBLEMS WITH ME BEING YOUR GRAMPS: ONE, I'M THIRTEEN.
TWO, YOU'RE BLACK.
BLACK-ISH. MAYBE A GOOD TAN...
PUT ON THE WATCH, PETEY.
THIS GOOFY THING? I'M THIRTEEN, NOT FIVE.
AND NOW YOU'RE HOMELESS. C'MON, GRAMPA--
--TIME'S WASTING.

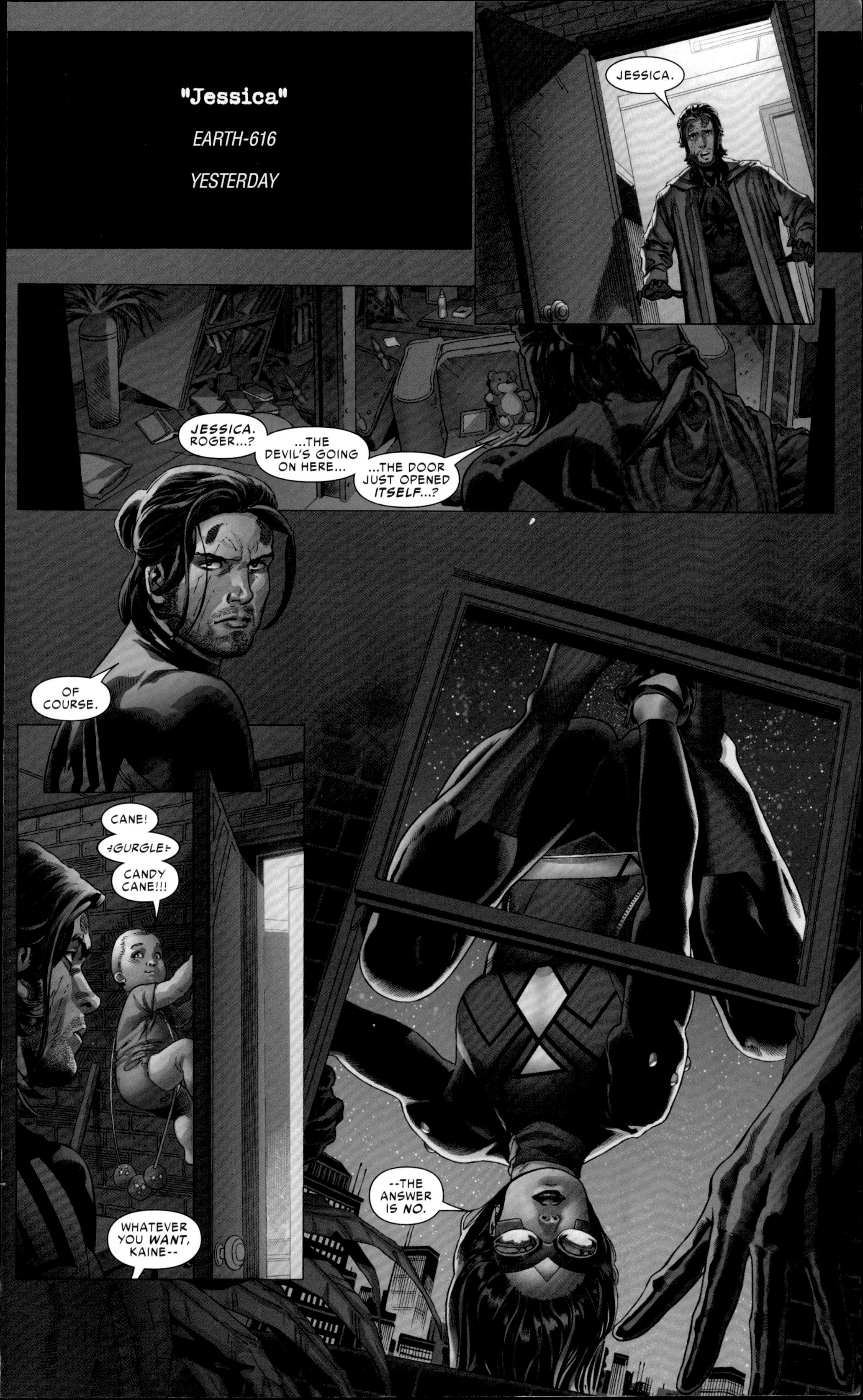
"Jessica"
EARTH-616
YESTERDAY
JESSICA.
JESSICA. ROGER...?
...THE DEVIL'S GOING ON HERE...
...THE DOOR JUST OPENED ITSELF...?
OF COURSE.
CANE!
-GURGLE-
CANDY CANE!!!
WHATEVER YOU *WANT*, KAINE--
--THE ANSWER IS *NO*.

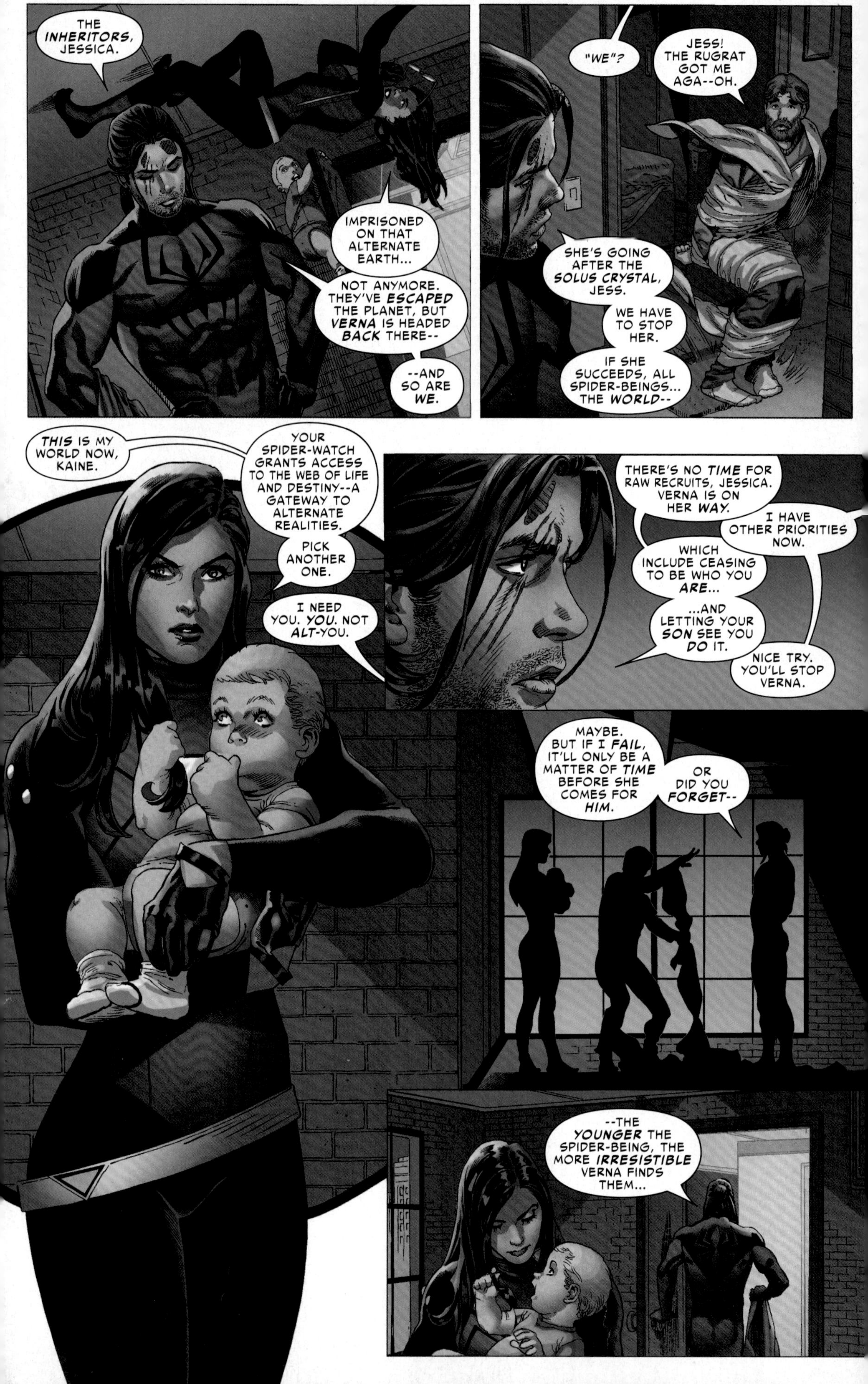
THE INHERITORS, JESSICA.
IMPRISONED ON THAT ALTERNATE EARTH...
NOT ANYMORE. THEY'VE ESCAPED THE PLANET, BUT VERNA IS HEADED BACK THERE--
--AND SO ARE WE.
"WE"?
JESS! THE RUGRAT GOT ME AGA--OH.
SHE'S GOING AFTER THE SOLUS CRYSTAL, JESS.
WE HAVE TO STOP HER.
IF SHE SUCCEEDS, ALL SPIDER-BEINGS... THE WORLD--
THIS IS MY WORLD NOW, KAINE.
YOUR SPIDER-WATCH GRANTS ACCESS TO THE WEB OF LIFE AND DESTINY--A GATEWAY TO ALTERNATE REALITIES.
PICK ANOTHER ONE.
I NEED YOU. YOU. NOT ALT-YOU.
THERE'S NO TIME FOR RAW RECRUITS, JESSICA. VERNA IS ON HER WAY.
I HAVE OTHER PRIORITIES NOW.
WHICH INCLUDE CEASING TO BE WHO YOU ARE...
...AND LETTING YOUR SON SEE YOU DO IT.
NICE TRY. YOU'LL STOP VERNA.
MAYBE. BUT IF I FAIL, IT'LL ONLY BE A MATTER OF TIME BEFORE SHE COMES FOR HIM.
OR DID YOU FORGET--
--THE YOUNGER THE SPIDER-BEING, THE MORE IRRESISTIBLE VERNA FINDS THEM...

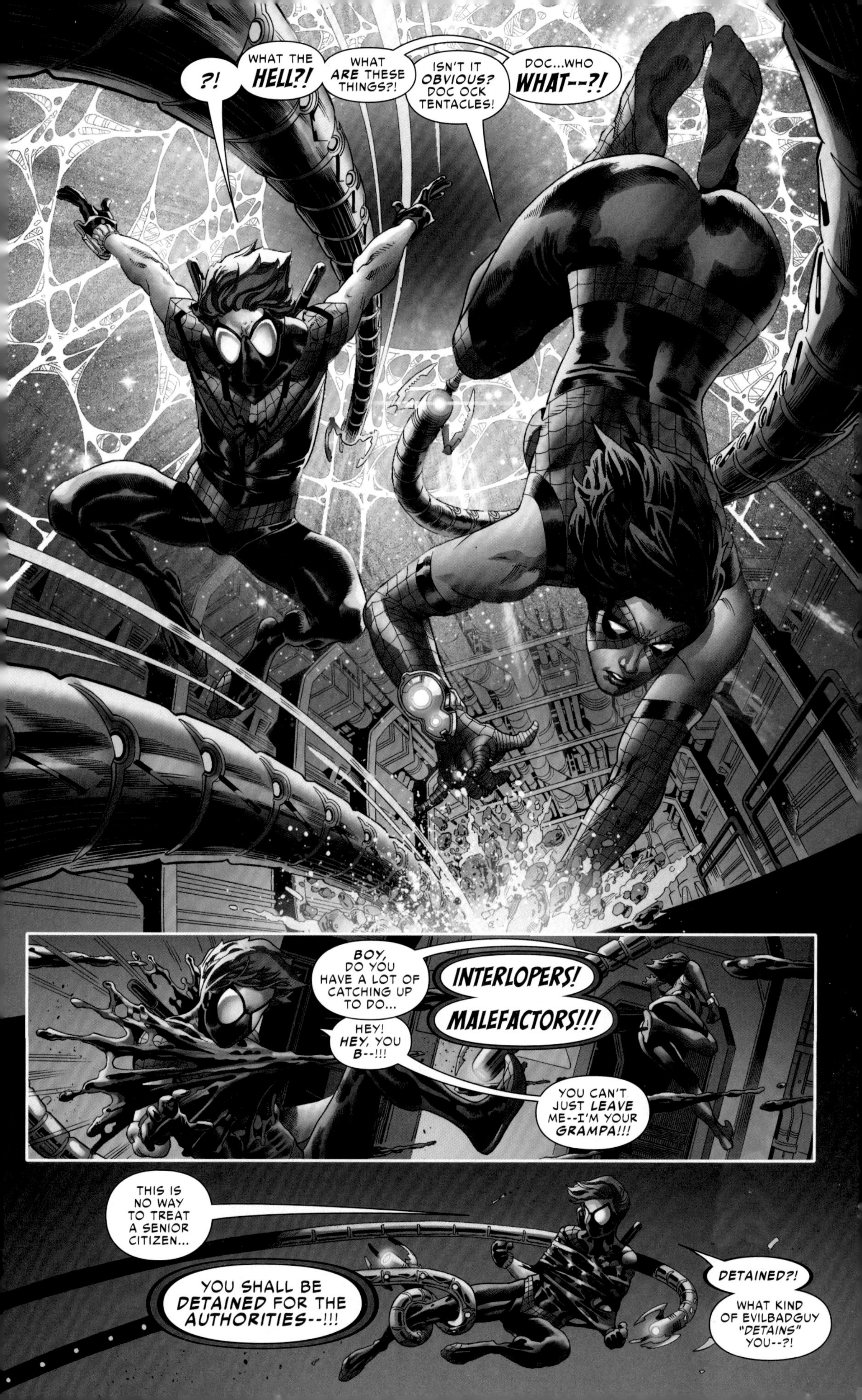
?!
WHAT THE HELL?!
WHAT ARE THESE THINGS?!
ISN'T IT OBVIOUS? DOC OCK TENTACLES!
DOC...WHO WHAT--?!
BOY, DO YOU HAVE A LOT OF CATCHING UP TO DO...
INTERLOPERS!
MALEFACTORS!!!
HEY! HEY, YOU B--!!!
YOU CAN'T JUST LEAVE ME--I'M YOUR GRAMPA!!!
THIS IS NO WAY TO TREAT A SENIOR CITIZEN...
YOU SHALL BE DETAINED FOR THE AUTHORITIES--!!!
DETAINED?!
WHAT KIND OF EVILBADGUY "DETAINS" YOU--?!

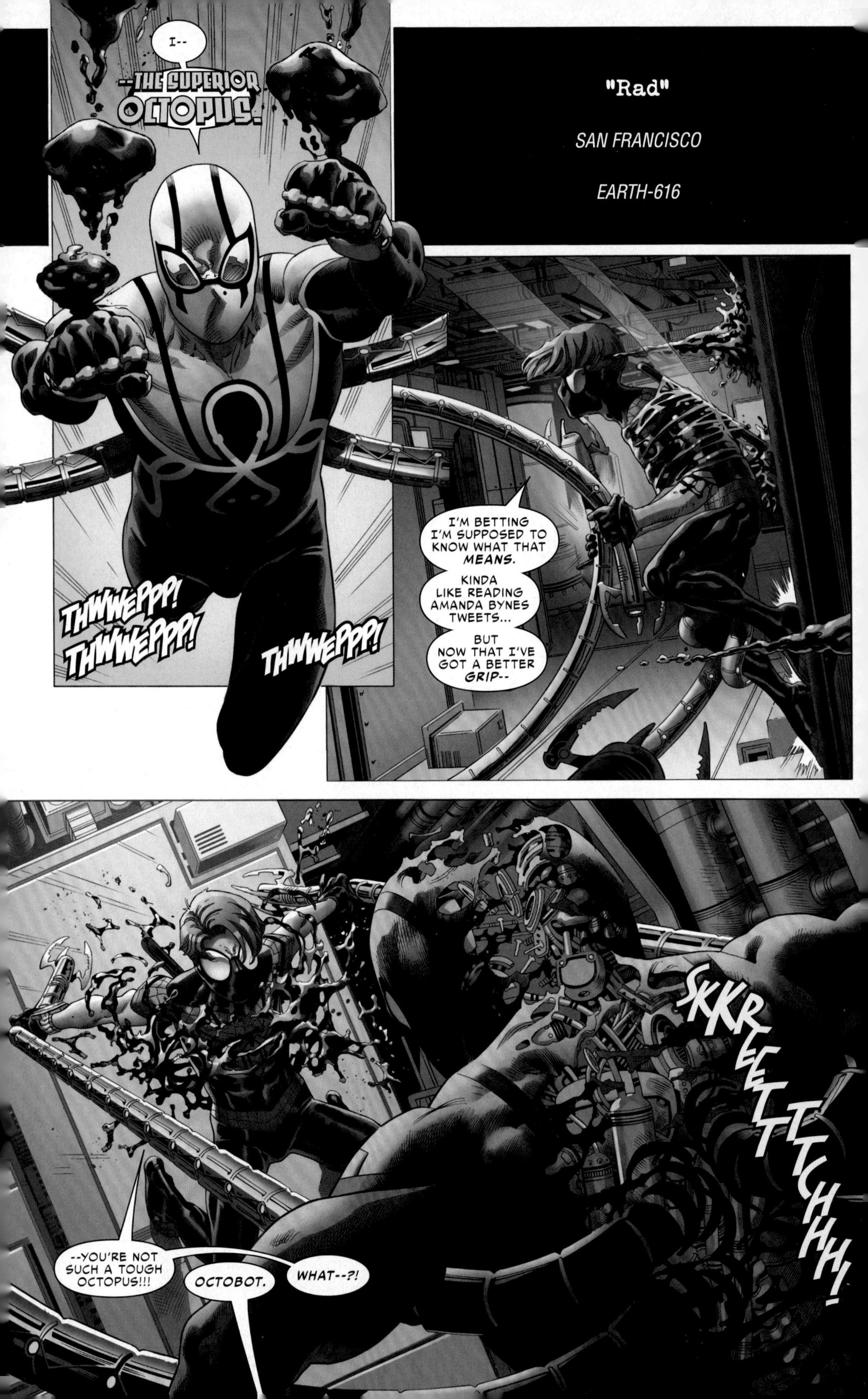

I--
--THE SUPERIOR OCTOPUS!
"Rad"
SAN FRANCISCO
EARTH-616
THWWEPPP! THWWEPPP!
THWWEPPP!
I'M BETTING I'M SUPPOSED TO KNOW WHAT THAT MEANS.
KINDA LIKE READING AMANDA BYNES TWEETS...
BUT NOW THAT I'VE GOT A BETTER GRIP--
--YOU'RE NOT SUCH A TOUGH OCTOPUS!!!
OCTOBOT.
WHAT--?!
SKKREETTTCHHH!

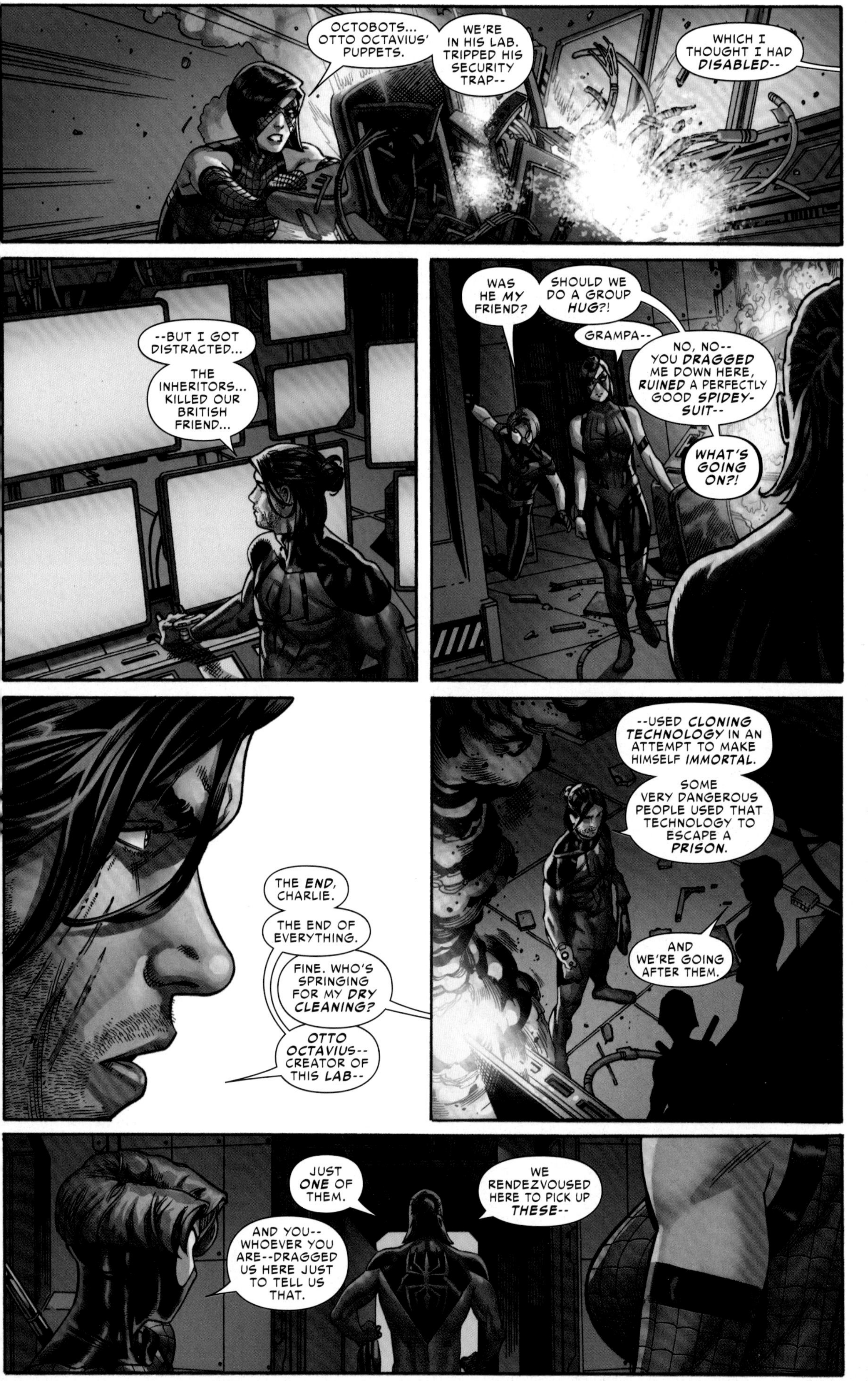
OCTOBOTS... OTTO OCTAVIUS' PUPPETS.
WE'RE IN HIS LAB. TRIPPED HIS SECURITY TRAP--
WHICH I THOUGHT I HAD DISABLED--
--BUT I GOT DISTRACTED...
THE INHERITORS... KILLED OUR BRITISH FRIEND...
WAS HE MY FRIEND?
SHOULD WE DO A GROUP HUG?!
GRAMPA--
NO, NO-- YOU DRAGGED ME DOWN HERE, RUINED A PERFECTLY GOOD SPIDEY-SUIT--
WHAT'S GOING ON?!
THE END, CHARLIE.
THE END OF EVERYTHING.
FINE. WHO'S SPRINGING FOR MY DRY CLEANING?
OTTO OCTAVIUS-- CREATOR OF THIS LAB--
--USED CLONING TECHNOLOGY IN AN ATTEMPT TO MAKE HIMSELF IMMORTAL.
SOME VERY DANGEROUS PEOPLE USED THAT TECHNOLOGY TO ESCAPE A PRISON.
AND WE'RE GOING AFTER THEM.
JUST ONE OF THEM.
AND YOU-- WHOEVER YOU ARE--DRAGGED US HERE JUST TO TELL US THAT.
WE RENDEZVOUSED HERE TO PICK UP THESE--

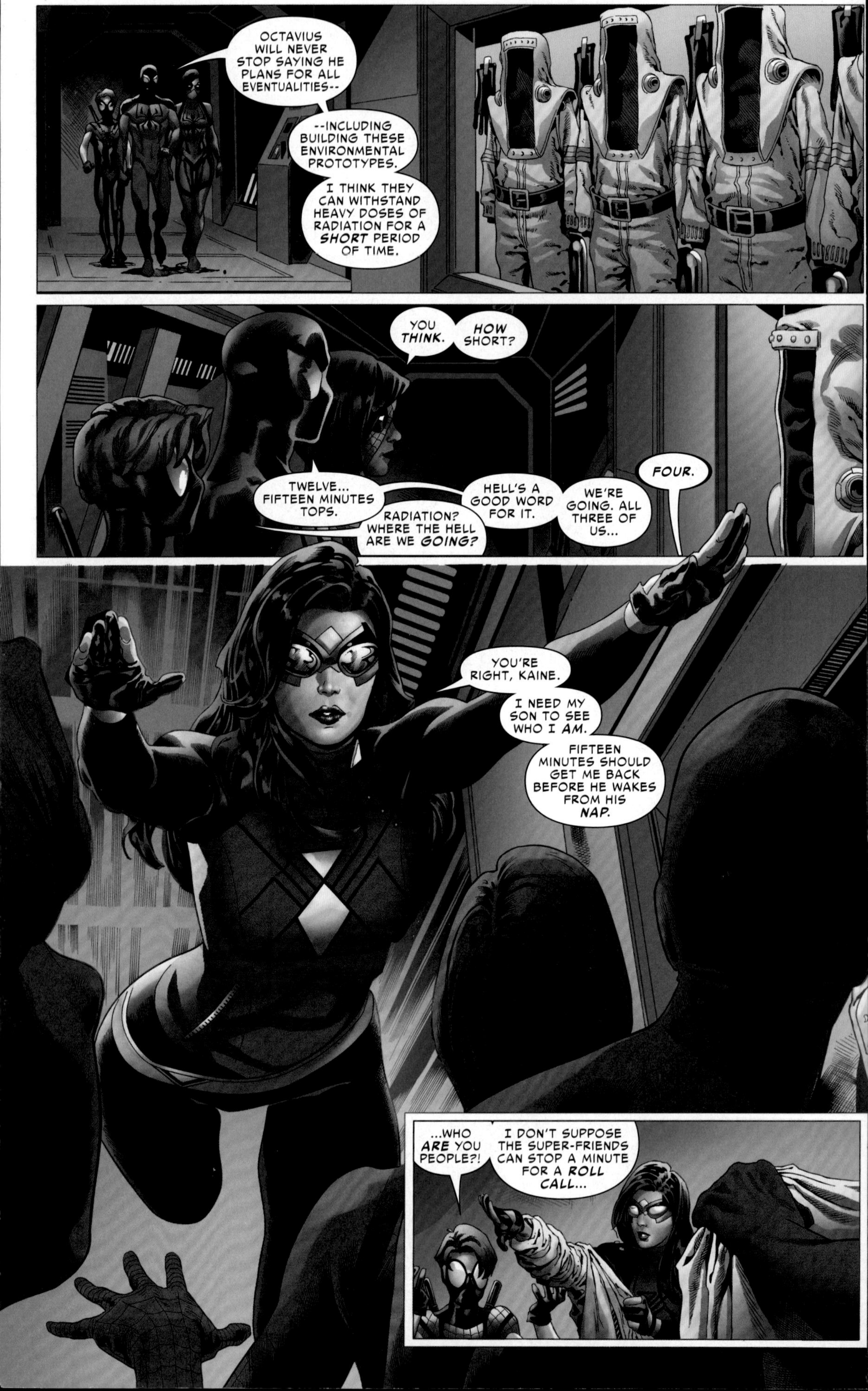
OCTAVIUS WILL NEVER STOP SAYING HE PLANS FOR ALL EVENTUALITIES--
--INCLUDING BUILDING THESE ENVIRONMENTAL PROTOTYPES.
I THINK THEY CAN WITHSTAND HEAVY DOSES OF RADIATION FOR A SHORT PERIOD OF TIME.
YOU THINK.
HOW SHORT?
TWELVE... FIFTEEN MINUTES TOPS.
RADIATION? WHERE THE HELL ARE WE GOING?
HELL'S A GOOD WORD FOR IT.
WE'RE GOING. ALL THREE OF US...
FOUR.
YOU'RE RIGHT, KAINE.
I NEED MY SON TO SEE WHO I AM.
FIFTEEN MINUTES SHOULD GET ME BACK BEFORE HE WAKES FROM HIS NAP.
I DON'T SUPPOSE THE SUPER-FRIENDS CAN STOP A MINUTE FOR A ROLL CALL...
...WHO ARE YOU PEOPLE?!

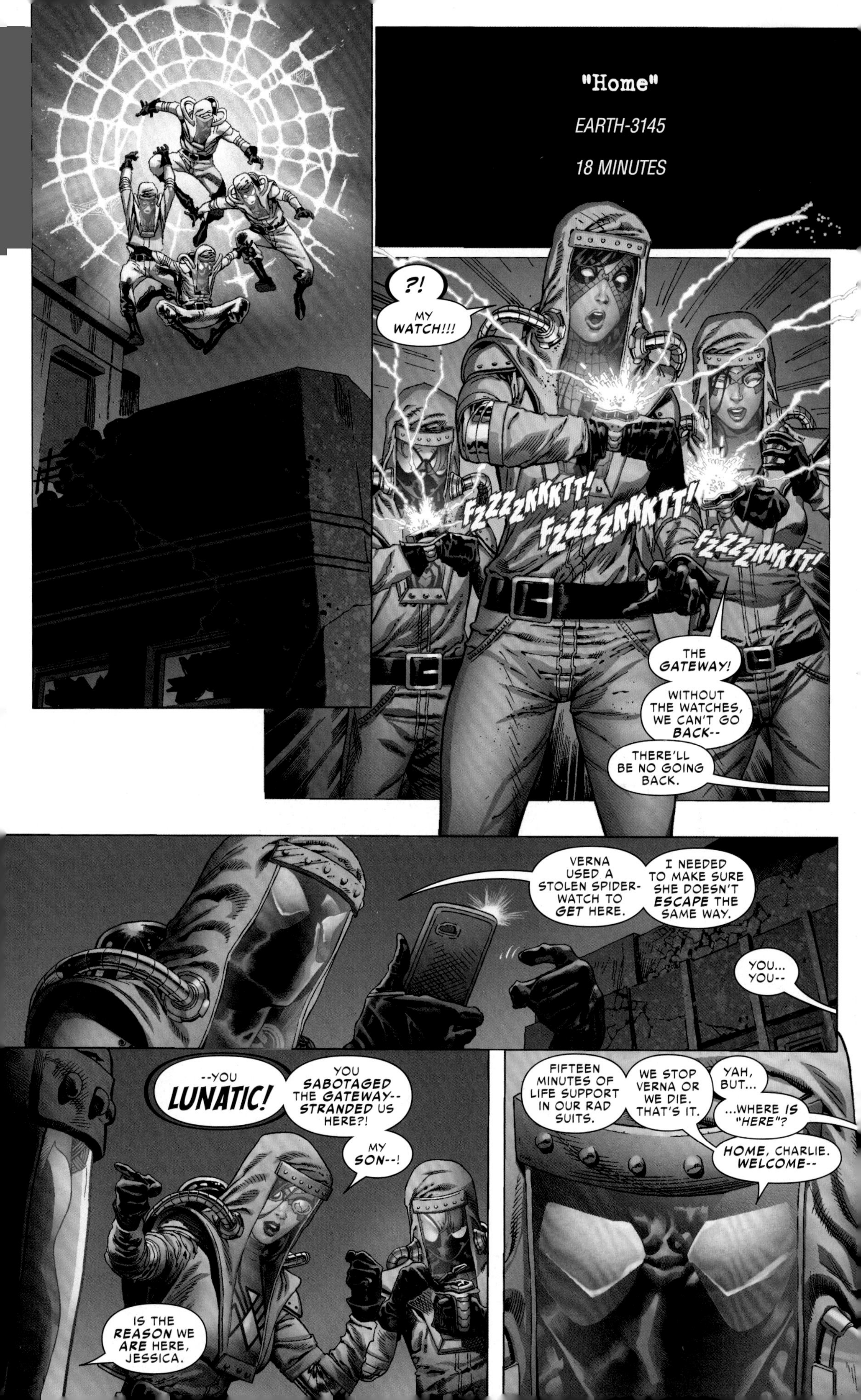
"Home"
EARTH-3145
18 MINUTES
?! MY WATCH!!!
FZZZZKKKTT! FZZZZKKKTT! FZZZZKKKTT!
THE GATEWAY!
WITHOUT THE WATCHES, WE CAN'T GO BACK--
THERE'LL BE NO GOING BACK.
VERNA USED A STOLEN SPIDER-WATCH TO GET HERE.
I NEEDED TO MAKE SURE SHE DOESN'T ESCAPE THE SAME WAY.
YOU... YOU--
--YOU LUNATIC!
YOU SABOTAGED THE GATEWAY--STRANDED US HERE?!
MY SON--!
IS THE REASON WE ARE HERE, JESSICA.
FIFTEEN MINUTES OF LIFE SUPPORT IN OUR RAD SUITS.
WE STOP VERNA OR WE DIE. THAT'S IT.
YAH, BUT...
...WHERE IS "HERE"?
HOME, CHARLIE. WELCOME--

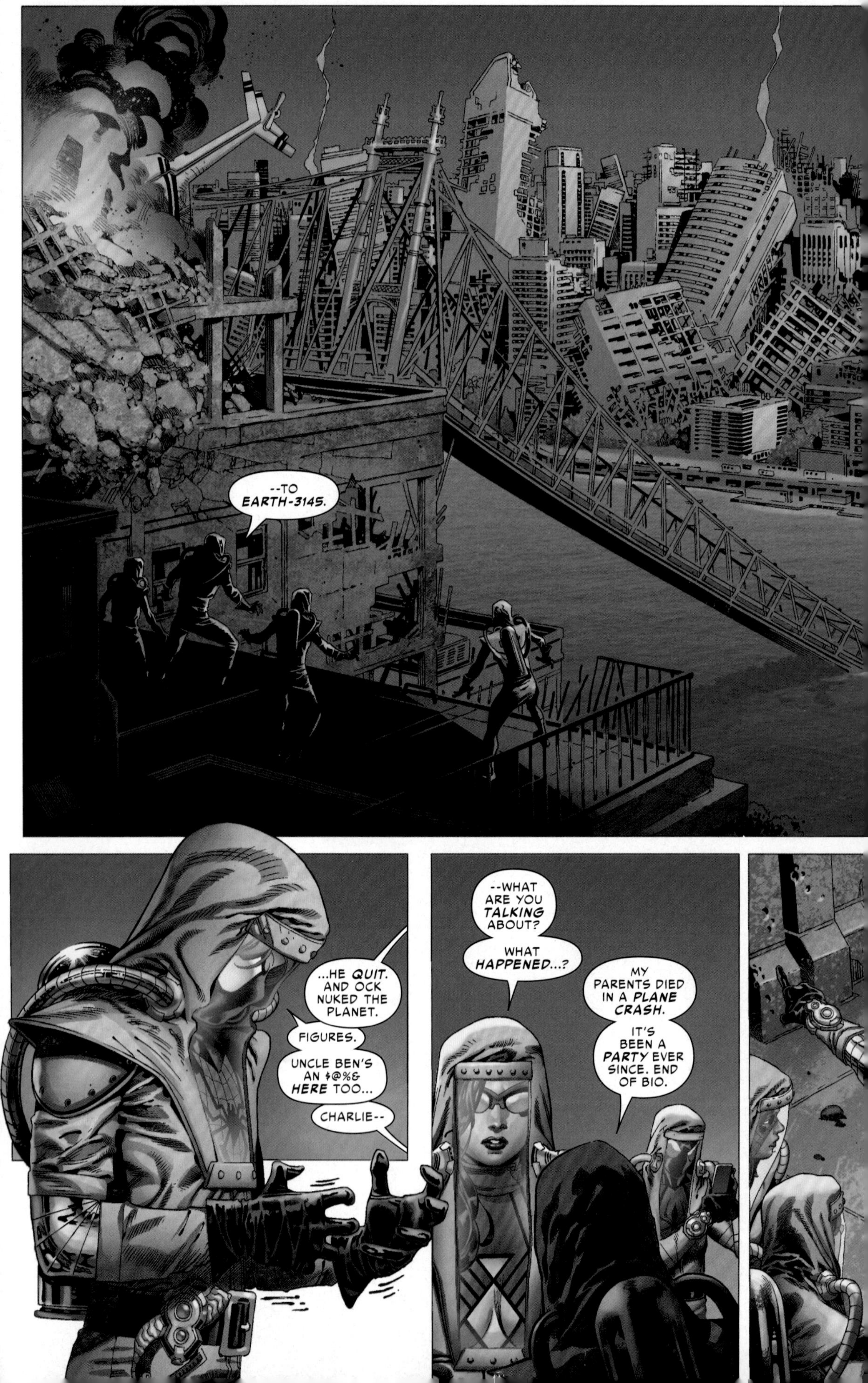
--TO *EARTH-3145.*
...HE *QUIT.* AND OCK NUKED THE PLANET.
FIGURES.
UNCLE BEN'S AN $@%& *HERE* TOO...
CHARLIE--
--WHAT ARE YOU *TALKING* ABOUT?
WHAT *HAPPENED...?*
MY PARENTS DIED IN A *PLANE CRASH.*
IT'S BEEN A *PARTY* EVER SINCE. END OF BIO.

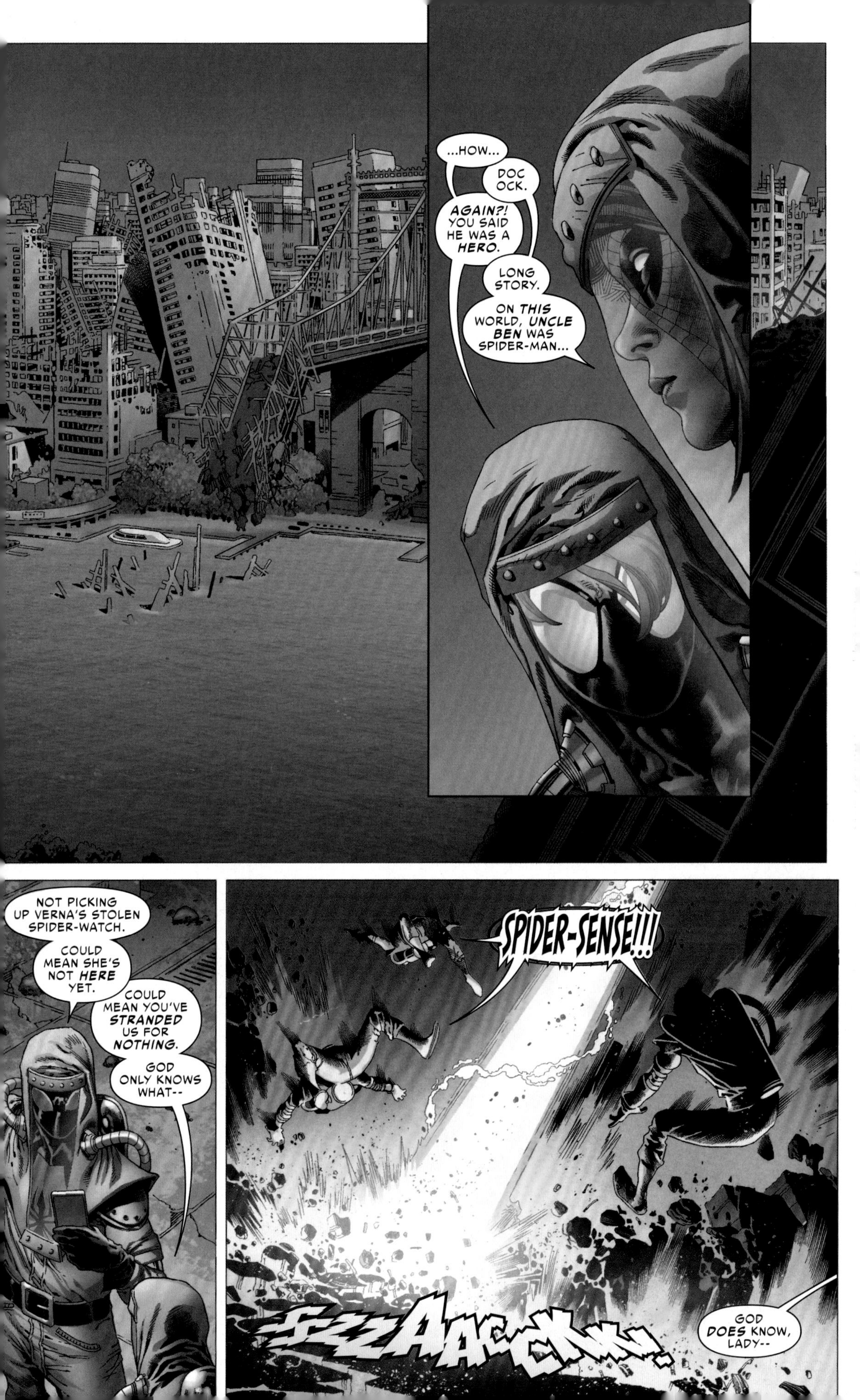

...HOW...
DOC OCK.
AGAIN?! YOU SAID HE WAS A HERO.
LONG STORY.
ON THIS WORLD, UNCLE BEN WAS SPIDER-MAN...
NOT PICKING UP VERNA'S STOLEN SPIDER-WATCH.
COULD MEAN SHE'S NOT HERE YET.
COULD MEAN YOU'VE STRANDED US FOR NOTHING.
GOD ONLY KNOWS WHAT--
SPIDER-SENSE!!!
FZZZAACKK!!
GOD DOES KNOW, LADY--

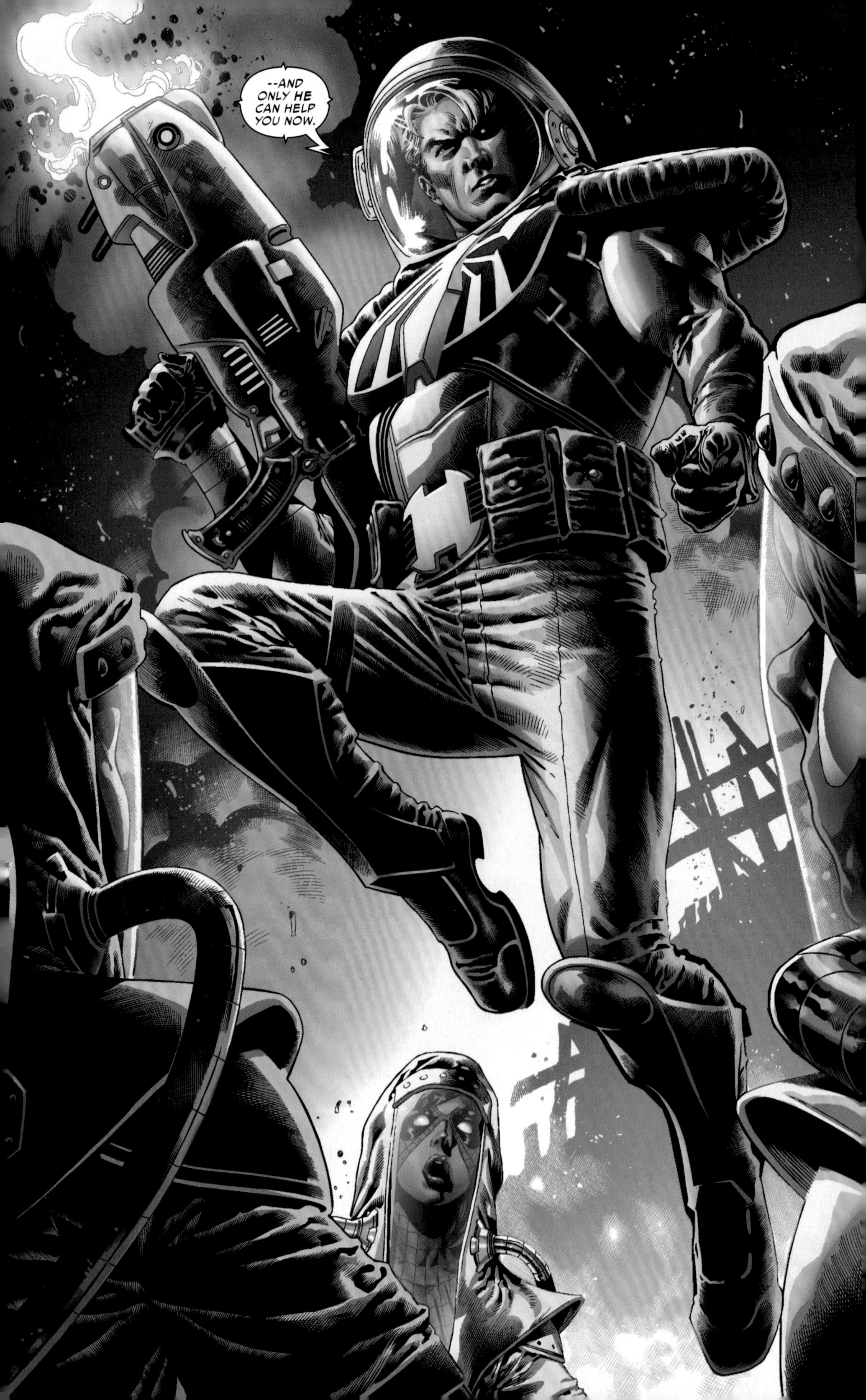
--AND ONLY HE CAN HELP YOU NOW.

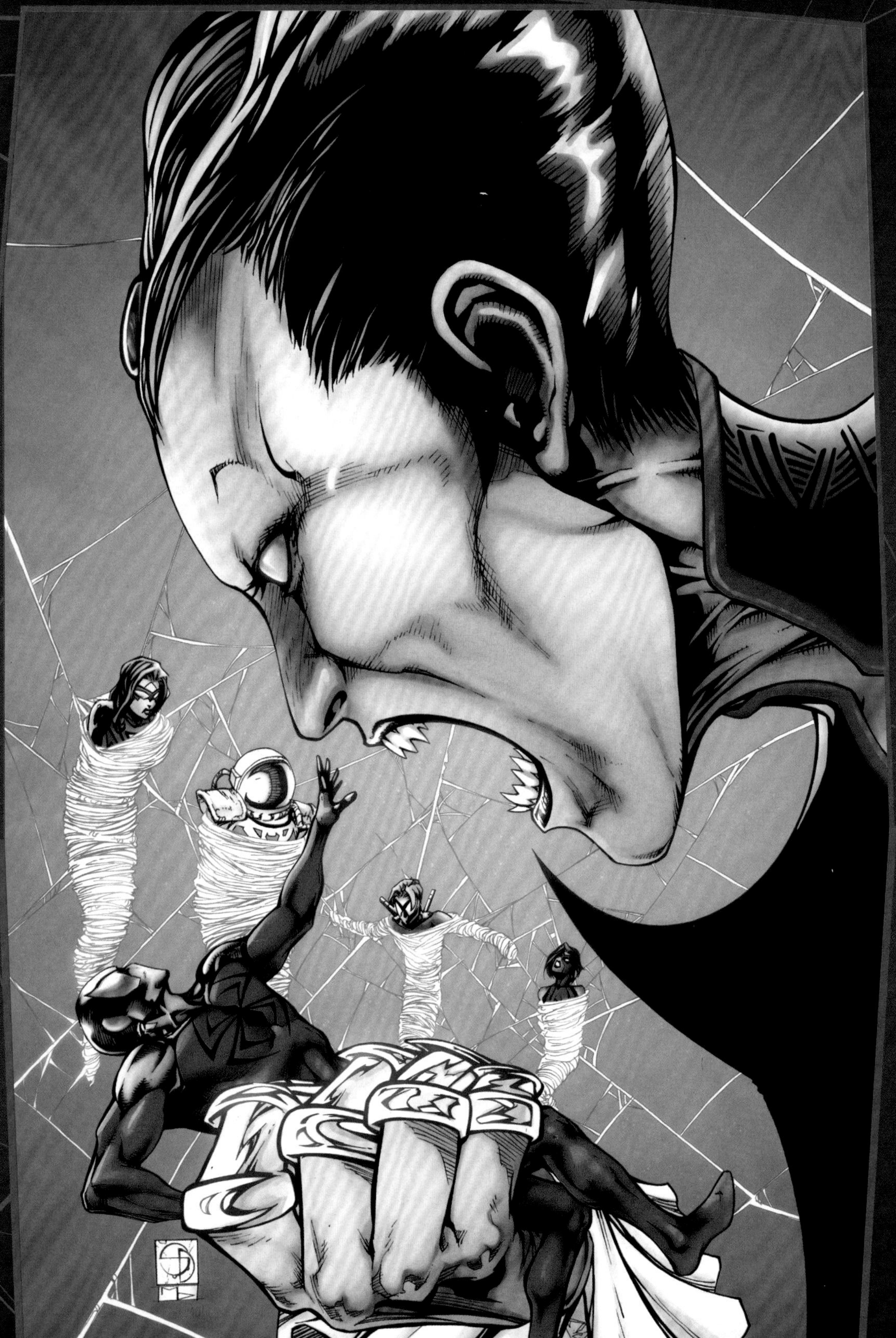

SPIDER-FORCE #2

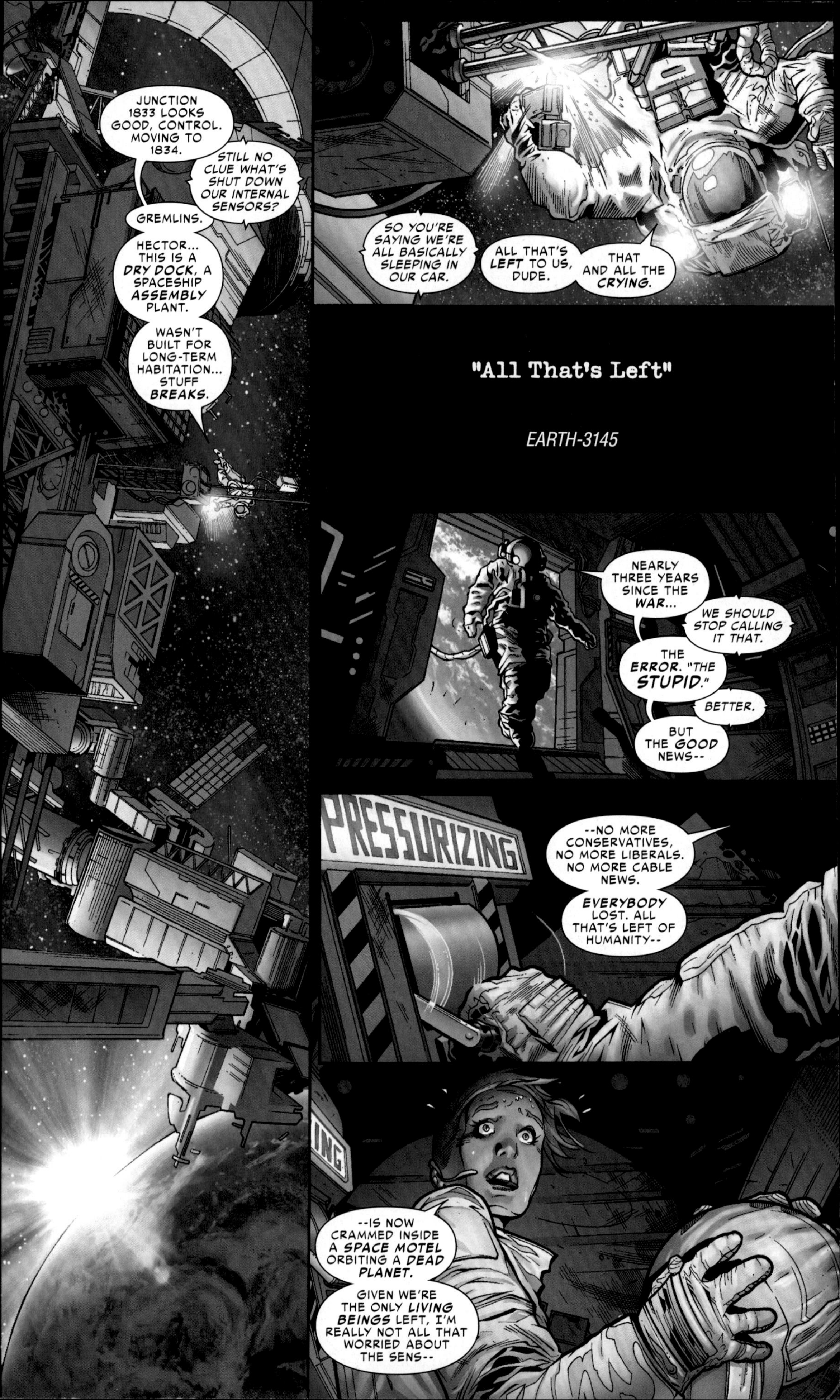
JUNCTION 1833 LOOKS GOOD, CONTROL. MOVING TO 1834.
STILL NO CLUE WHAT'S SHUT DOWN OUR INTERNAL SENSORS?
GREMLINS.
HECTOR... THIS IS A DRY DOCK, A SPACESHIP ASSEMBLY PLANT.
WASN'T BUILT FOR LONG-TERM HABITATION... STUFF BREAKS.
SO YOU'RE SAYING WE'RE ALL BASICALLY SLEEPING IN OUR CAR.
ALL THAT'S LEFT TO US, DUDE.
THAT AND ALL THE CRYING.
"All That's Left"
EARTH-3145
NEARLY THREE YEARS SINCE THE WAR...
WE SHOULD STOP CALLING IT THAT.
THE ERROR. "THE STUPID."
BETTER.
BUT THE GOOD NEWS--
PRESSURIZING
--NO MORE CONSERVATIVES, NO MORE LIBERALS. NO MORE CABLE NEWS.
EVERYBODY LOST. ALL THAT'S LEFT OF HUMANITY--
--IS NOW CRAMMED INSIDE A SPACE MOTEL ORBITING A DEAD PLANET.
GIVEN WE'RE THE ONLY LIVING BEINGS LEFT, I'M REALLY NOT ALL THAT WORRIED ABOUT THE SENS--

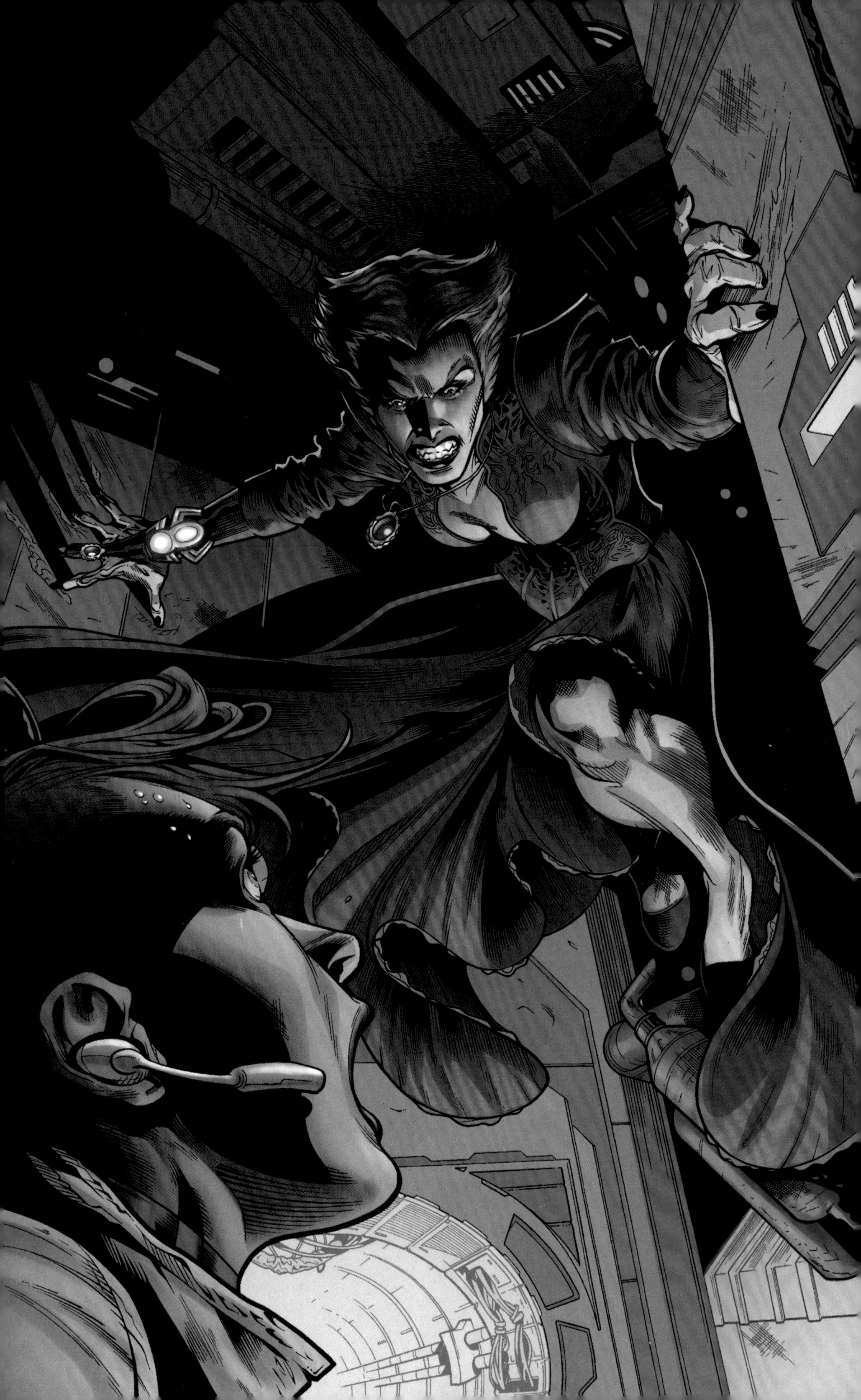

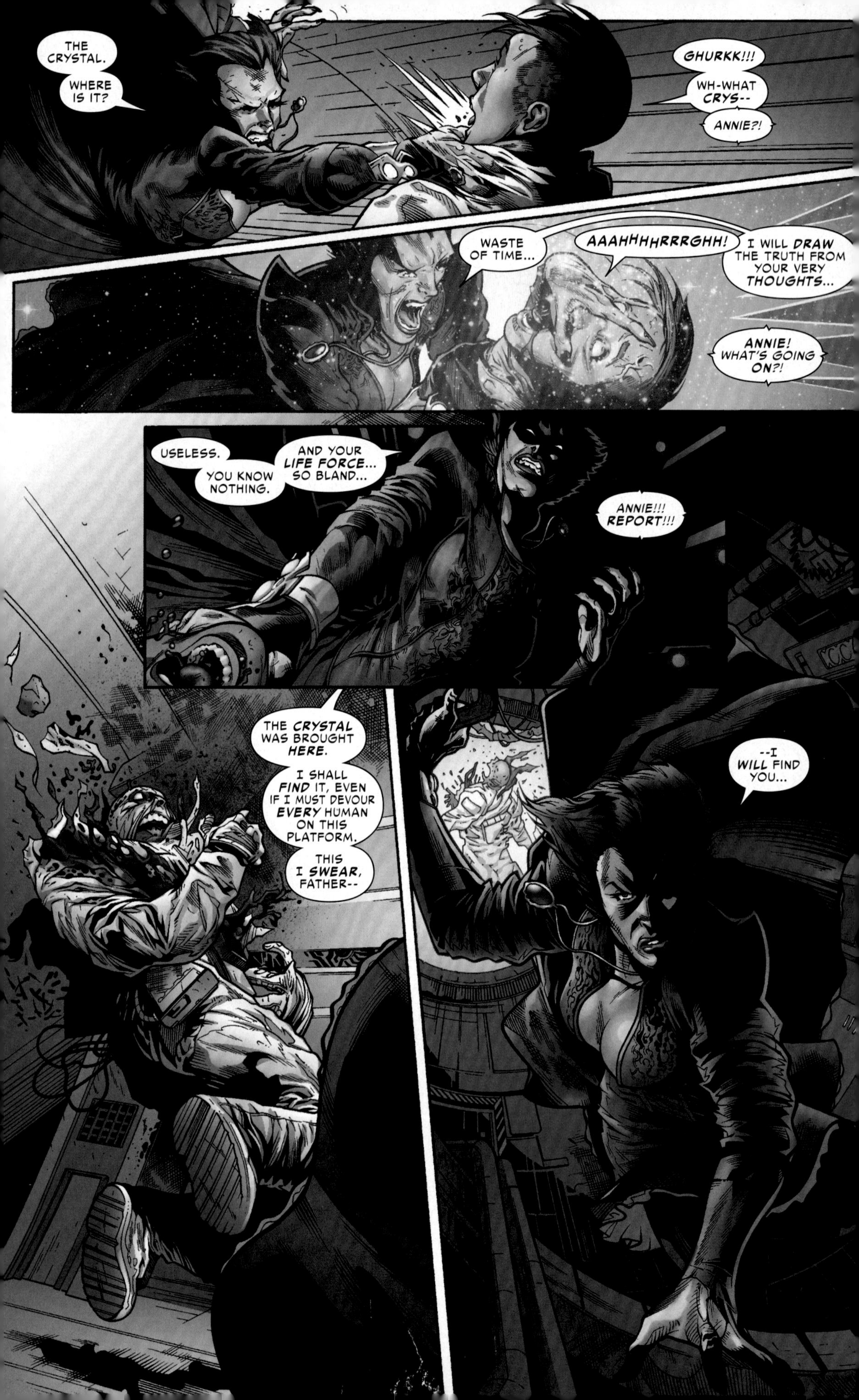
THE CRYSTAL.
WHERE IS IT?
GHURKK!!!
WH-WHAT CRYS--
ANNIE?!
WASTE OF TIME...
AAAHHHHRRRGHH!
I WILL DRAW THE TRUTH FROM YOUR VERY THOUGHTS...
ANNIE! WHAT'S GOING ON?!
USELESS.
YOU KNOW NOTHING.
AND YOUR LIFE FORCE... SO BLAND...
ANNIE!!! REPORT!!!
THE CRYSTAL WAS BROUGHT HERE.
I SHALL FIND IT, EVEN IF I MUST DEVOUR EVERY HUMAN ON THIS PLATFORM.
THIS I SWEAR, FATHER--
--I WILL FIND YOU...

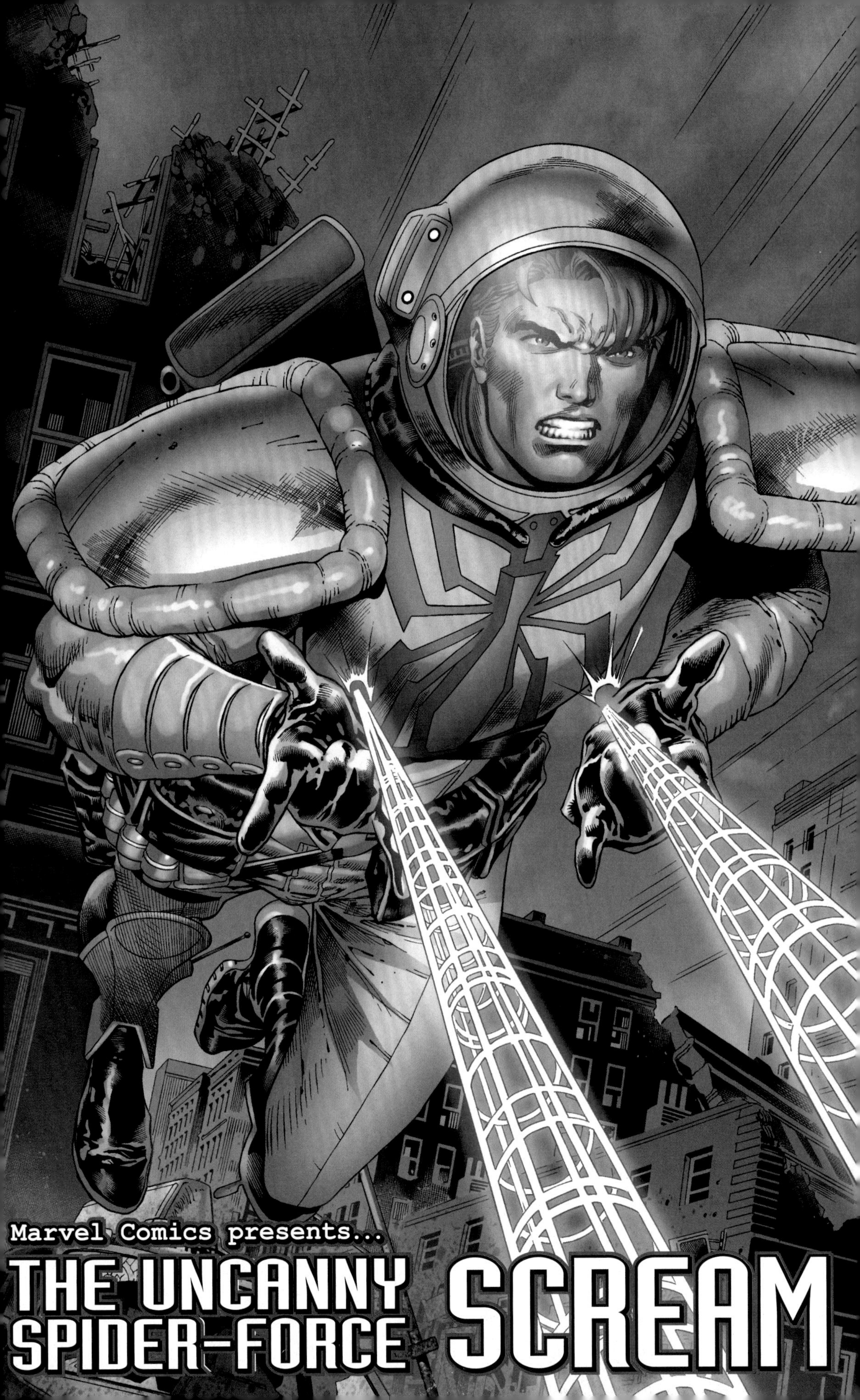
Marvel Comics presents...
THE UNCANNY SPIDER-FORCE
SCREAM

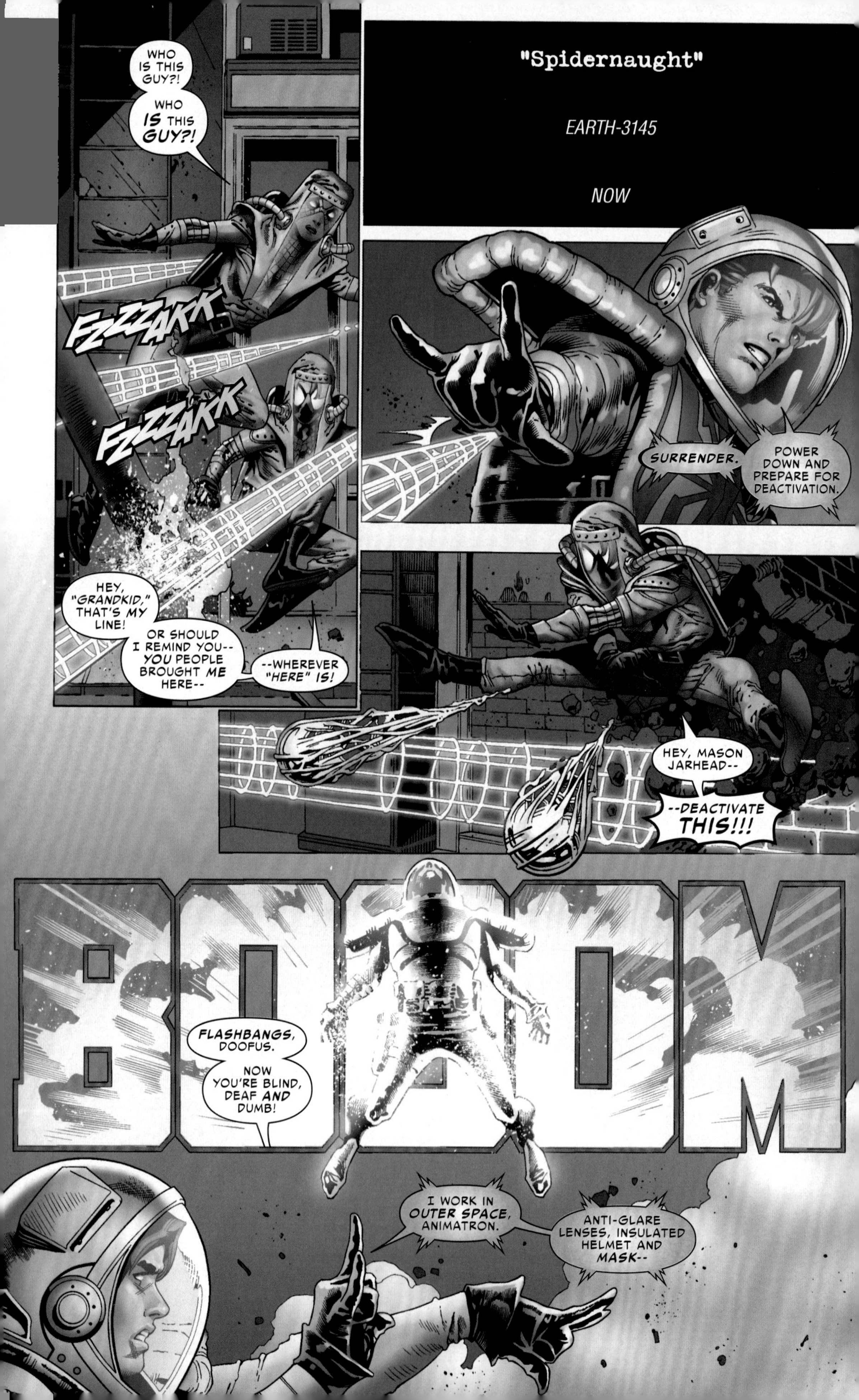

WHO IS THIS GUY?!
WHO IS THIS GUY?!
"Spidernaught"
EARTH-3145
NOW
FZZZAKK
FZZZAKK
SURRENDER.
POWER DOWN AND PREPARE FOR DEACTIVATION.
HEY, "GRANDKID," THAT'S MY LINE!
OR SHOULD I REMIND YOU-- YOU PEOPLE BROUGHT ME HERE--
--WHEREVER "HERE" IS!
HEY, MASON JARHEAD--
--DEACTIVATE THIS!!!
BOOOM
FLASHBANGS, DOOFUS.
NOW YOU'RE BLIND, DEAF AND DUMB!
I WORK IN OUTER SPACE, ANIMATRON.
ANTI-GLARE LENSES, INSULATED HELMET AND MASK--

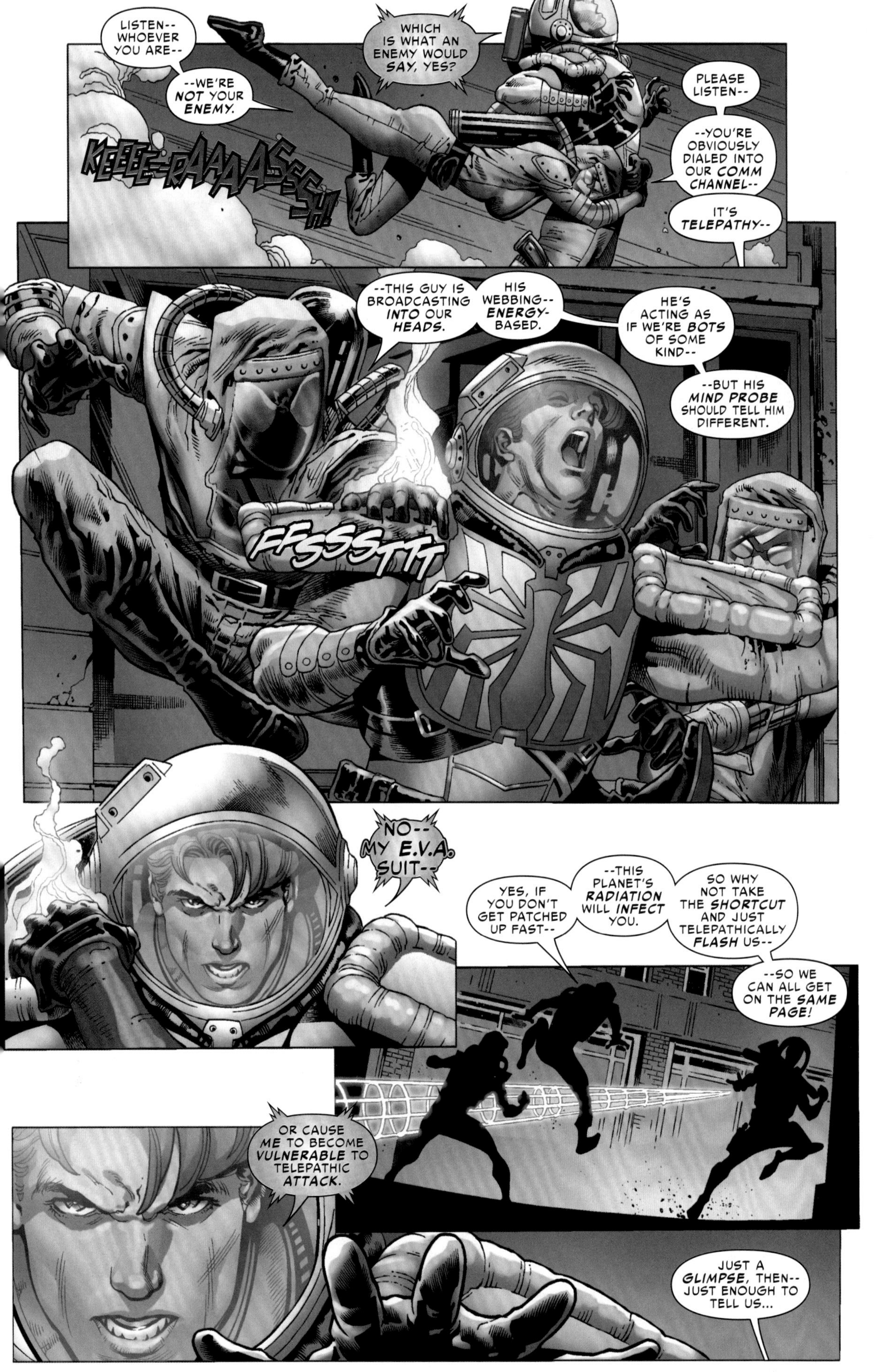

LISTEN-- WHOEVER YOU ARE--
--WE'RE NOT YOUR ENEMY.
WHICH IS WHAT AN ENEMY WOULD SAY, YES?
KEEEE-RAAAASSSH!
PLEASE LISTEN--
--YOU'RE OBVIOUSLY DIALED INTO OUR COMM CHANNEL--
IT'S TELEPATHY--
--THIS GUY IS BROADCASTING INTO OUR HEADS.
HIS WEBBING-- ENERGY-BASED.
HE'S ACTING AS IF WE'RE BOTS OF SOME KIND--
--BUT HIS MIND PROBE SHOULD TELL HIM DIFFERENT.
FFSSSTTT
NO-- MY E.V.A. SUIT--
YES, IF YOU DON'T GET PATCHED UP FAST--
--THIS PLANET'S RADIATION WILL INFECT YOU.
SO WHY NOT TAKE THE SHORTCUT AND JUST TELEPATHICALLY FLASH US--
--SO WE CAN ALL GET ON THE SAME PAGE!
OR CAUSE ME TO BECOME VULNERABLE TO TELEPATHIC ATTACK.
JUST A GLIMPSE, THEN-- JUST ENOUGH TO TELL US...

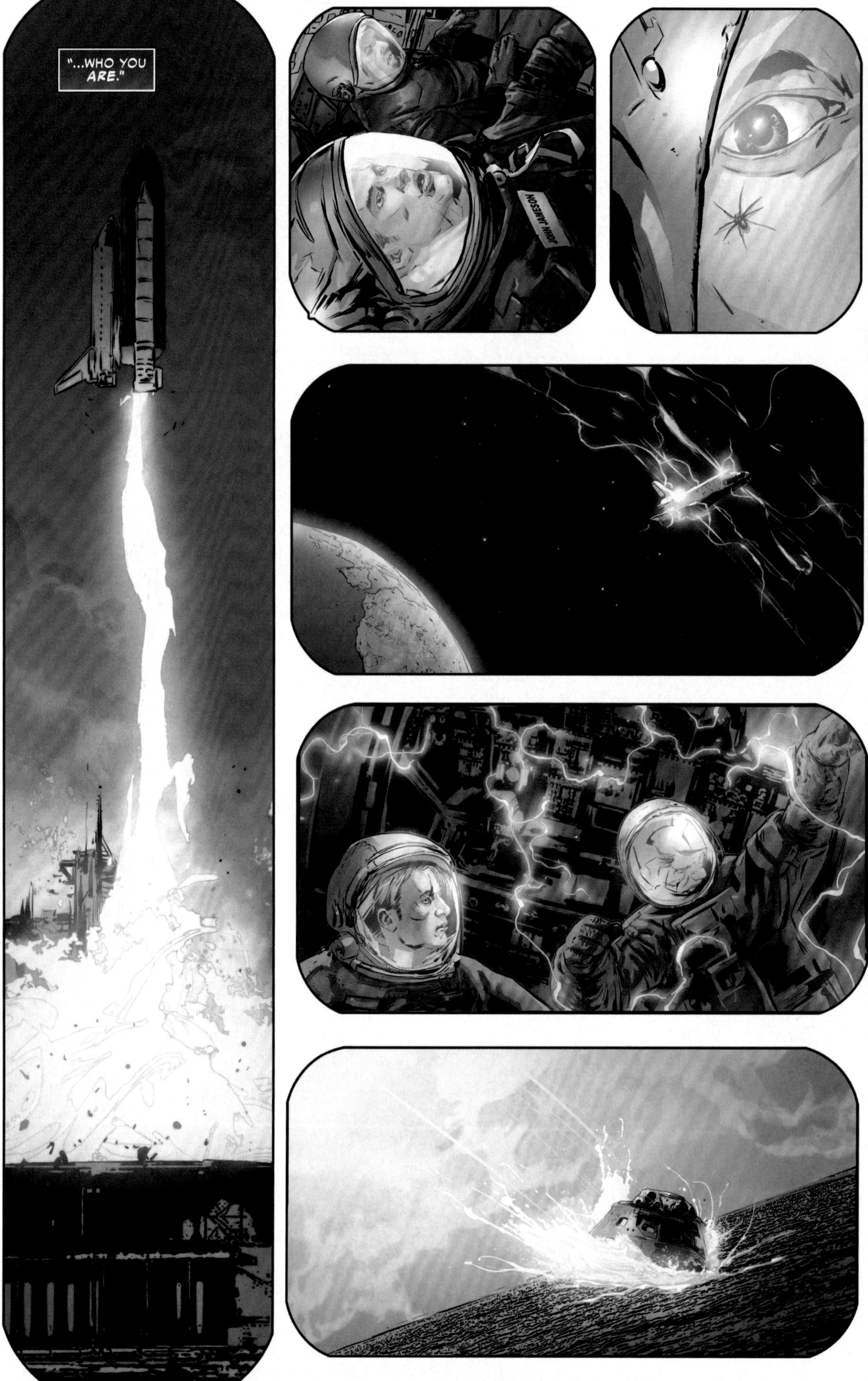
"...WHO YOU ARE."
JOHN JAMESON

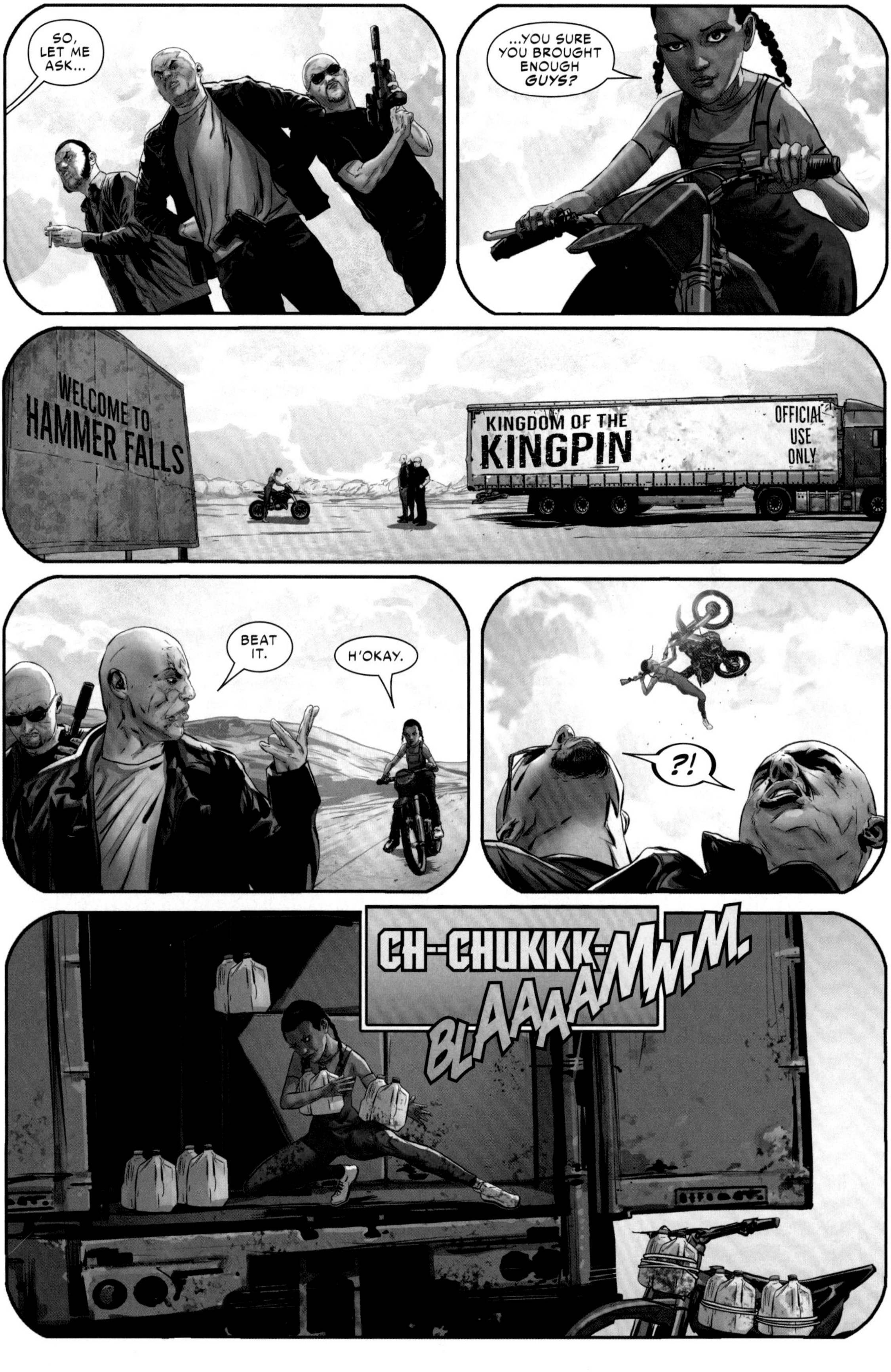
SO, LET ME ASK...
...YOU SURE YOU BROUGHT ENOUGH GUYS?
WELCOME TO HAMMER FALLS
KINGDOM OF THE KINGPIN
OFFICIAL USE ONLY
BEAT IT.
H'OKAY.
?!
CH-CHUKKK-BLAAAAMMM.

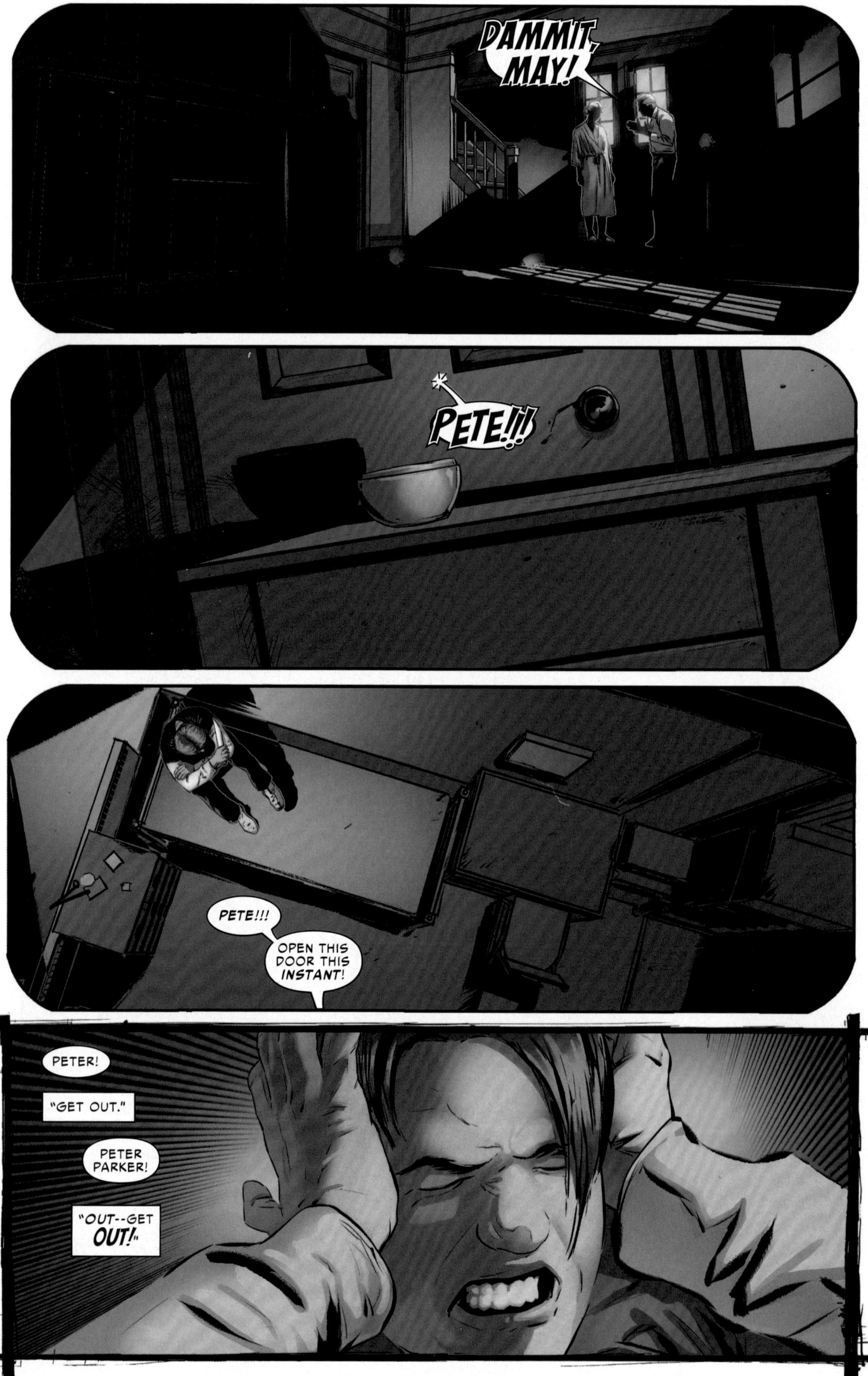

DAMMIT, MAY!
PETE!!!
PETE!!!
OPEN THIS DOOR THIS INSTANT!
PETER!
"GET OUT."
PETER PARKER!
"OUT--GET OUT!"

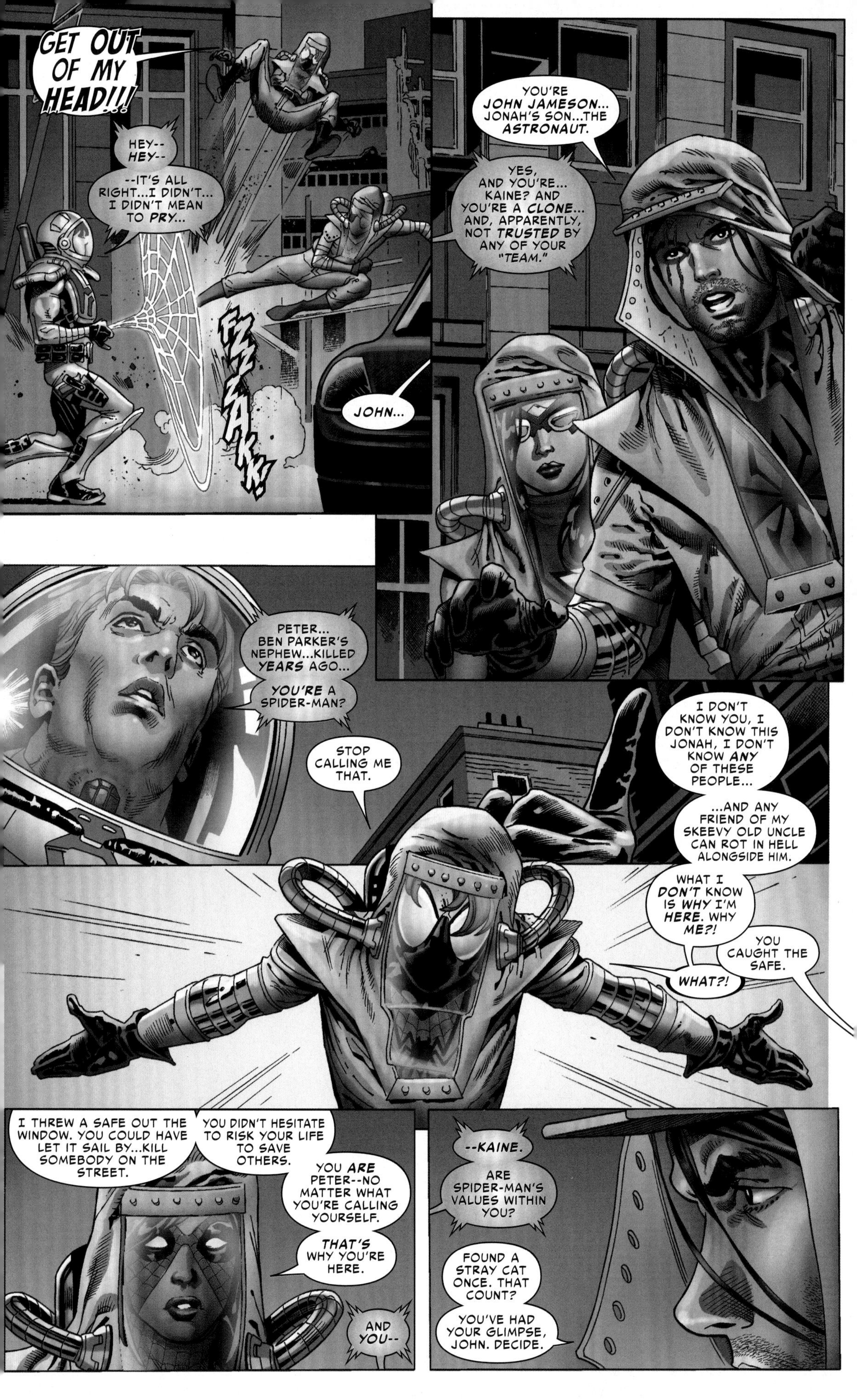
GET OUT OF MY HEAD!!!
HEY-- HEY--
--IT'S ALL RIGHT...I DIDN'T... I DIDN'T MEAN TO PRY...
FZZZAKK!
YOU'RE JOHN JAMESON... JONAH'S SON...THE ASTRONAUT.
YES, AND YOU'RE... KAINE? AND YOU'RE A CLONE... AND, APPARENTLY, NOT TRUSTED BY ANY OF YOUR "TEAM."
JOHN...
PETER... BEN PARKER'S NEPHEW...KILLED YEARS AGO...
YOU'RE A SPIDER-MAN?
STOP CALLING ME THAT.
I DON'T KNOW YOU, I DON'T KNOW THIS JONAH, I DON'T KNOW ANY OF THESE PEOPLE...
...AND ANY FRIEND OF MY SKEEVY OLD UNCLE CAN ROT IN HELL ALONGSIDE HIM.
WHAT I DON'T KNOW IS WHY I'M HERE. WHY ME?!
YOU CAUGHT THE SAFE.
WHAT?!
I THREW A SAFE OUT THE WINDOW. YOU COULD HAVE LET IT SAIL BY...KILL SOMEBODY ON THE STREET.
YOU DIDN'T HESITATE TO RISK YOUR LIFE TO SAVE OTHERS.
YOU ARE PETER--NO MATTER WHAT YOU'RE CALLING YOURSELF.
THAT'S WHY YOU'RE HERE.
AND YOU--
--KAINE.
ARE SPIDER-MAN'S VALUES WITHIN YOU?
FOUND A STRAY CAT ONCE. THAT COUNT?
YOU'VE HAD YOUR GLIMPSE, JOHN. DECIDE.

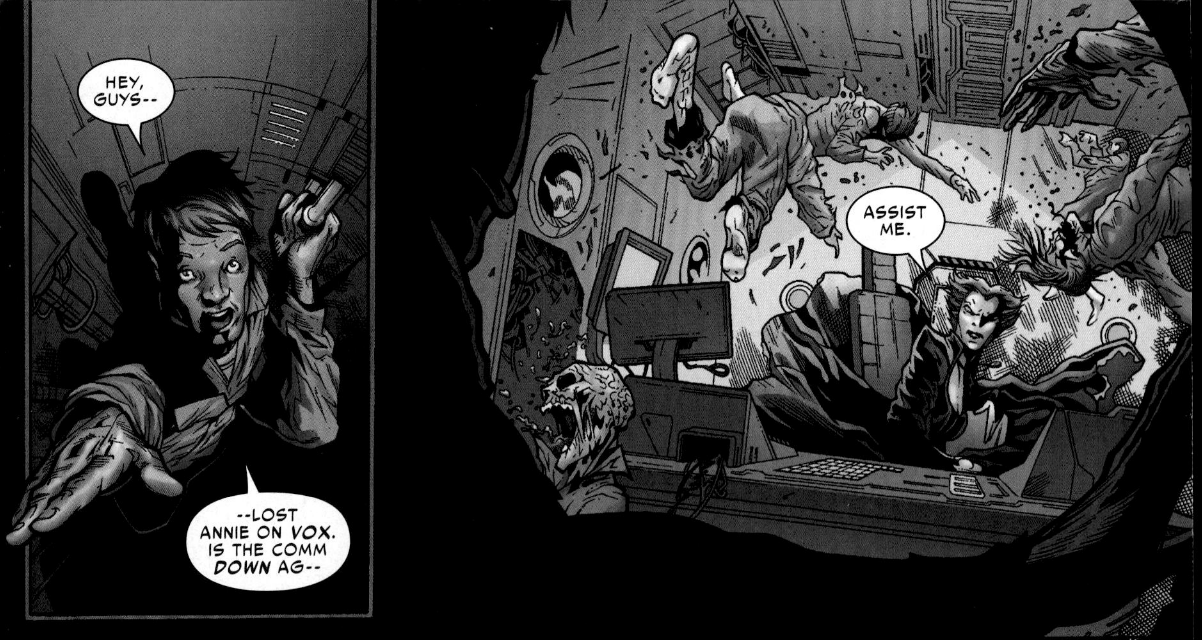
HEY, GUYS--
--LOST ANNIE ON VOX. IS THE COMM DOWN AG--
ASSIST ME.

"Aristokratia"

NAUTILUS OPS CENTER

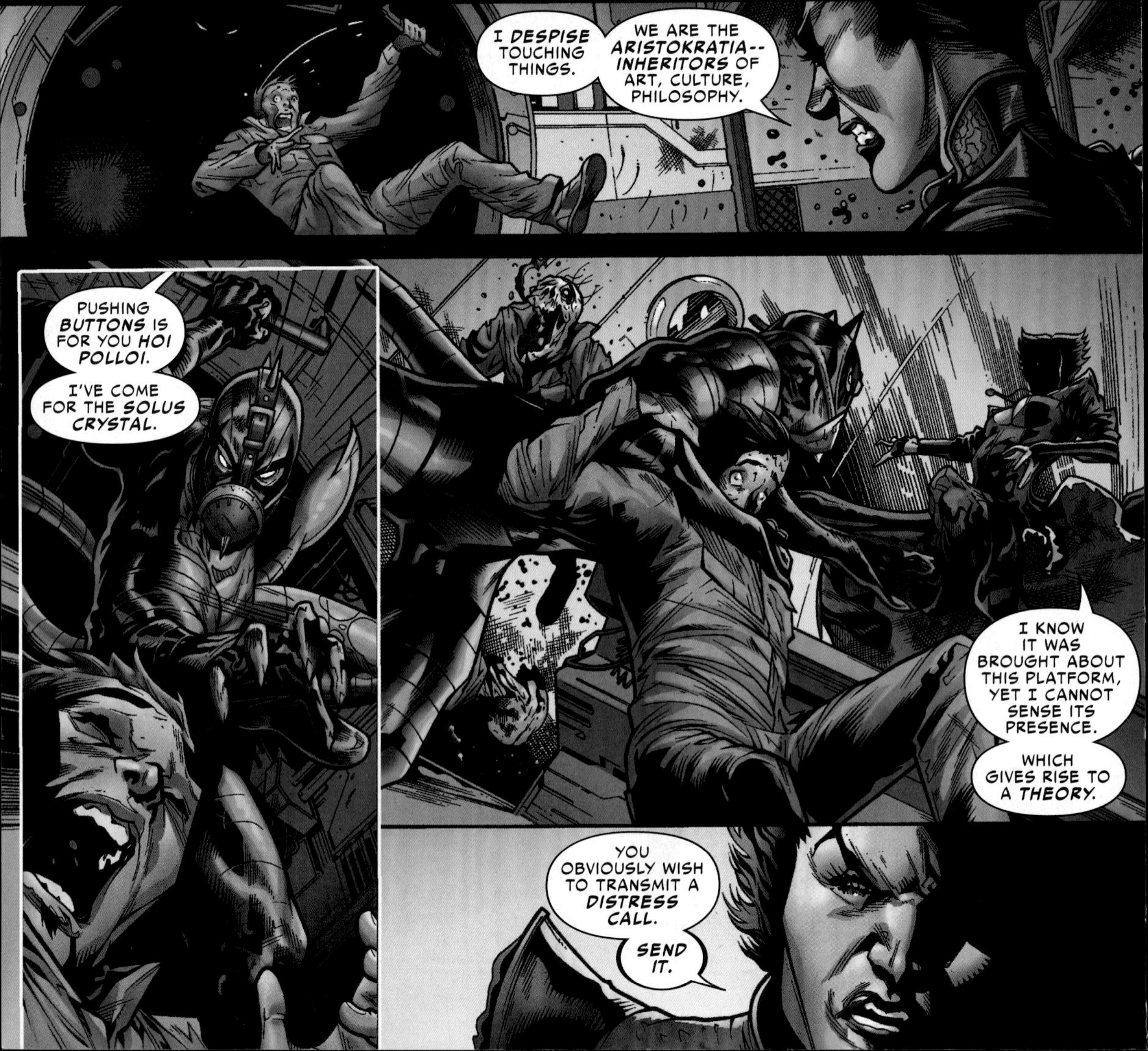
I DESPISE TOUCHING THINGS.
WE ARE THE ARISTOKRATIA-- INHERITORS OF ART, CULTURE, PHILOSOPHY.
PUSHING BUTTONS IS FOR YOU HOI POLLOI.
I'VE COME FOR THE SOLUS CRYSTAL.
I KNOW IT WAS BROUGHT ABOUT THIS PLATFORM, YET I CANNOT SENSE ITS PRESENCE.
WHICH GIVES RISE TO A THEORY.
YOU OBVIOUSLY WISH TO TRANSMIT A DISTRESS CALL.
SEND IT.

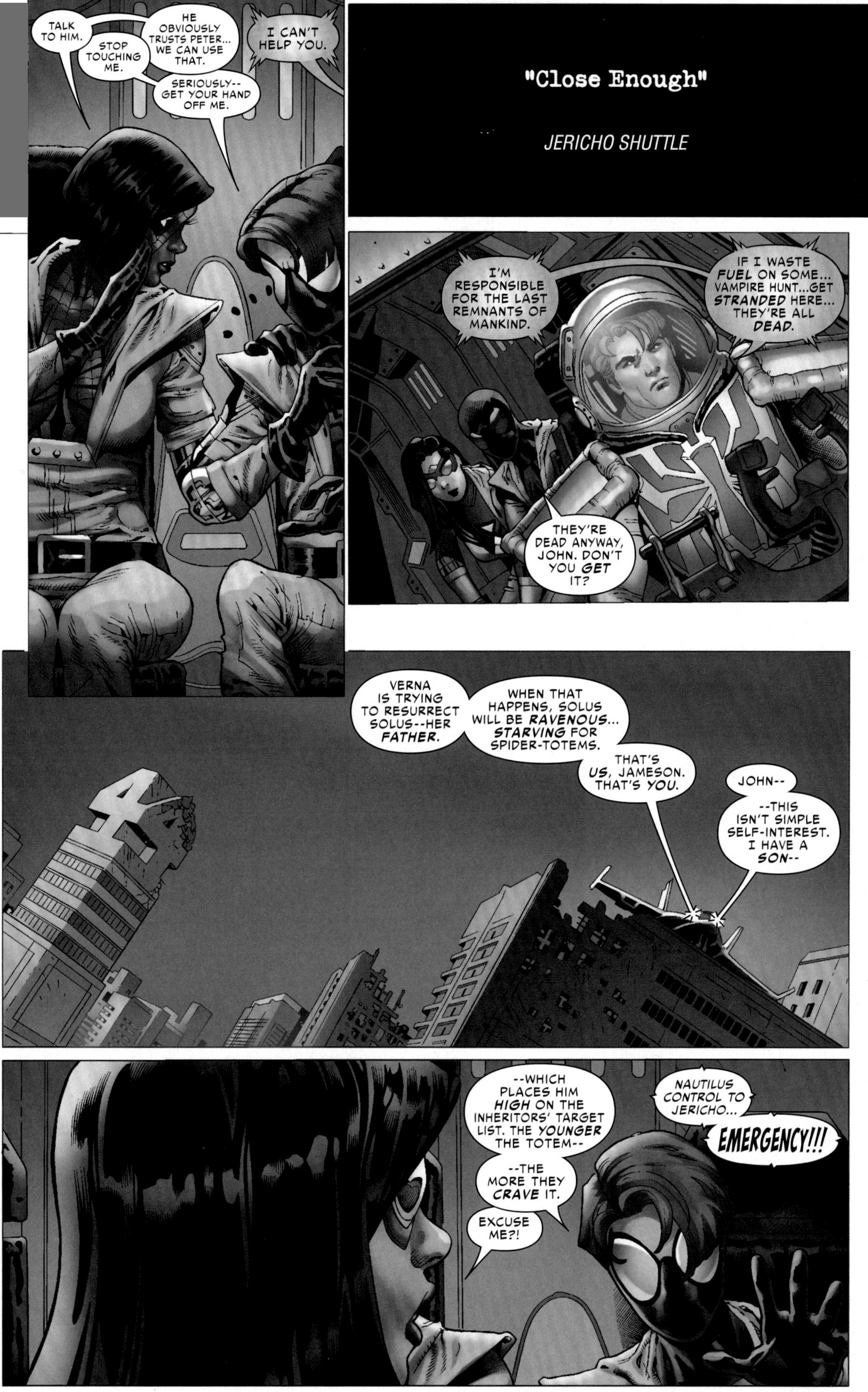
TALK TO HIM.
HE OBVIOUSLY TRUSTS PETER... WE CAN USE THAT.
STOP TOUCHING ME.
SERIOUSLY-- GET YOUR HAND OFF ME.
I CAN'T HELP YOU.
"Close Enough"
JERICHO SHUTTLE
I'M RESPONSIBLE FOR THE LAST REMNANTS OF MANKIND.
IF I WASTE FUEL ON SOME... VAMPIRE HUNT...GET STRANDED HERE... THEY'RE ALL DEAD.
THEY'RE DEAD ANYWAY, JOHN. DON'T YOU GET IT?
VERNA IS TRYING TO RESURRECT SOLUS--HER FATHER.
WHEN THAT HAPPENS, SOLUS WILL BE RAVENOUS... STARVING FOR SPIDER-TOTEMS.
THAT'S US, JAMESON. THAT'S YOU.
JOHN--
--THIS ISN'T SIMPLE SELF-INTEREST. I HAVE A SON--
--WHICH PLACES HIM HIGH ON THE INHERITORS' TARGET LIST. THE YOUNGER THE TOTEM--
--THE MORE THEY CRAVE IT.
EXCUSE ME?!
NAUTILUS CONTROL TO JERICHO...
EMERGENCY!!!

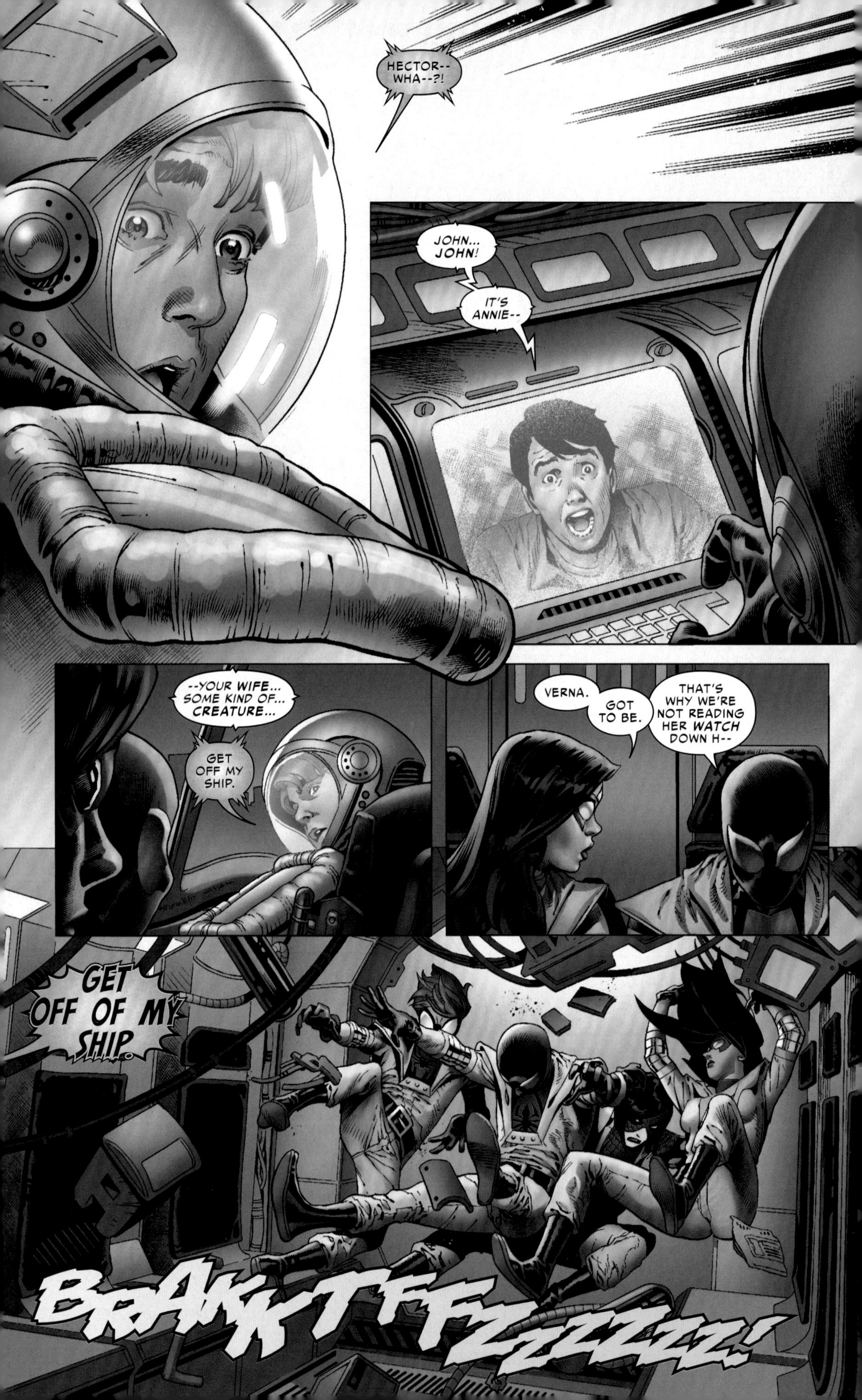
HECTOR-- WHA--?!
JOHN... JOHN!
IT'S ANNIE--
--YOUR WIFE... SOME KIND OF... CREATURE...
GET OFF MY SHIP.
VERNA.
GOT TO BE.
THAT'S WHY WE'RE NOT READING HER WATCH DOWN H--
GET OFF OF MY SHIP
BRAKKTTFFZZZZZZZ!

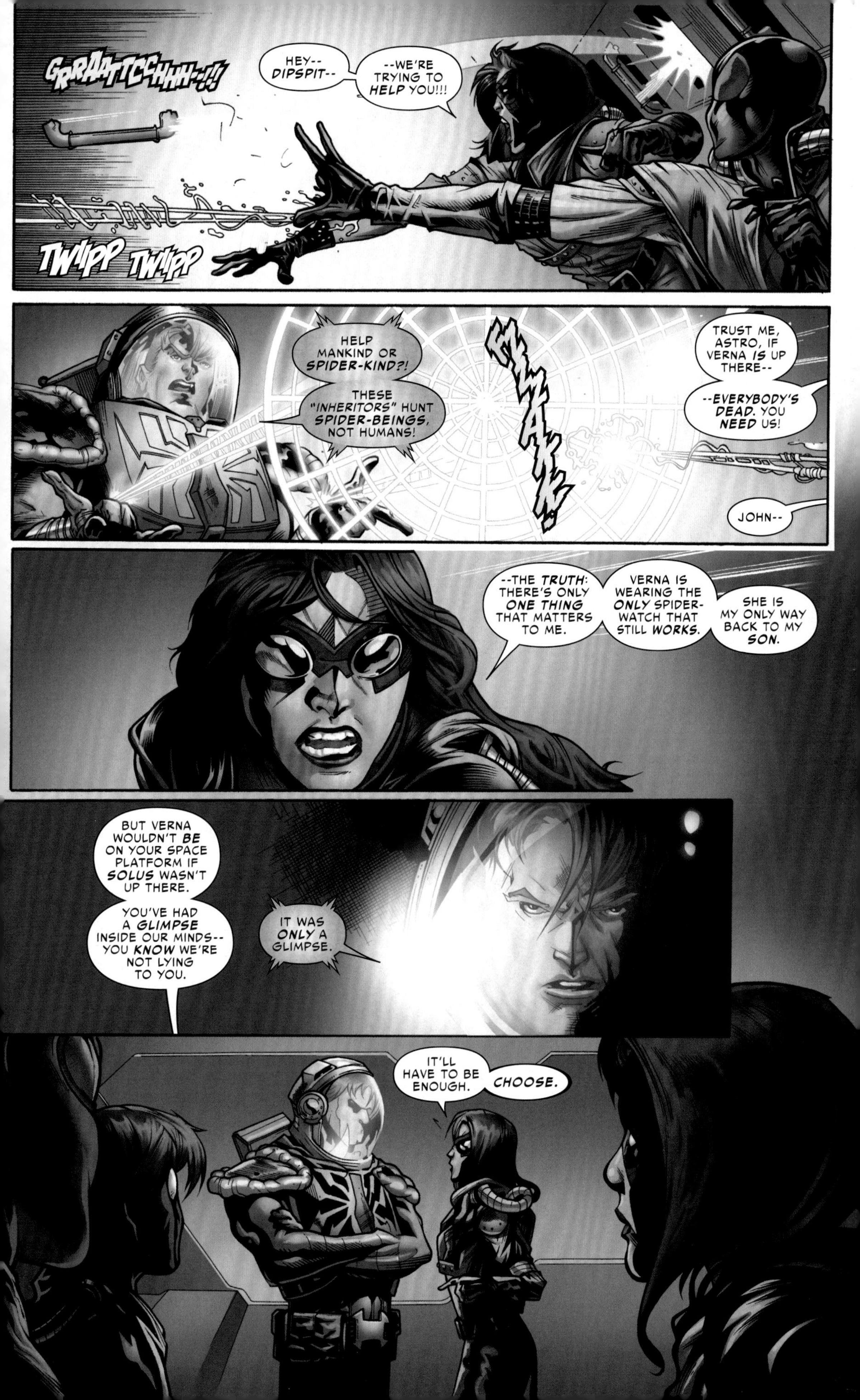

GRRAATTCCHHH--!!!
HEY-- DIPSPIT--
--WE'RE TRYING TO HELP YOU!!!
TWIPP TWIPP
HELP MANKIND OR SPIDER-KIND?!
THESE "INHERITORS" HUNT SPIDER-BEINGS, NOT HUMANS!
KNAKK!
TRUST ME, ASTRO, IF VERNA IS UP THERE--
--EVERYBODY'S DEAD. YOU NEED US!
JOHN--
--THE TRUTH: THERE'S ONLY ONE THING THAT MATTERS TO ME.
VERNA IS WEARING THE ONLY SPIDER-WATCH THAT STILL WORKS.
SHE IS MY ONLY WAY BACK TO MY SON.
BUT VERNA WOULDN'T BE ON YOUR SPACE PLATFORM IF SOLUS WASN'T UP THERE.
YOU'VE HAD A GLIMPSE INSIDE OUR MINDS-- YOU KNOW WE'RE NOT LYING TO YOU.
IT WAS ONLY A GLIMPSE.
IT'LL HAVE TO BE ENOUGH.
CHOOSE.

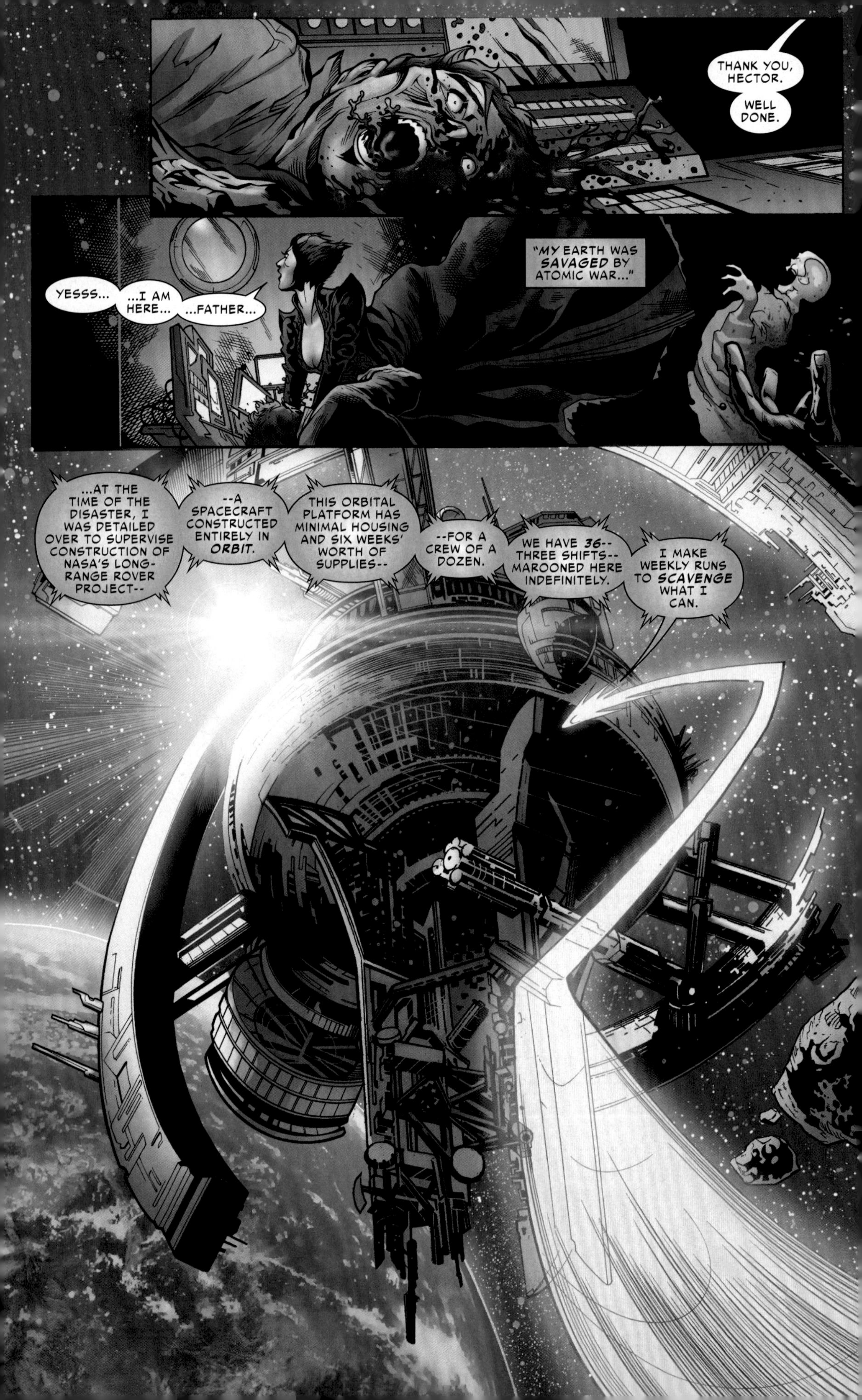
THANK YOU, HECTOR.
WELL DONE.
YESSS...
...I AM HERE...
...FATHER...
"MY EARTH WAS SAVAGED BY ATOMIC WAR..."
...AT THE TIME OF THE DISASTER, I WAS DETAILED OVER TO SUPERVISE CONSTRUCTION OF NASA'S LONG-RANGE ROVER PROJECT--
--A SPACECRAFT CONSTRUCTED ENTIRELY IN ORBIT.
THIS ORBITAL PLATFORM HAS MINIMAL HOUSING AND SIX WEEKS' WORTH OF SUPPLIES--
--FOR A CREW OF A DOZEN.
WE HAVE 36-- THREE SHIFTS-- MAROONED HERE INDEFINITELY.
I MAKE WEEKLY RUNS TO SCAVENGE WHAT I CAN.

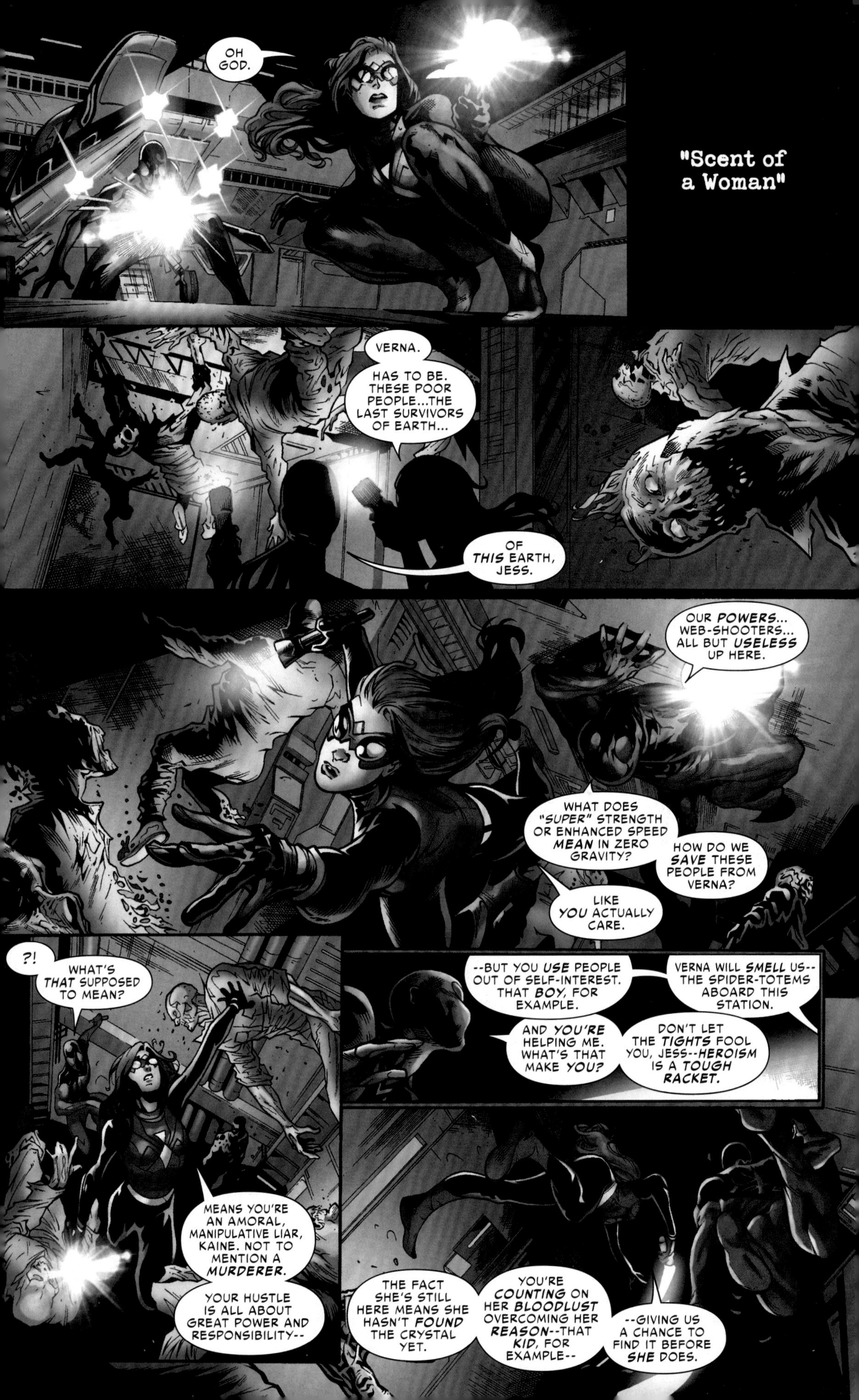
OH GOD.
"Scent of a Woman"
VERNA.
HAS TO BE. THESE POOR PEOPLE...THE LAST SURVIVORS OF EARTH...
OF THIS EARTH, JESS.
OUR POWERS... WEB-SHOOTERS... ALL BUT USELESS UP HERE.
WHAT DOES "SUPER" STRENGTH OR ENHANCED SPEED MEAN IN ZERO GRAVITY?
HOW DO WE SAVE THESE PEOPLE FROM VERNA?
LIKE YOU ACTUALLY CARE.
?!
WHAT'S THAT SUPPOSED TO MEAN?
MEANS YOU'RE AN AMORAL, MANIPULATIVE LIAR, KAINE. NOT TO MENTION A MURDERER.
YOUR HUSTLE IS ALL ABOUT GREAT POWER AND RESPONSIBILITY--
--BUT YOU USE PEOPLE OUT OF SELF-INTEREST. THAT BOY, FOR EXAMPLE.
AND YOU'RE HELPING ME. WHAT'S THAT MAKE YOU?
VERNA WILL SMELL US-- THE SPIDER-TOTEMS ABOARD THIS STATION.
DON'T LET THE TIGHTS FOOL YOU, JESS--HEROISM IS A TOUGH RACKET.
THE FACT SHE'S STILL HERE MEANS SHE HASN'T FOUND THE CRYSTAL YET.
YOU'RE COUNTING ON HER BLOODLUST OVERCOMING HER REASON--THAT KID, FOR EXAMPLE--
--GIVING US A CHANCE TO FIND IT BEFORE SHE DOES.

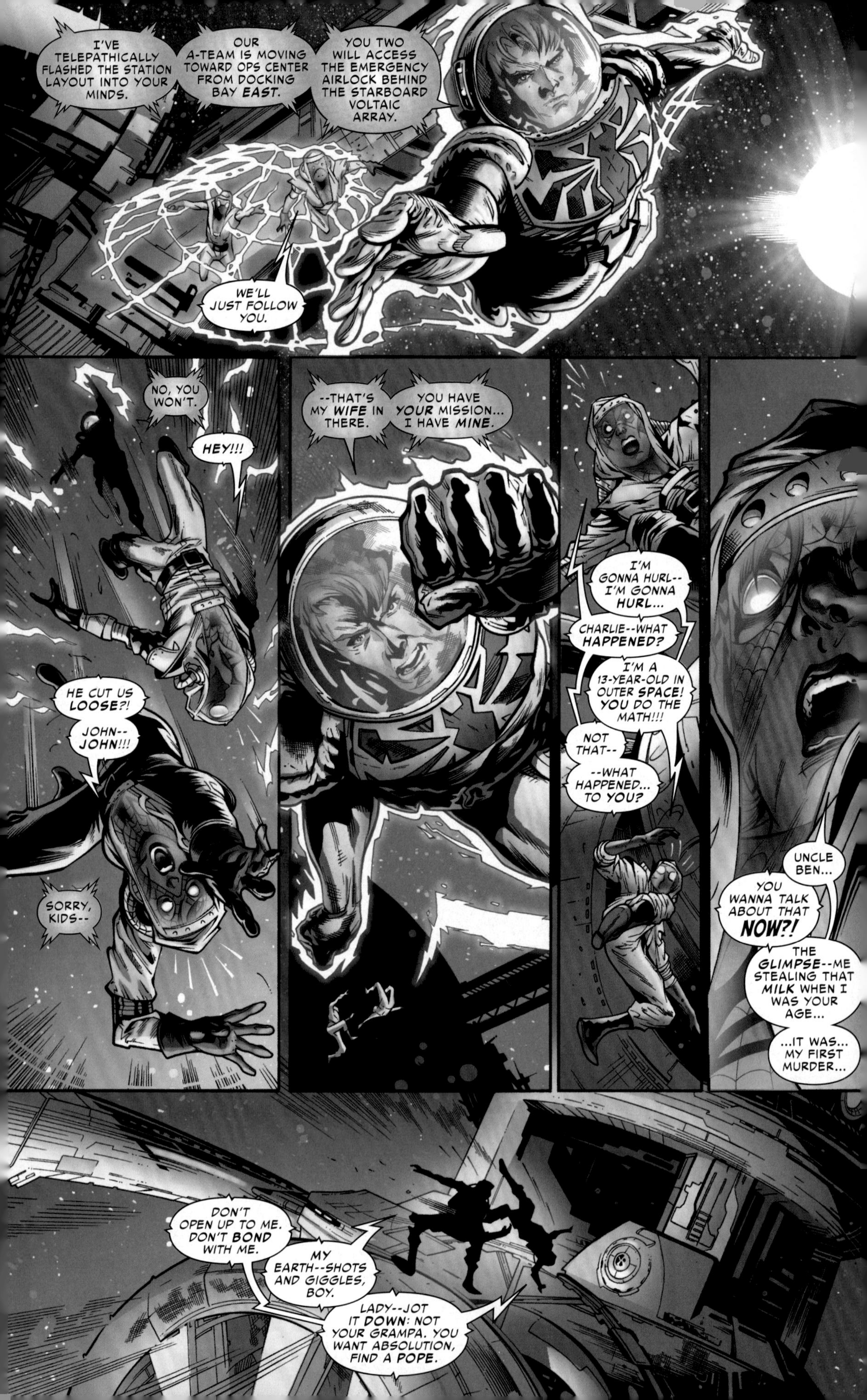
I'VE TELEPATHICALLY FLASHED THE STATION LAYOUT INTO YOUR MINDS.
OUR A-TEAM IS MOVING TOWARD OPS CENTER FROM DOCKING BAY EAST.
YOU TWO WILL ACCESS THE EMERGENCY AIRLOCK BEHIND THE STARBOARD VOLTAIC ARRAY.
WE'LL JUST FOLLOW YOU.
NO, YOU WON'T.
HEY!!!
HE CUT US LOOSE?!
JOHN-- JOHN!!!
SORRY, KIDS--
--THAT'S MY WIFE IN THERE.
YOU HAVE YOUR MISSION... I HAVE MINE.
I'M GONNA HURL-- I'M GONNA HURL...
CHARLIE--WHAT HAPPENED?
I'M A 13-YEAR-OLD IN OUTER SPACE! YOU DO THE MATH!!!
NOT THAT--
--WHAT HAPPENED... TO YOU?
UNCLE BEN...
YOU WANNA TALK ABOUT THAT NOW?!
THE GLIMPSE--ME STEALING THAT MILK WHEN I WAS YOUR AGE...
...IT WAS... MY FIRST MURDER...
DON'T OPEN UP TO ME. DON'T BOND WITH ME.
MY EARTH--SHOTS AND GIGGLES, BOY.
LADY--JOT IT DOWN: NOT YOUR GRAMPA. YOU WANT ABSOLUTION, FIND A POPE.

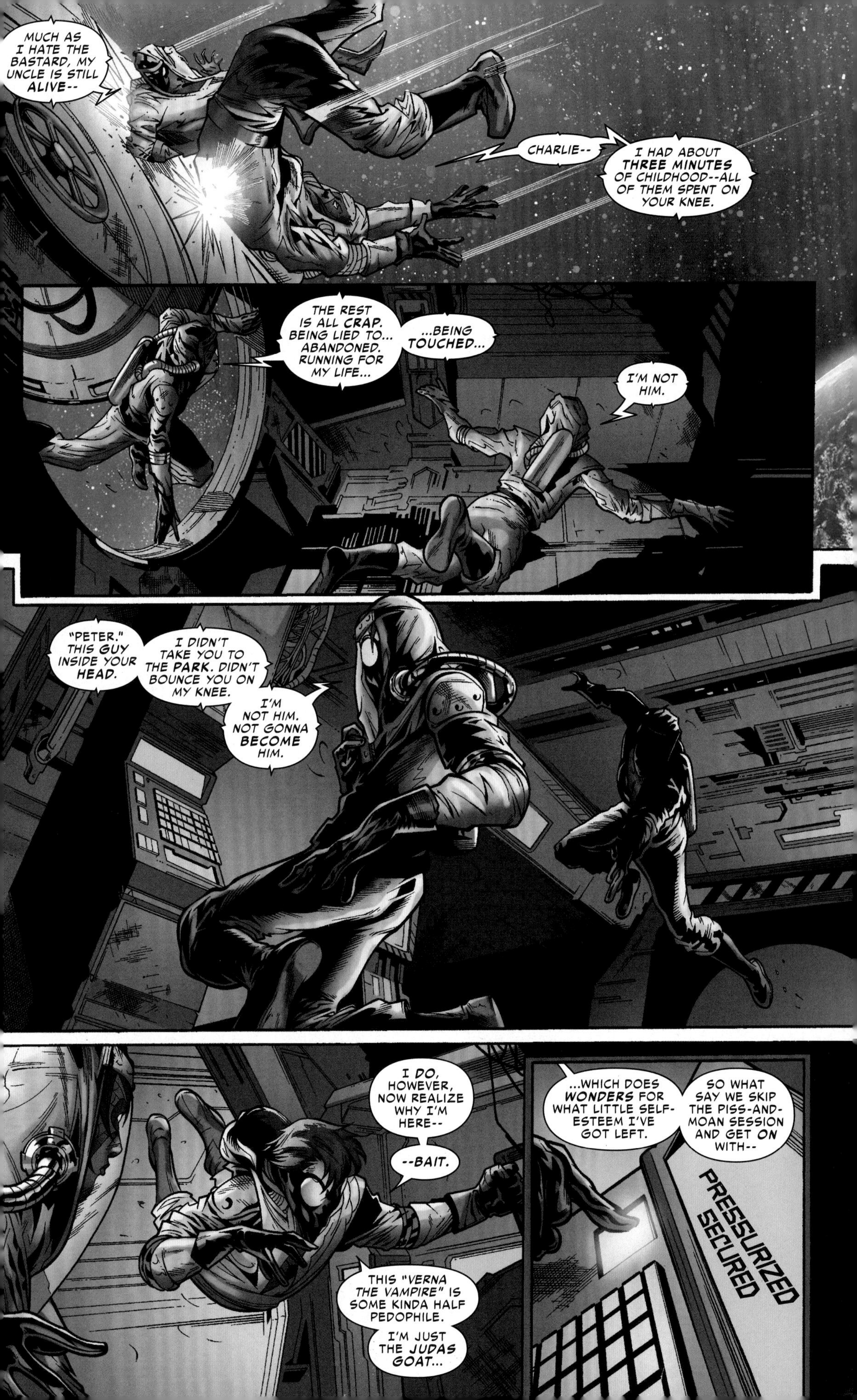
MUCH AS I HATE THE BASTARD, MY UNCLE IS STILL ALIVE--
CHARLIE--
I HAD ABOUT THREE MINUTES OF CHILDHOOD--ALL OF THEM SPENT ON YOUR KNEE.
THE REST IS ALL CRAP. BEING LIED TO... ABANDONED. RUNNING FOR MY LIFE...
...BEING TOUCHED...
I'M NOT HIM.
"PETER." THIS GUY INSIDE YOUR HEAD.
I DIDN'T TAKE YOU TO THE PARK. DIDN'T BOUNCE YOU ON MY KNEE.
I'M NOT HIM. NOT GONNA BECOME HIM.
I DO, HOWEVER, NOW REALIZE WHY I'M HERE--
--BAIT.
THIS "VERNA THE VAMPIRE" IS SOME KINDA HALF PEDOPHILE.
I'M JUST THE JUDAS GOAT...
...WHICH DOES WONDERS FOR WHAT LITTLE SELF-ESTEEM I'VE GOT LEFT.
SO WHAT SAY WE SKIP THE PISS-AND-MOAN SESSION AND GET ON WITH--
PRESSURIZED SECURED

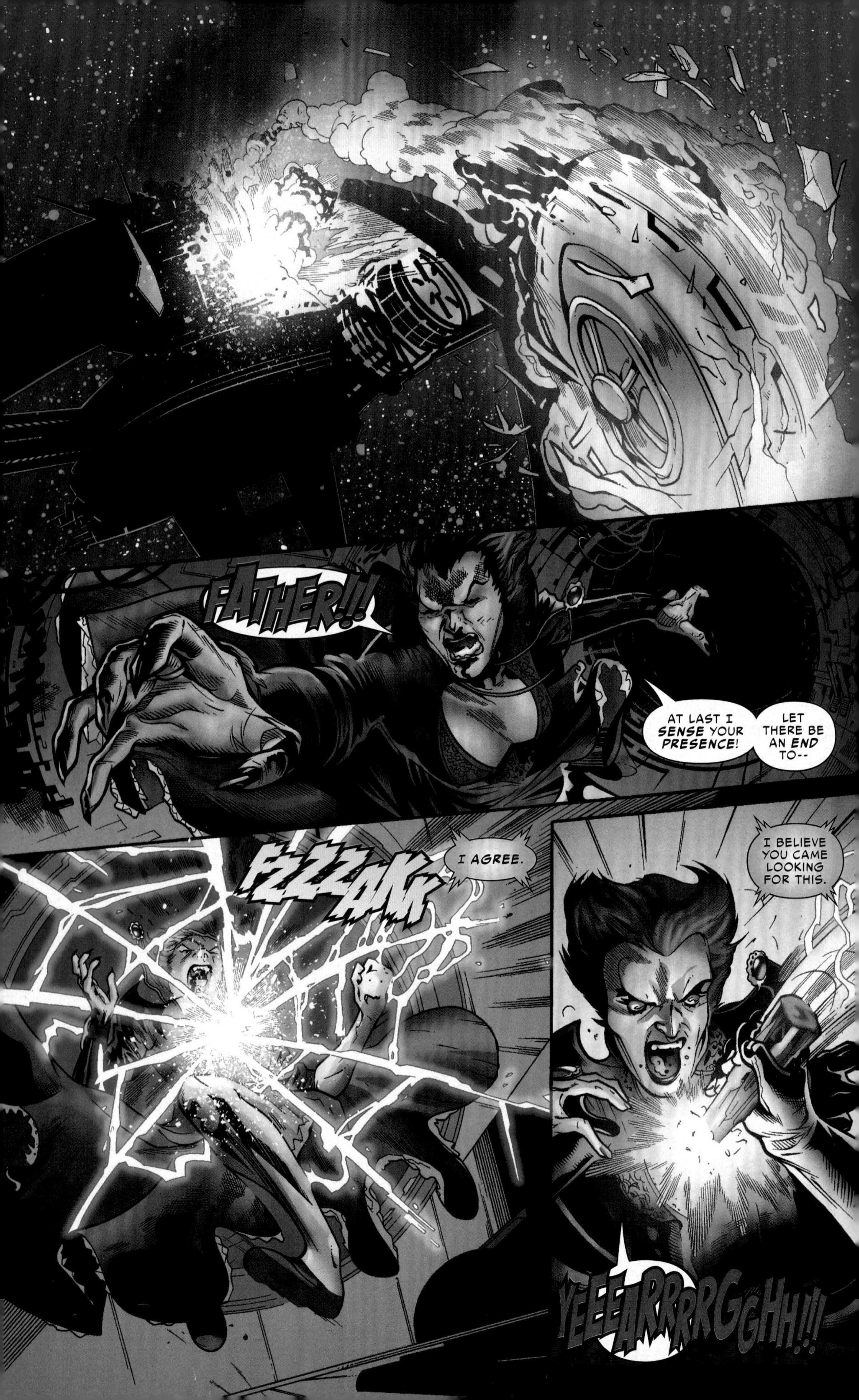

FATHER!!!
AT LAST I SENSE YOUR PRESENCE!
LET THERE BE AN END TO--
FZZZAK
I AGREE.
I BELIEVE YOU CAME LOOKING FOR THIS.
YEEEARRRRRGGHH!!!

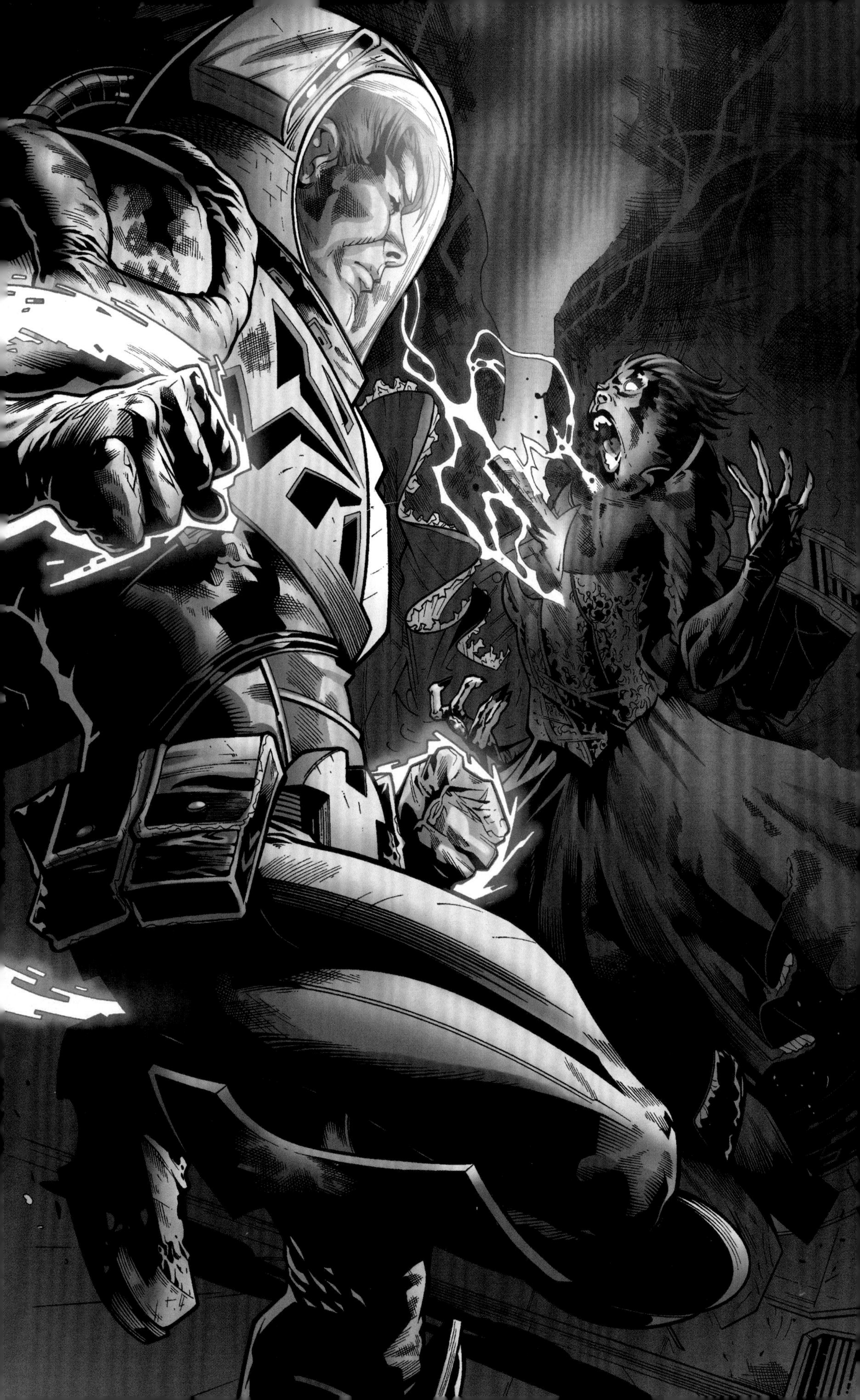

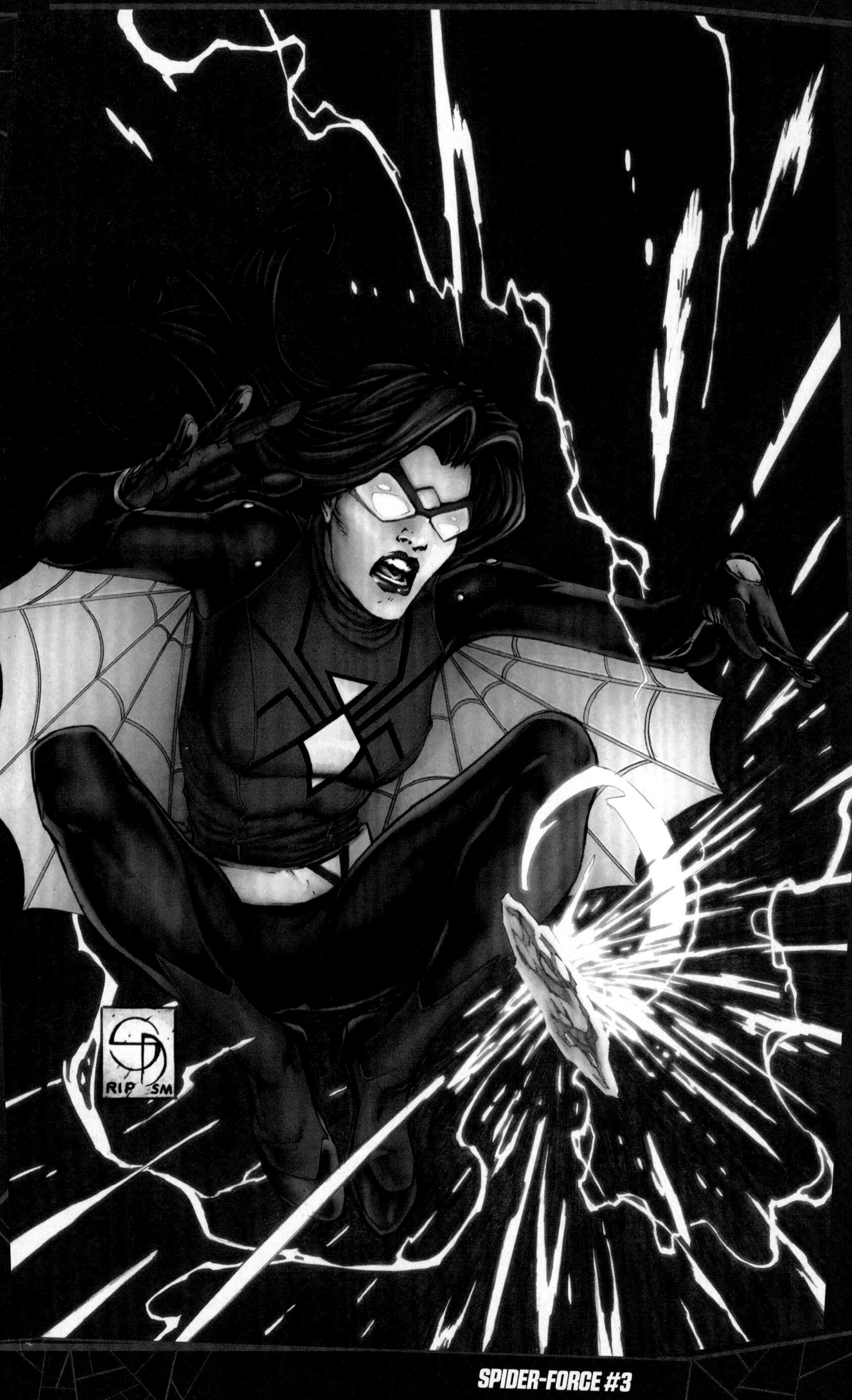

SPIDER-FORCE #3

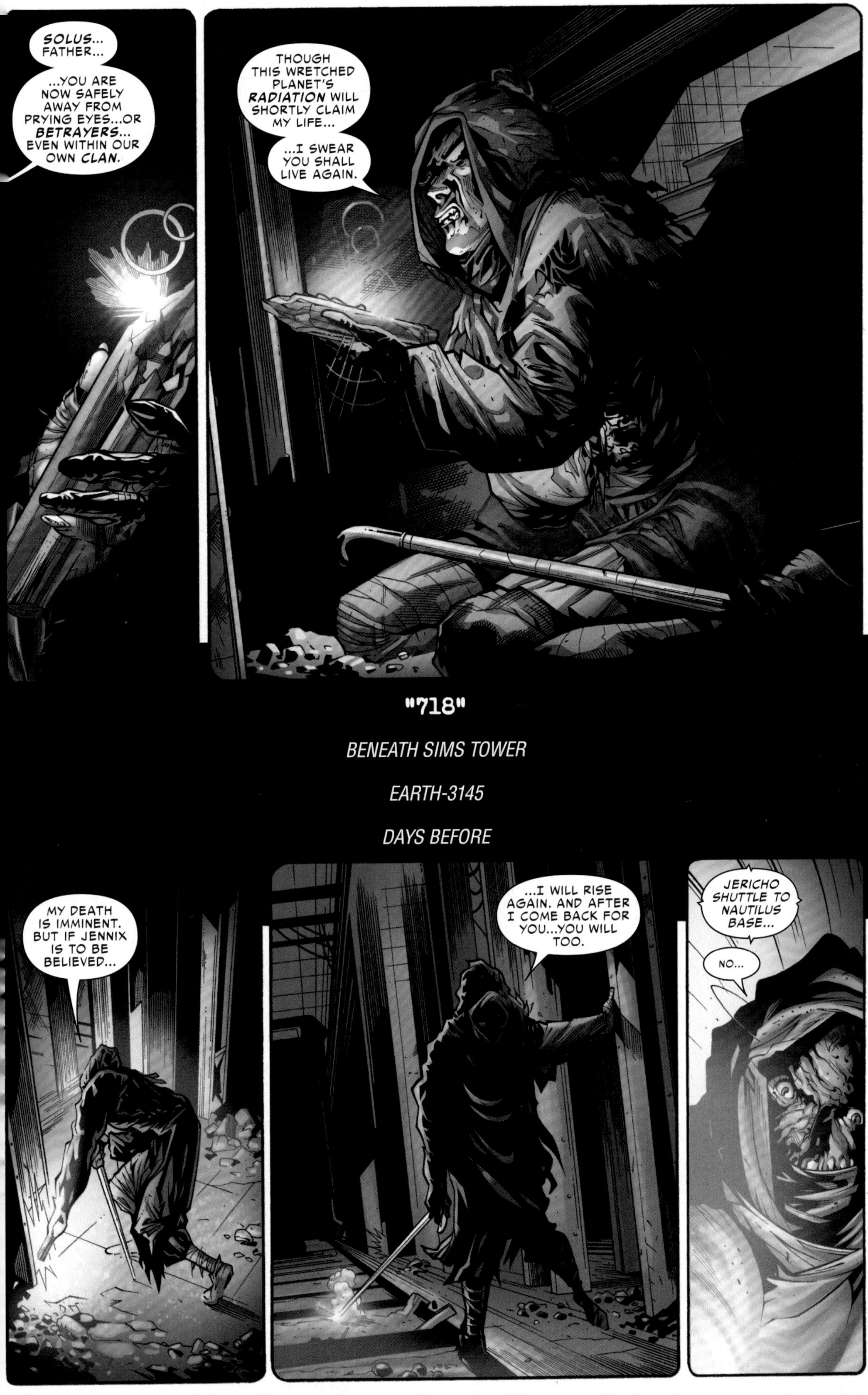
SOLUS... FATHER...
...YOU ARE NOW SAFELY AWAY FROM PRYING EYES...OR BETRAYERS... EVEN WITHIN OUR OWN CLAN.
THOUGH THIS WRETCHED PLANET'S RADIATION WILL SHORTLY CLAIM MY LIFE...
...I SWEAR YOU SHALL LIVE AGAIN.
"718"
BENEATH SIMS TOWER
EARTH-3145
DAYS BEFORE
MY DEATH IS IMMINENT. BUT IF JENNIX IS TO BE BELIEVED...
...I WILL RISE AGAIN. AND AFTER I COME BACK FOR YOU...YOU WILL TOO.
JERICHO SHUTTLE TO NAUTILUS BASE...
NO...

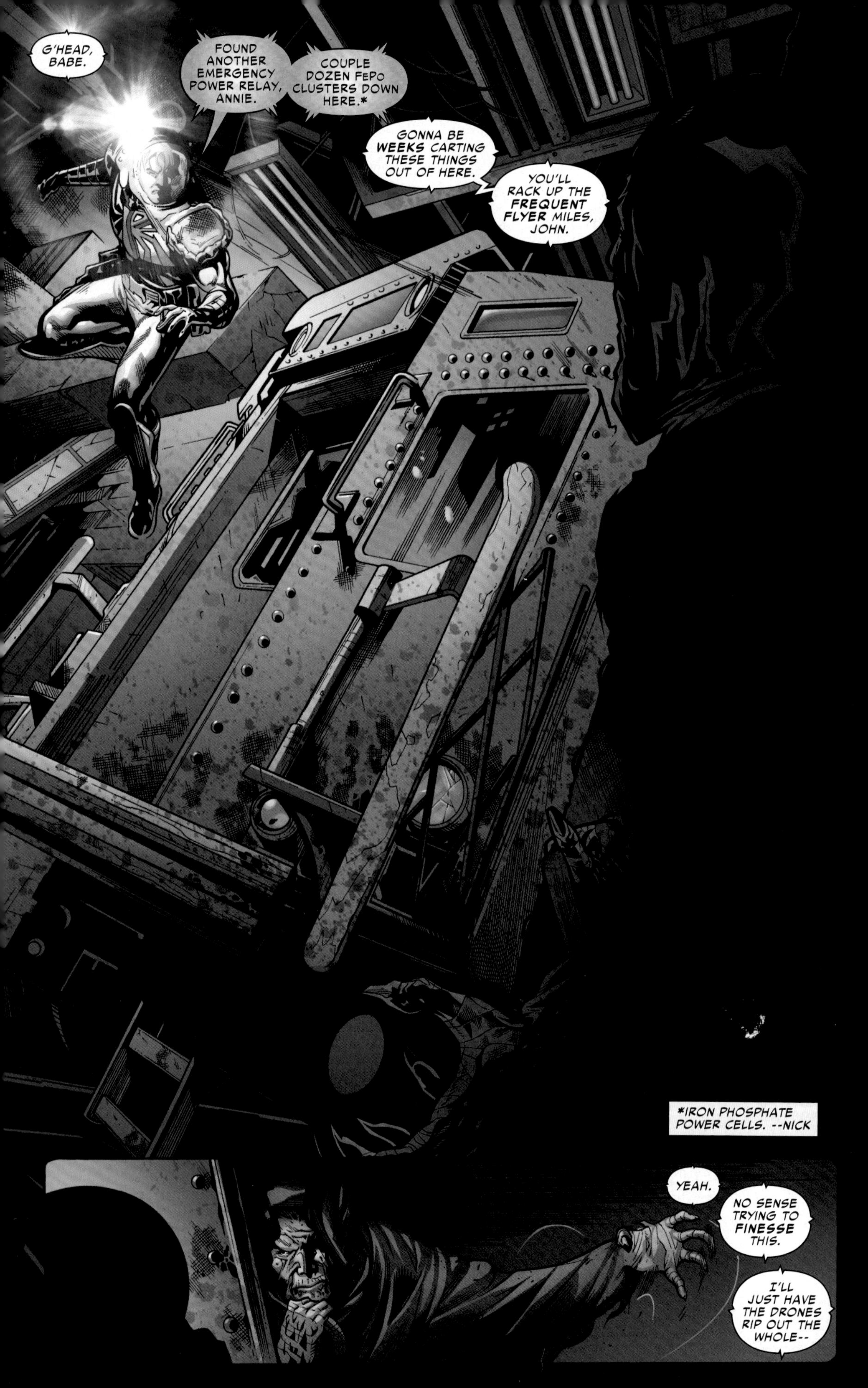
G'HEAD, BABE.
FOUND ANOTHER EMERGENCY POWER RELAY, ANNIE.
COUPLE DOZEN FePo CLUSTERS DOWN HERE.*
GONNA BE WEEKS CARTING THESE THINGS OUT OF HERE.
YOU'LL RACK UP THE FREQUENT FLYER MILES, JOHN.
*IRON PHOSPHATE POWER CELLS. --NICK
YEAH.
NO SENSE TRYING TO FINESSE THIS.
I'LL JUST HAVE THE DRONES RIP OUT THE WHOLE--

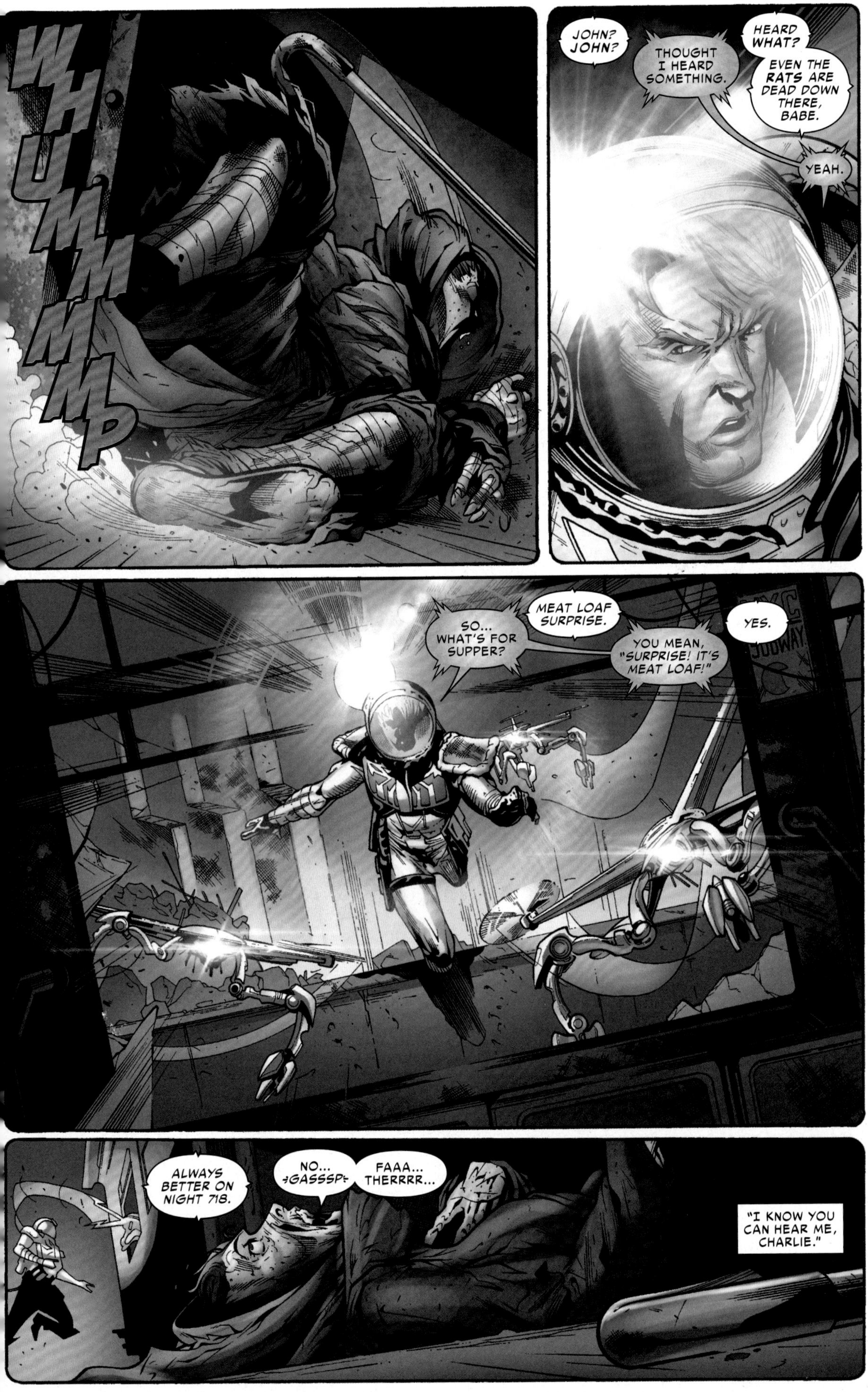
WHUMMMMP
JOHN? JOHN?
THOUGHT I HEARD SOMETHING.
HEARD WHAT?
EVEN THE RATS ARE DEAD DOWN THERE, BABE.
YEAH.
SO... WHAT'S FOR SUPPER?
MEAT LOAF SURPRISE.
YOU MEAN, "SURPRISE! IT'S MEAT LOAF!"
YES.
ALWAYS BETTER ON NIGHT 718.
NO... -GASSSP-
FAAA... THERRRR...
"I KNOW YOU CAN HEAR ME, CHARLIE."

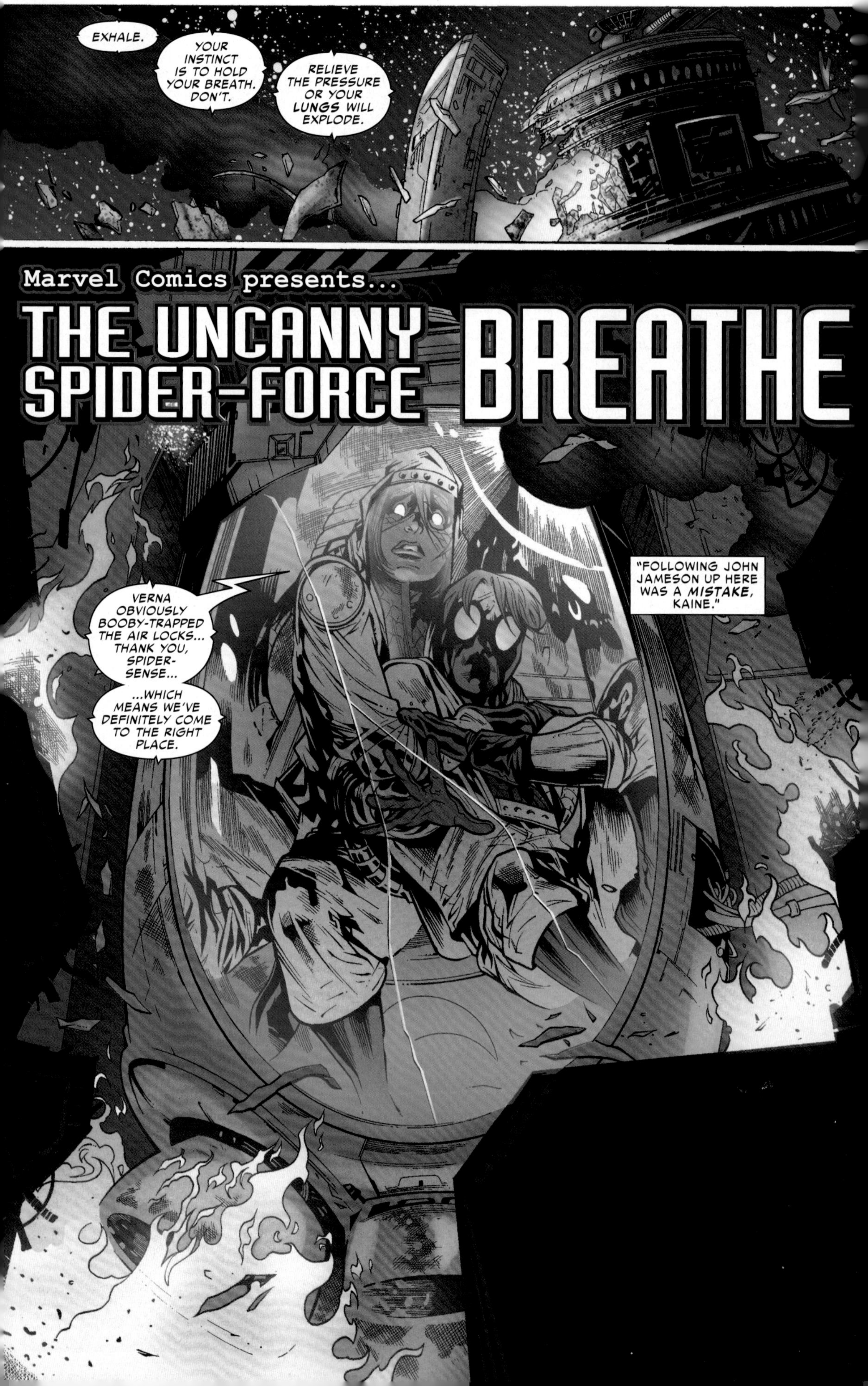

EXHALE.
YOUR INSTINCT IS TO HOLD YOUR BREATH. DON'T.
RELIEVE THE PRESSURE OR YOUR LUNGS WILL EXPLODE.
Marvel Comics presents...
THE UNCANNY SPIDER-FORCE
BREATHE
"FOLLOWING JOHN JAMESON UP HERE WAS A MISTAKE, KAINE."
VERNA OBVIOUSLY BOOBY-TRAPPED THE AIR LOCKS... THANK YOU, SPIDER-SENSE...
...WHICH MEANS WE'VE DEFINITELY COME TO THE RIGHT PLACE.

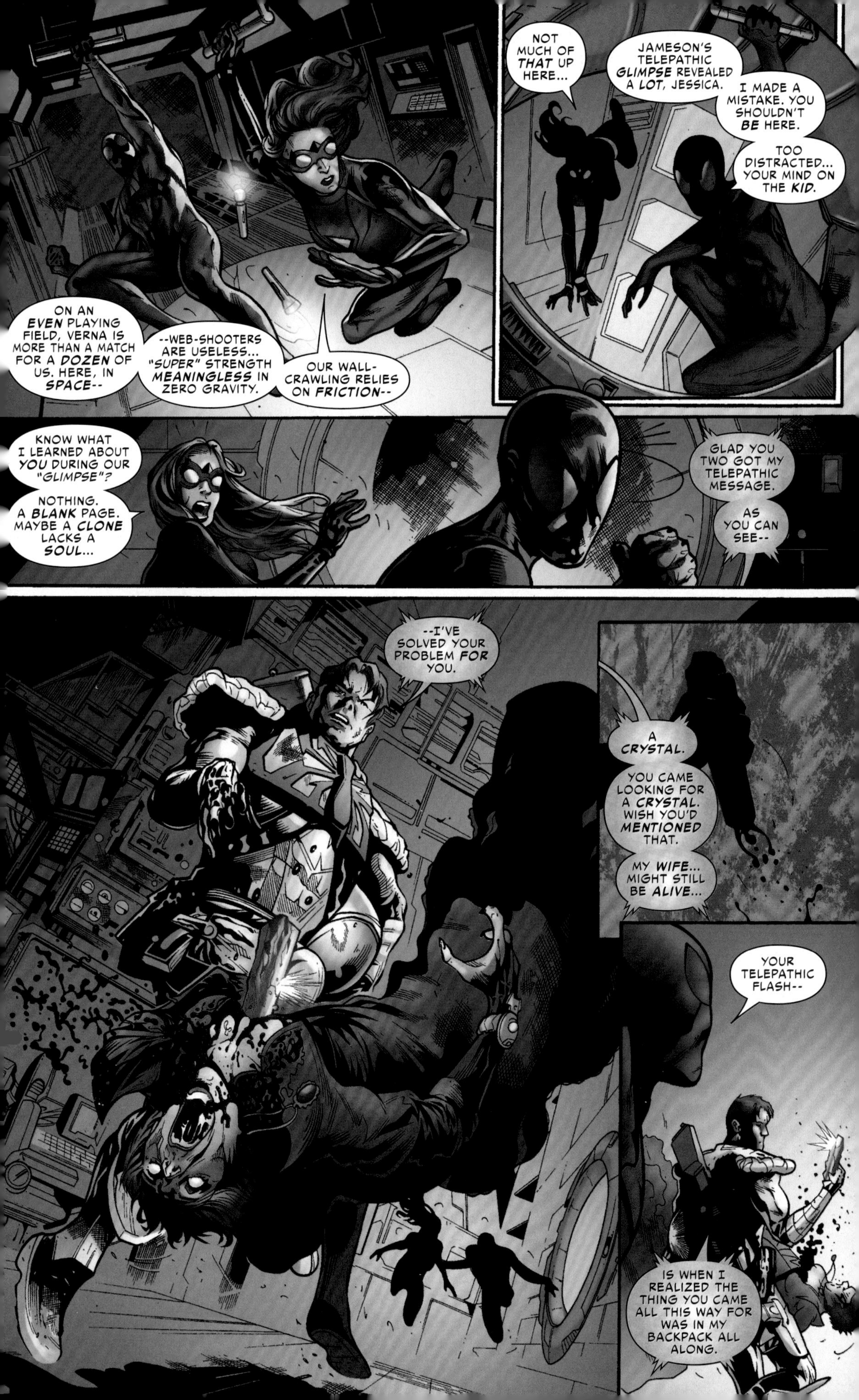
ON AN EVEN PLAYING FIELD, VERNA IS MORE THAN A MATCH FOR A DOZEN OF US. HERE, IN SPACE--
--WEB-SHOOTERS ARE USELESS... "SUPER" STRENGTH MEANINGLESS IN ZERO GRAVITY.
OUR WALL-CRAWLING RELIES ON FRICTION--
NOT MUCH OF THAT UP HERE...
JAMESON'S TELEPATHIC GLIMPSE REVEALED A LOT, JESSICA.
I MADE A MISTAKE. YOU SHOULDN'T BE HERE.
TOO DISTRACTED... YOUR MIND ON THE KID.
KNOW WHAT I LEARNED ABOUT YOU DURING OUR "GLIMPSE"?
NOTHING. A BLANK PAGE. MAYBE A CLONE LACKS A SOUL...
GLAD YOU TWO GOT MY TELEPATHIC MESSAGE.
AS YOU CAN SEE--
--I'VE SOLVED YOUR PROBLEM FOR YOU.
A CRYSTAL.
YOU CAME LOOKING FOR A CRYSTAL. WISH YOU'D MENTIONED THAT.
MY WIFE... MIGHT STILL BE ALIVE...
YOUR TELEPATHIC FLASH--
IS WHEN I REALIZED THE THING YOU CAME ALL THIS WAY FOR WAS IN MY BACKPACK ALL ALONG.

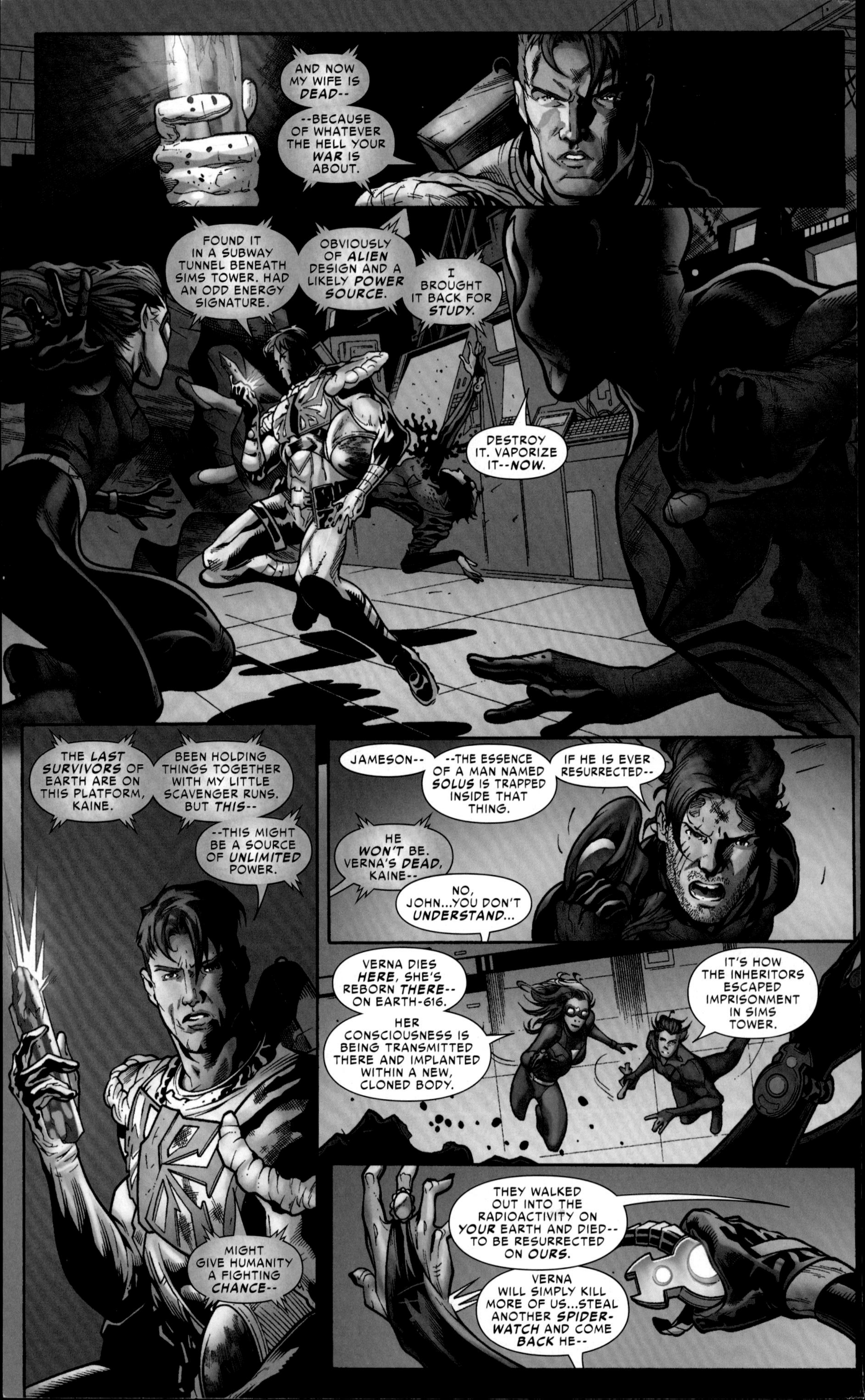
AND NOW MY WIFE IS DEAD--
--BECAUSE OF WHATEVER THE HELL YOUR WAR IS ABOUT.
FOUND IT IN A SUBWAY TUNNEL BENEATH SIMS TOWER. HAD AN ODD ENERGY SIGNATURE.
OBVIOUSLY OF ALIEN DESIGN AND A LIKELY POWER SOURCE.
I BROUGHT IT BACK FOR STUDY.
DESTROY IT. VAPORIZE IT--NOW.
THE LAST SURVIVORS OF EARTH ARE ON THIS PLATFORM, KAINE.
BEEN HOLDING THINGS TOGETHER WITH MY LITTLE SCAVENGER RUNS. BUT THIS--
--THIS MIGHT BE A SOURCE OF UNLIMITED POWER.
MIGHT GIVE HUMANITY A FIGHTING CHANCE--
JAMESON--
--THE ESSENCE OF A MAN NAMED SOLUS IS TRAPPED INSIDE THAT THING.
IF HE IS EVER RESURRECTED--
HE WON'T BE. VERNA'S DEAD, KAINE--
NO, JOHN...YOU DON'T UNDERSTAND...
VERNA DIES HERE, SHE'S REBORN THERE-- ON EARTH-616.
HER CONSCIOUSNESS IS BEING TRANSMITTED THERE AND IMPLANTED WITHIN A NEW, CLONED BODY.
IT'S HOW THE INHERITORS ESCAPED IMPRISONMENT IN SIMS TOWER.
THEY WALKED OUT INTO THE RADIOACTIVITY ON YOUR EARTH AND DIED-- TO BE RESURRECTED ON OURS.
VERNA WILL SIMPLY KILL MORE OF US...STEAL ANOTHER SPIDER-WATCH AND COME BACK HE--

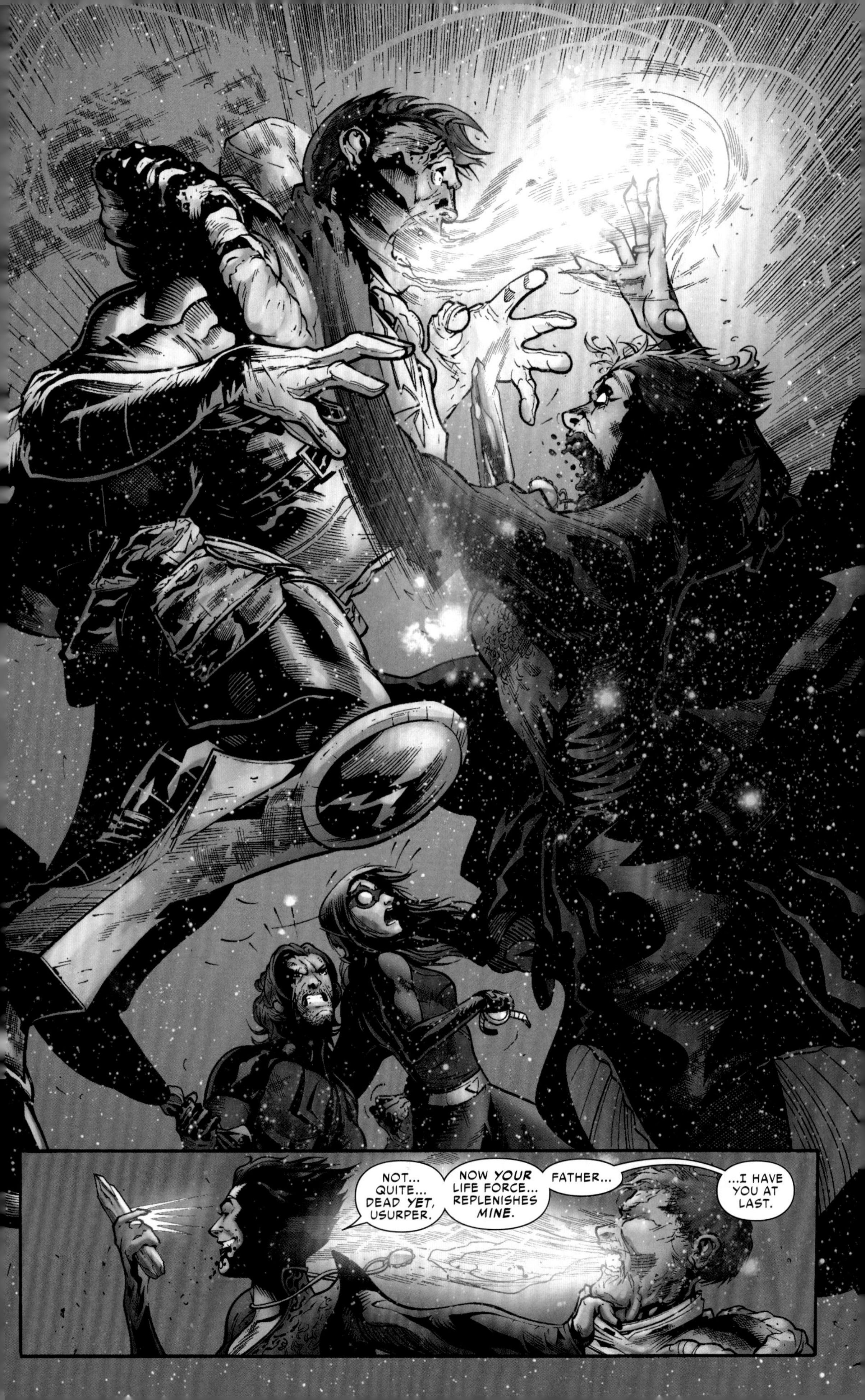
NOT... QUITE... DEAD YET, USURPER.
NOW YOUR LIFE FORCE... REPLENISHES MINE.
FATHER...
...I HAVE YOU AT LAST.

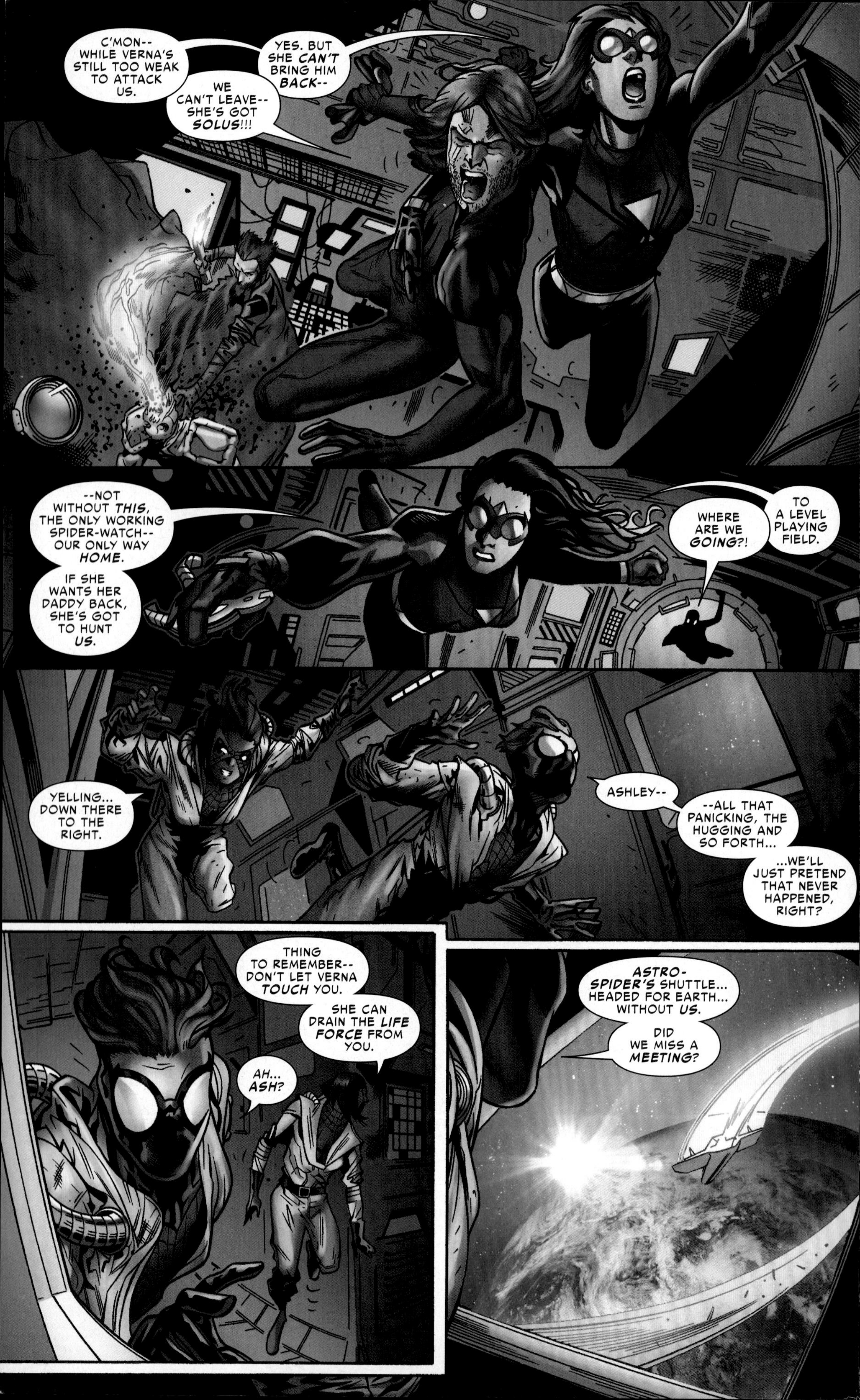
C'MON-- WHILE VERNA'S STILL TOO WEAK TO ATTACK US.
YES. BUT SHE CAN'T BRING HIM BACK--
WE CAN'T LEAVE-- SHE'S GOT SOLUS!!!
--NOT WITHOUT THIS, THE ONLY WORKING SPIDER-WATCH-- OUR ONLY WAY HOME.
IF SHE WANTS HER DADDY BACK, SHE'S GOT TO HUNT US.
WHERE ARE WE GOING?!
TO A LEVEL PLAYING FIELD.
YELLING... DOWN THERE TO THE RIGHT.
ASHLEY--
--ALL THAT PANICKING, THE HUGGING AND SO FORTH...
...WE'LL JUST PRETEND THAT NEVER HAPPENED, RIGHT?
THING TO REMEMBER-- DON'T LET VERNA TOUCH YOU.
SHE CAN DRAIN THE LIFE FORCE FROM YOU.
AH... ASH?
ASTRO-SPIDER'S SHUTTLE... HEADED FOR EARTH... WITHOUT US.
DID WE MISS A MEETING?

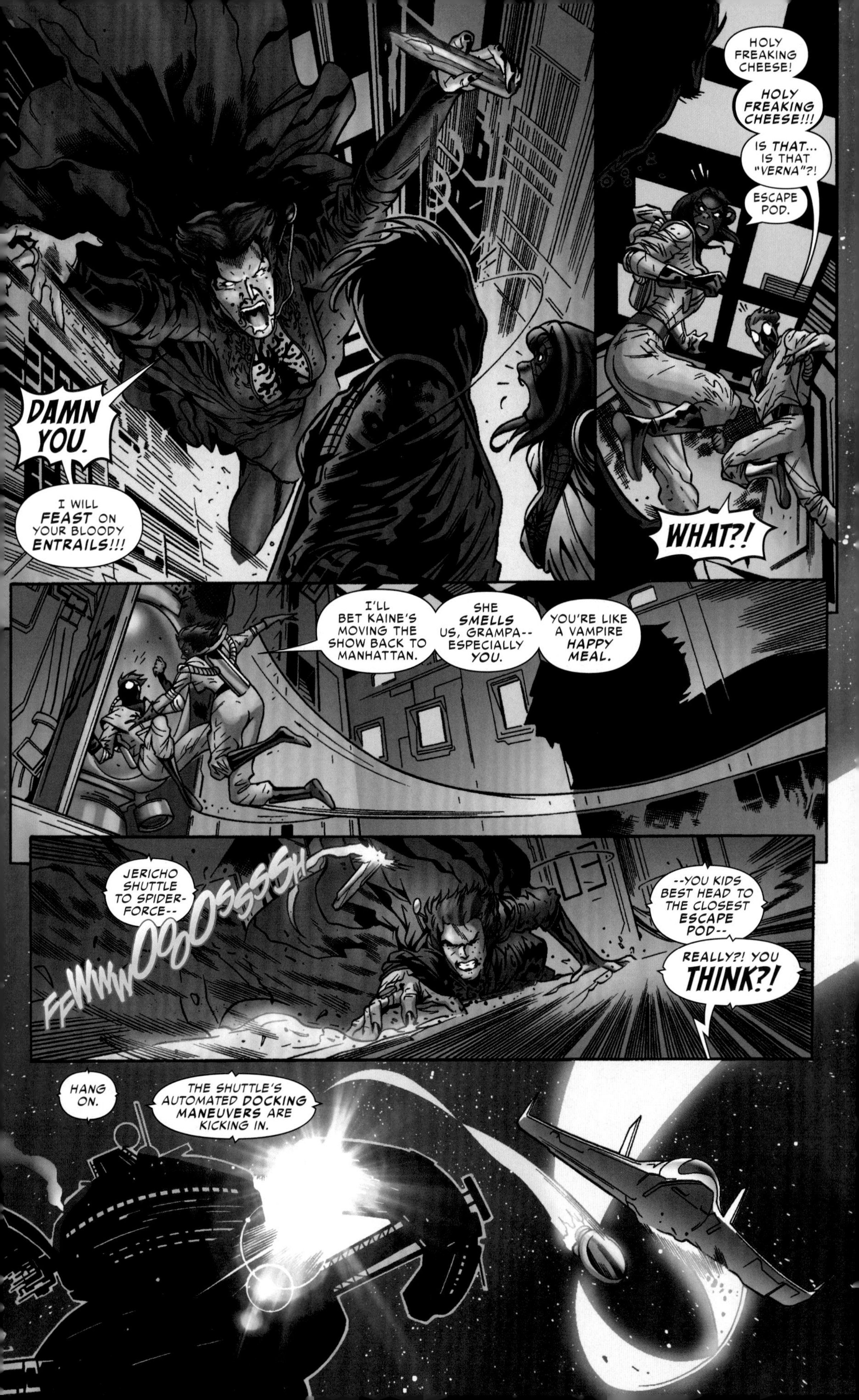
DAMN YOU.
I WILL FEAST ON YOUR BLOODY ENTRAILS!!!
HOLY FREAKING CHEESE!
HOLY FREAKING CHEESE!!!
IS THAT... IS THAT "VERNA"?!
ESCAPE POD.
WHAT?!
I'LL BET KAINE'S MOVING THE SHOW BACK TO MANHATTAN.
SHE SMELLS US, GRAMPA-- ESPECIALLY YOU.
YOU'RE LIKE A VAMPIRE HAPPY MEAL.
JERICHO SHUTTLE TO SPIDER-FORCE--
FFWWWOOOOSSSSH
--YOU KIDS BEST HEAD TO THE CLOSEST ESCAPE POD--
REALLY?! YOU THINK?!
HANG ON.
THE SHUTTLE'S AUTOMATED DOCKING MANEUVERS ARE KICKING IN.

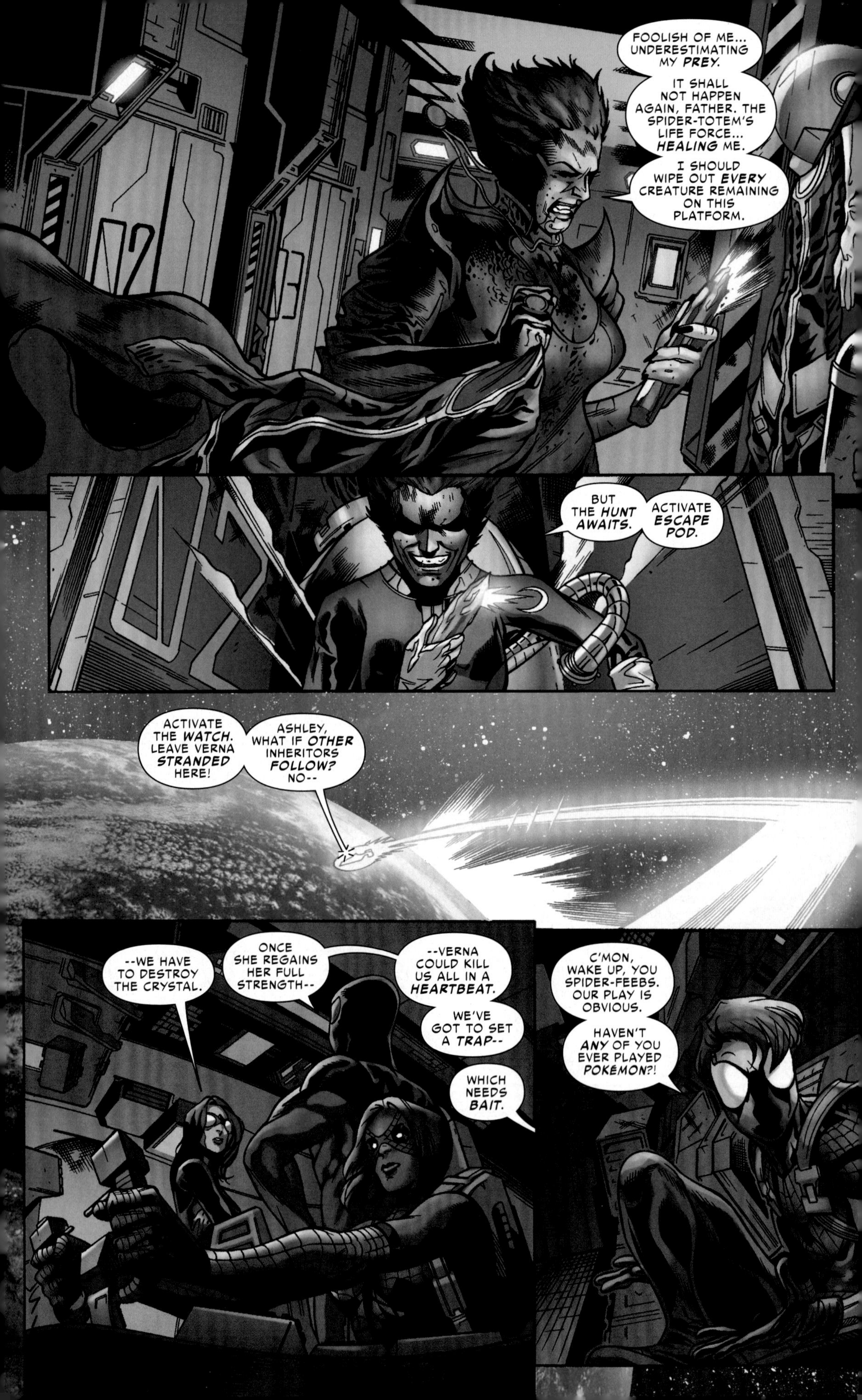
FOOLISH OF ME... UNDERESTIMATING MY PREY.
IT SHALL NOT HAPPEN AGAIN, FATHER. THE SPIDER-TOTEM'S LIFE FORCE... HEALING ME.
I SHOULD WIPE OUT EVERY CREATURE REMAINING ON THIS PLATFORM.
BUT THE HUNT AWAITS.
ACTIVATE ESCAPE POD.
ACTIVATE THE WATCH. LEAVE VERNA STRANDED HERE!
ASHLEY, WHAT IF OTHER INHERITORS FOLLOW? NO--
--WE HAVE TO DESTROY THE CRYSTAL.
ONCE SHE REGAINS HER FULL STRENGTH--
--VERNA COULD KILL US ALL IN A HEARTBEAT.
WE'VE GOT TO SET A TRAP--
WHICH NEEDS BAIT.
C'MON, WAKE UP, YOU SPIDER-FEEBS. OUR PLAY IS OBVIOUS.
HAVEN'T ANY OF YOU EVER PLAYED POKÉMON?!

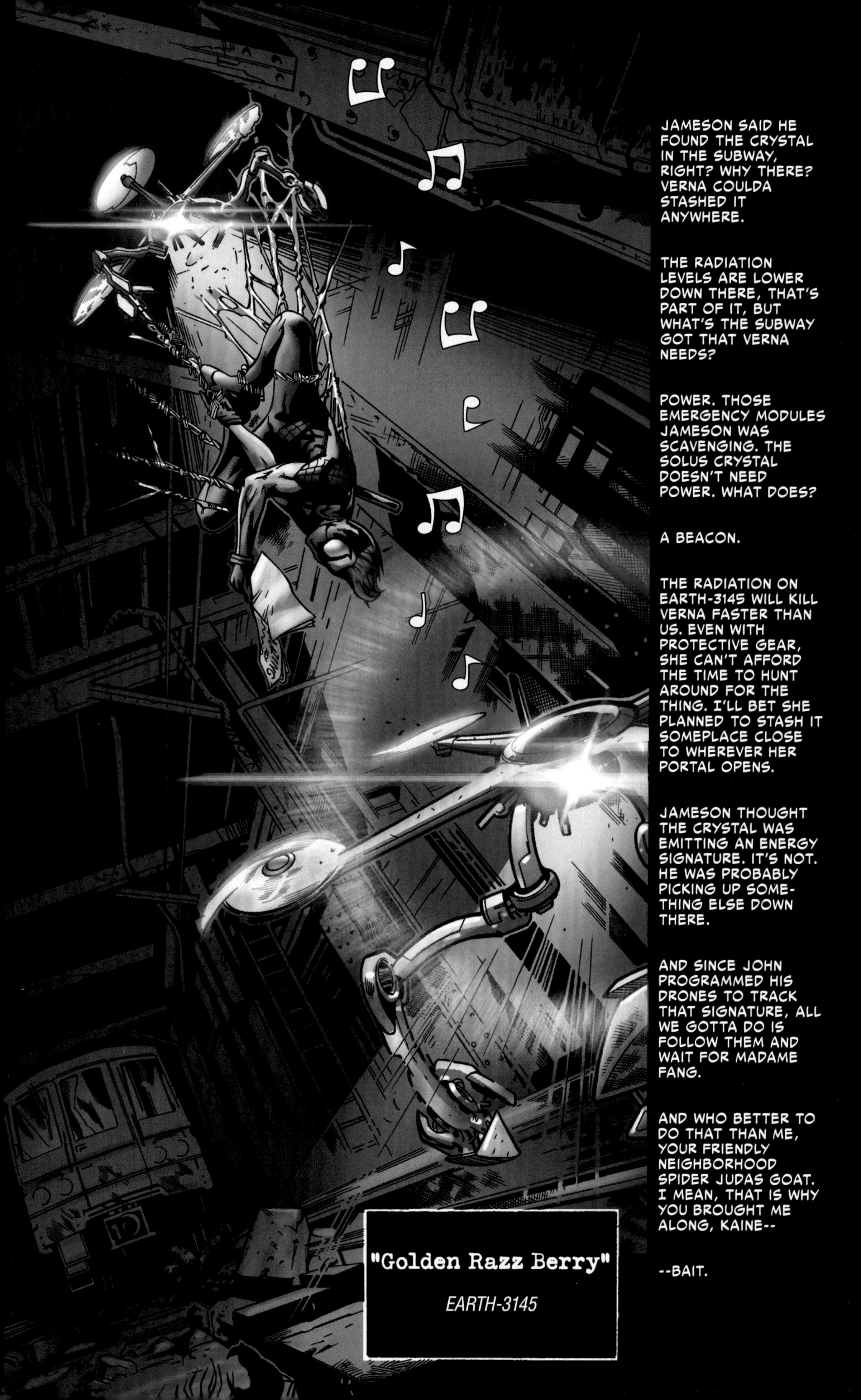
"Golden Razz Berry"
EARTH-3145
JAMESON SAID HE FOUND THE CRYSTAL IN THE SUBWAY, RIGHT? WHY THERE? VERNA COULDA STASHED IT ANYWHERE.
THE RADIATION LEVELS ARE LOWER DOWN THERE, THAT'S PART OF IT, BUT WHAT'S THE SUBWAY GOT THAT VERNA NEEDS?
POWER. THOSE EMERGENCY MODULES JAMESON WAS SCAVENGING. THE SOLUS CRYSTAL DOESN'T NEED POWER. WHAT DOES?
A BEACON.
THE RADIATION ON EARTH-3145 WILL KILL VERNA FASTER THAN US. EVEN WITH PROTECTIVE GEAR, SHE CAN'T AFFORD THE TIME TO HUNT AROUND FOR THE THING. I'LL BET SHE PLANNED TO STASH IT SOMEPLACE CLOSE TO WHEREVER HER PORTAL OPENS.
JAMESON THOUGHT THE CRYSTAL WAS EMITTING AN ENERGY SIGNATURE. IT'S NOT. HE WAS PROBABLY PICKING UP SOME-THING ELSE DOWN THERE.
AND SINCE JOHN PROGRAMMED HIS DRONES TO TRACK THAT SIGNATURE, ALL WE GOTTA DO IS FOLLOW THEM AND WAIT FOR MADAME FANG.
AND WHO BETTER TO DO THAT THAN ME, YOUR FRIENDLY NEIGHBORHOOD SPIDER JUDAS GOAT. I MEAN, THAT IS WHY YOU BROUGHT ME ALONG, KAINE--
--BAIT.

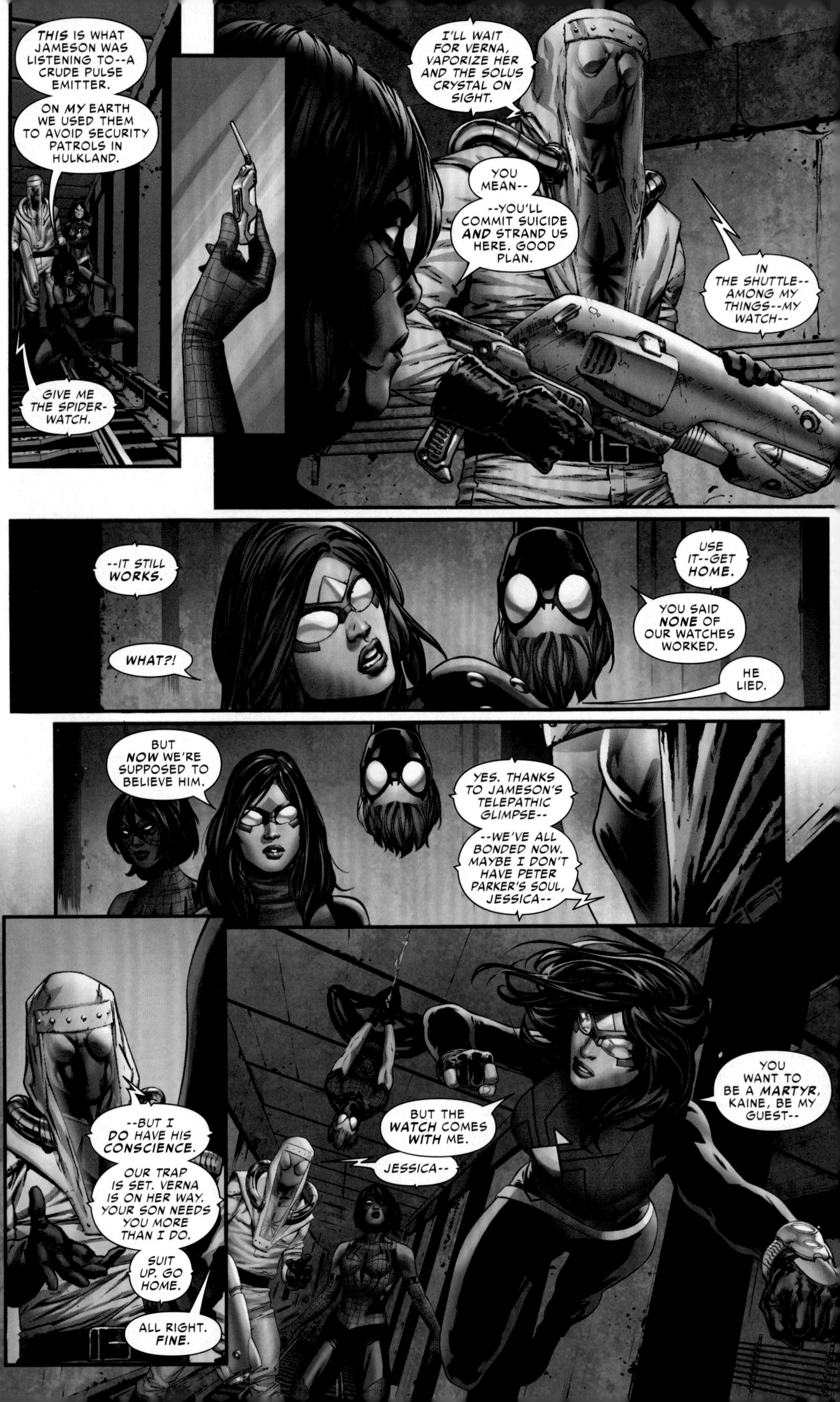
THIS IS WHAT JAMESON WAS LISTENING TO--A CRUDE PULSE EMITTER.
ON MY EARTH WE USED THEM TO AVOID SECURITY PATROLS IN HULKLAND.
GIVE ME THE SPIDER-WATCH.
I'LL WAIT FOR VERNA, VAPORIZE HER AND THE SOLUS CRYSTAL ON SIGHT.
YOU MEAN--
--YOU'LL COMMIT SUICIDE AND STRAND US HERE. GOOD PLAN.
IN THE SHUTTLE--AMONG MY THINGS--MY WATCH--
--IT STILL WORKS.
WHAT?!
USE IT--GET HOME.
YOU SAID NONE OF OUR WATCHES WORKED.
HE LIED.
BUT NOW WE'RE SUPPOSED TO BELIEVE HIM.
YES. THANKS TO JAMESON'S TELEPATHIC GLIMPSE--
--WE'VE ALL BONDED NOW. MAYBE I DON'T HAVE PETER PARKER'S SOUL, JESSICA--
--BUT I DO HAVE HIS CONSCIENCE.
OUR TRAP IS SET. VERNA IS ON HER WAY. YOUR SON NEEDS YOU MORE THAN I DO.
SUIT UP. GO HOME.
ALL RIGHT. FINE.
YOU WANT TO BE A MARTYR, KAINE, BE MY GUEST--
BUT THE WATCH COMES WITH ME.
JESSICA--

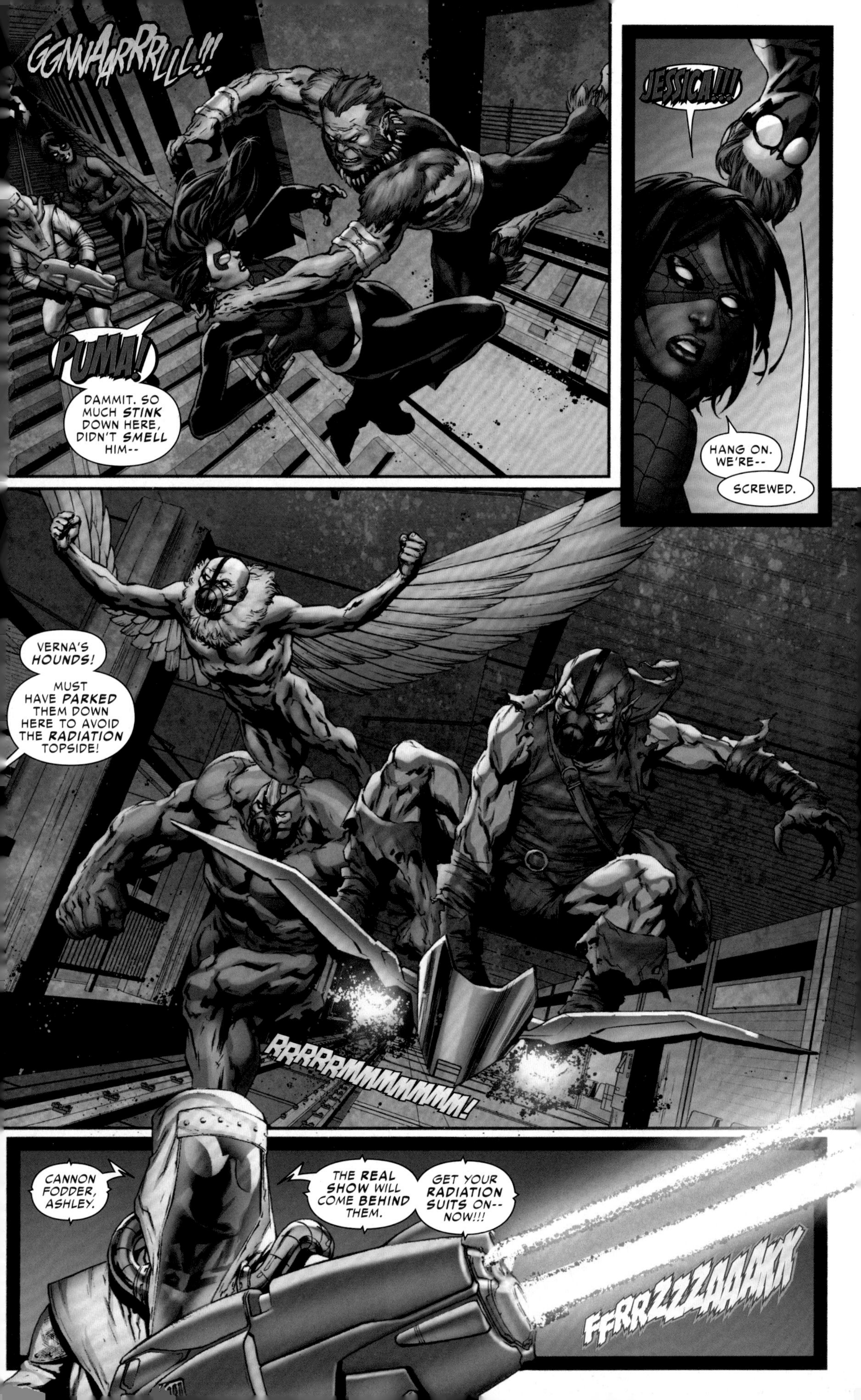
GGNNAARRRLLL!!!
PUMA!
DAMMIT. SO MUCH STINK DOWN HERE, DIDN'T SMELL HIM--
JESSICA!!!
HANG ON. WE'RE--
SCREWED.
VERNA'S HOUNDS!
MUST HAVE PARKED THEM DOWN HERE TO AVOID THE RADIATION TOPSIDE!
RRRRRMMMMMMM!
CANNON FODDER, ASHLEY.
THE REAL SHOW WILL COME BEHIND THEM.
GET YOUR RADIATION SUITS ON--NOW!!!
FFRRZZZAAAKK

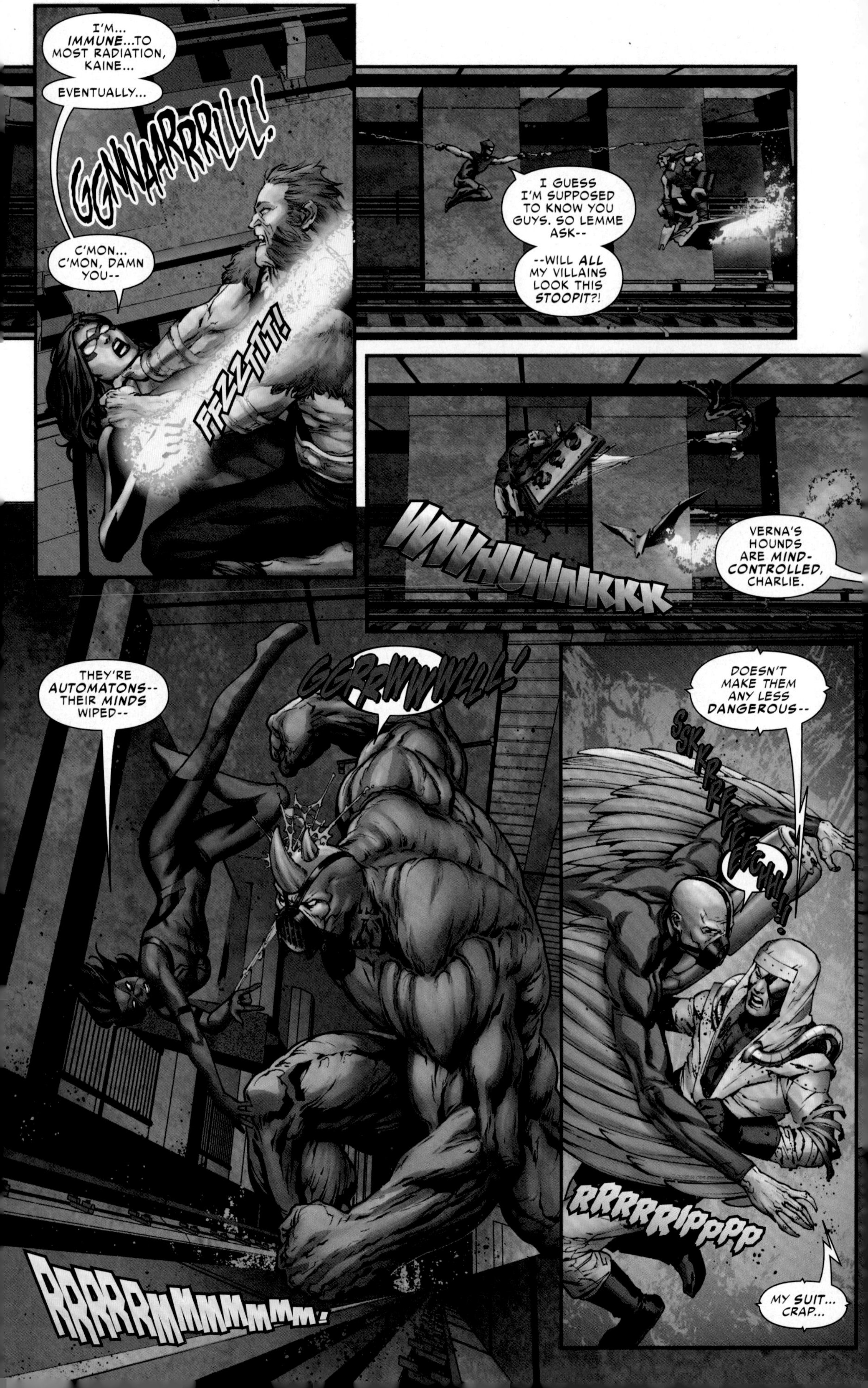
I'M... IMMUNE...TO MOST RADIATION, KAINE...
EVENTUALLY...
GGNNAARRRLLL!
C'MON... C'MON, DAMN YOU--
FFZZTTT!
I GUESS I'M SUPPOSED TO KNOW YOU GUYS. SO LEMME ASK--
--WILL ALL MY VILLAINS LOOK THIS STOOPIT?!
WWHUNNKKK
VERNA'S HOUNDS ARE MIND-CONTROLLED, CHARLIE.
THEY'RE AUTOMATONS-- THEIR MINDS WIPED--
GGRRWWLLL!
DOESN'T MAKE THEM ANY LESS DANGEROUS--
SSKKREEEEEGHH!
RRRRRRIPPPP
RRRRRMMMMMMM!
MY SUIT... CRAP...

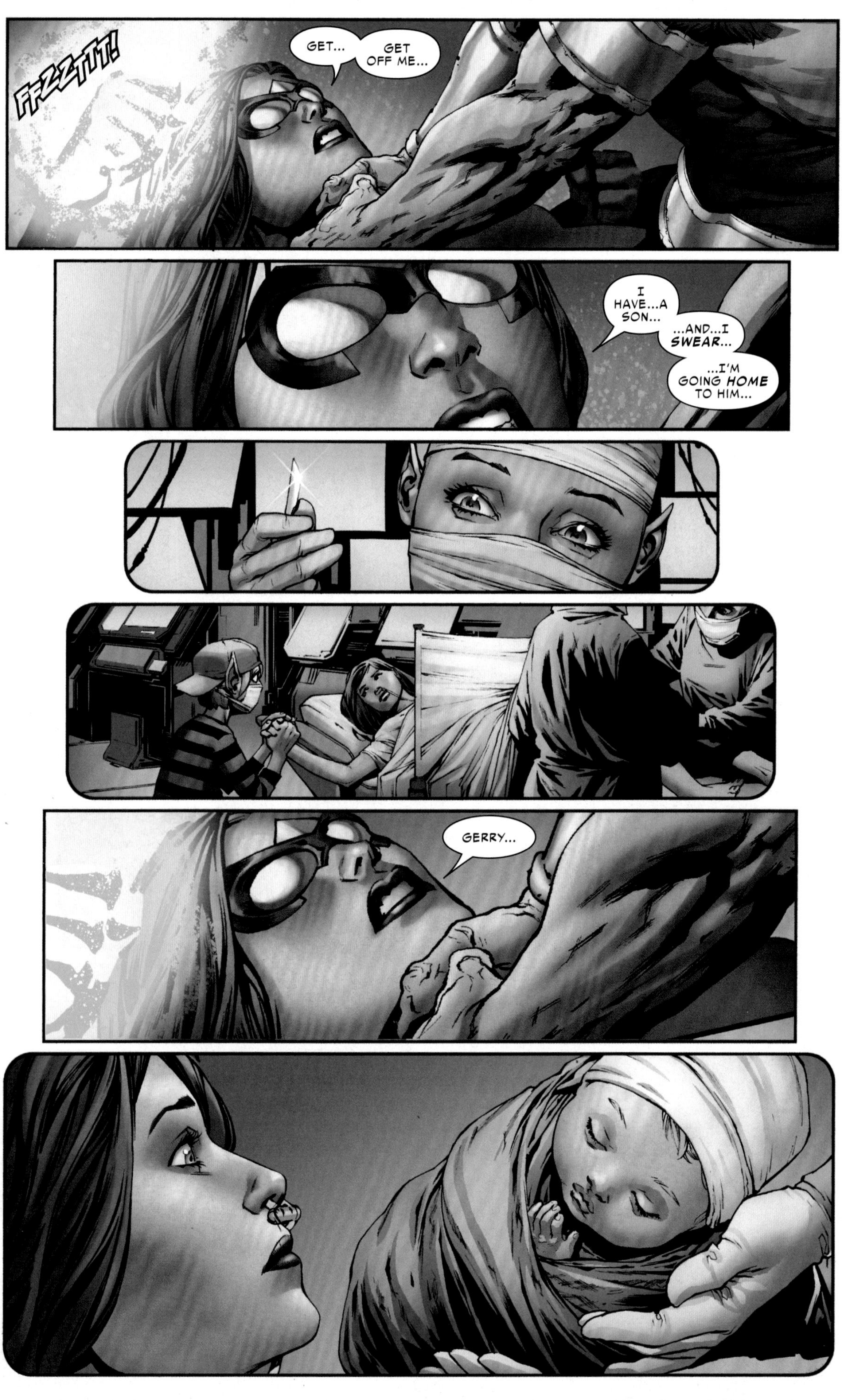
FFZZTTT!
GET...
GET OFF ME...
I HAVE...A SON...
...AND...I SWEAR...
...I'M GOING HOME TO HIM...
GERRY...

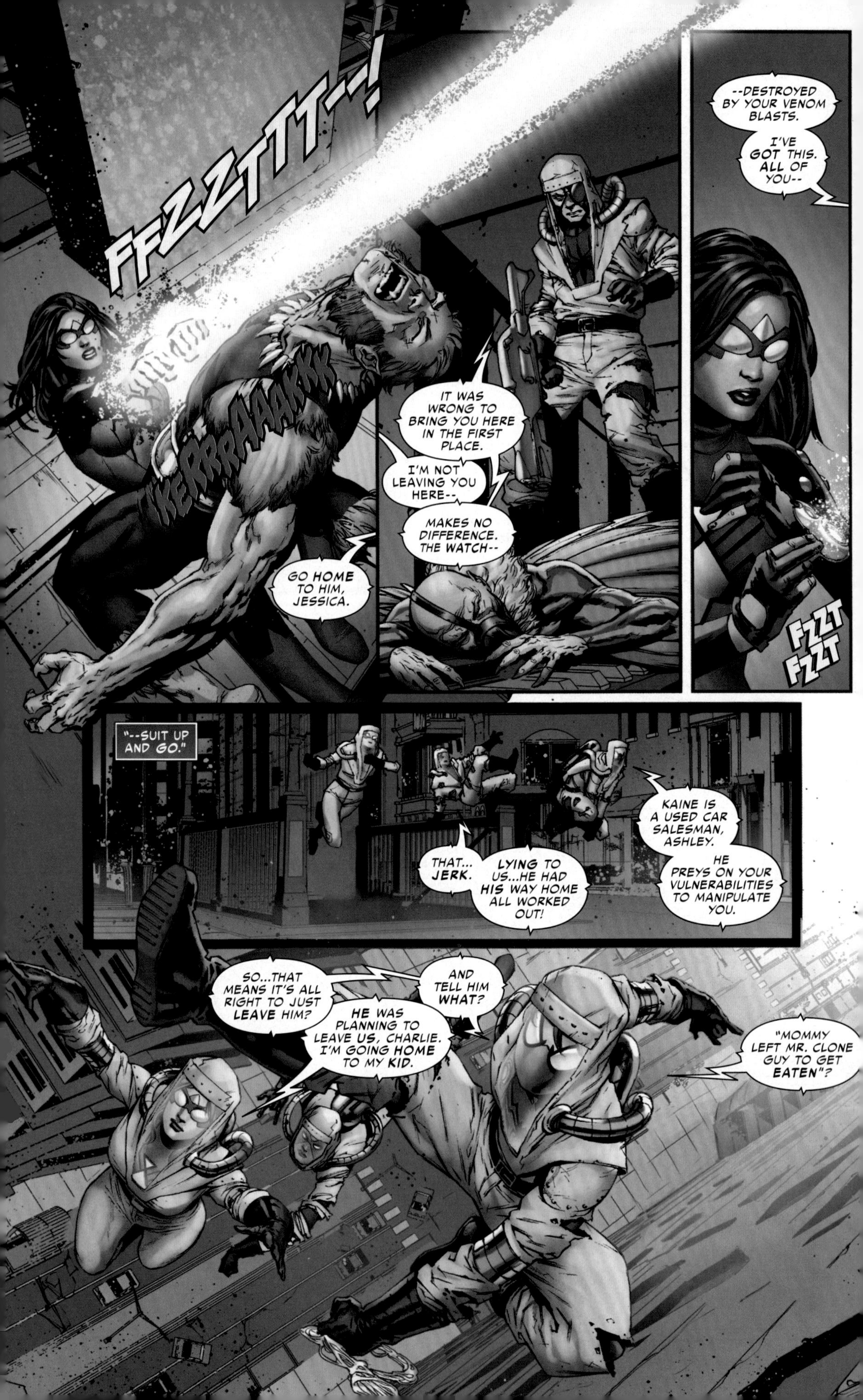
FFZZTTT--!
KERRRAAAKKK
GO HOME TO HIM, JESSICA.
IT WAS WRONG TO BRING YOU HERE IN THE FIRST PLACE.
I'M NOT LEAVING YOU HERE--
MAKES NO DIFFERENCE. THE WATCH--
--DESTROYED BY YOUR VENOM BLASTS.
I'VE GOT THIS. ALL OF YOU--
FZZT FZZT
"--SUIT UP AND GO."
KAINE IS A USED CAR SALESMAN, ASHLEY.
HE PREYS ON YOUR VULNERABILITIES TO MANIPULATE YOU.
THAT... JERK.
LYING TO US...HE HAD HIS WAY HOME ALL WORKED OUT!
SO...THAT MEANS IT'S ALL RIGHT TO JUST LEAVE HIM?
HE WAS PLANNING TO LEAVE US, CHARLIE. I'M GOING HOME TO MY KID.
AND TELL HIM WHAT?
"MOMMY LEFT MR. CLONE GUY TO GET EATEN"?

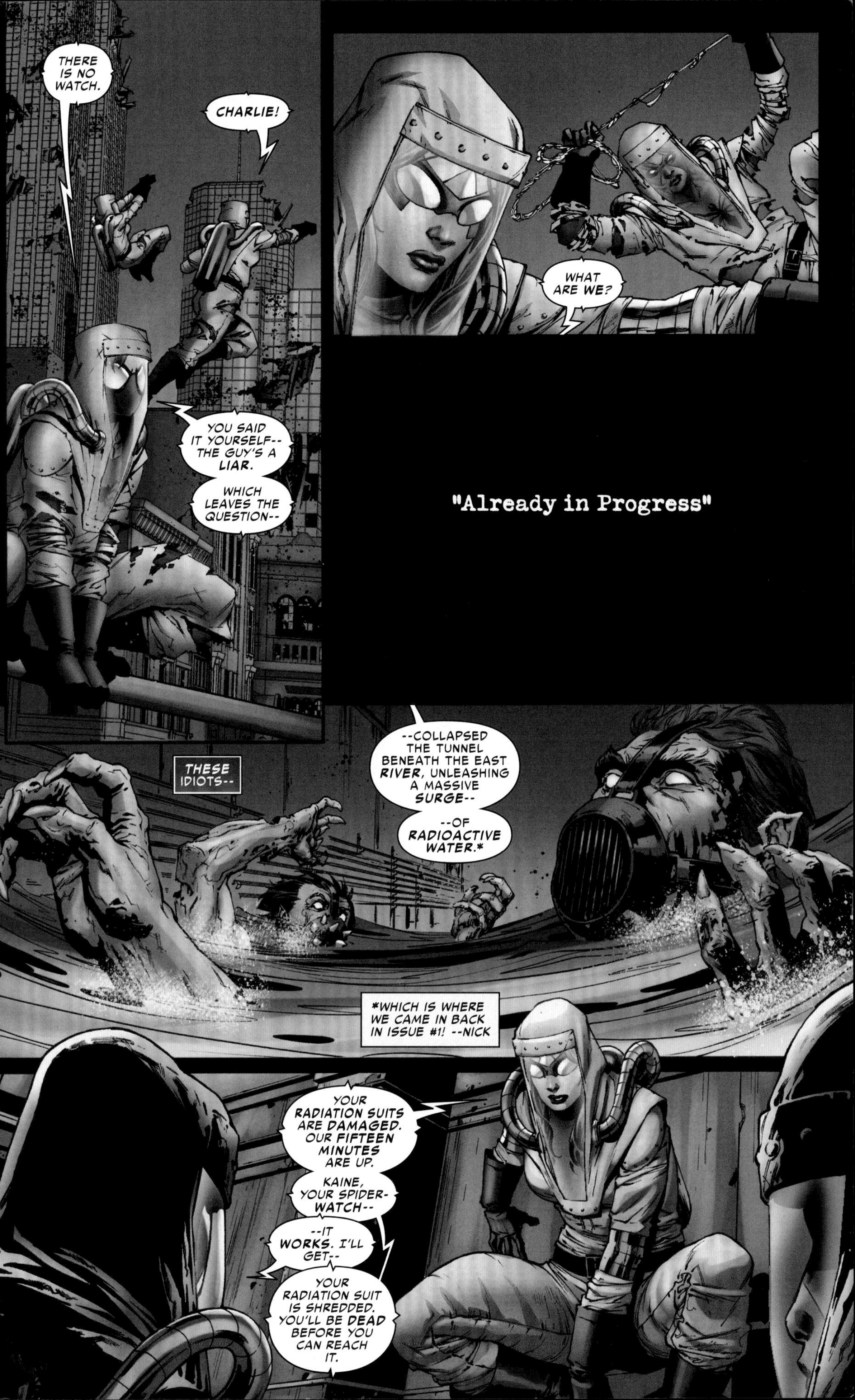

THERE IS NO WATCH.
CHARLIE!
WHAT ARE WE?
YOU SAID IT YOURSELF--THE GUY'S A LIAR.
WHICH LEAVES THE QUESTION--
"Already in Progress"
THESE IDIOTS--
--COLLAPSED THE TUNNEL BENEATH THE EAST RIVER, UNLEASHING A MASSIVE SURGE--
--OF RADIOACTIVE WATER.*
*WHICH IS WHERE WE CAME IN BACK IN ISSUE #1! --NICK
YOUR RADIATION SUITS ARE DAMAGED. OUR FIFTEEN MINUTES ARE UP.
KAINE, YOUR SPIDER-WATCH--
--IT WORKS. I'LL GET--
YOUR RADIATION SUIT IS SHREDDED. YOU'LL BE DEAD BEFORE YOU CAN REACH IT.

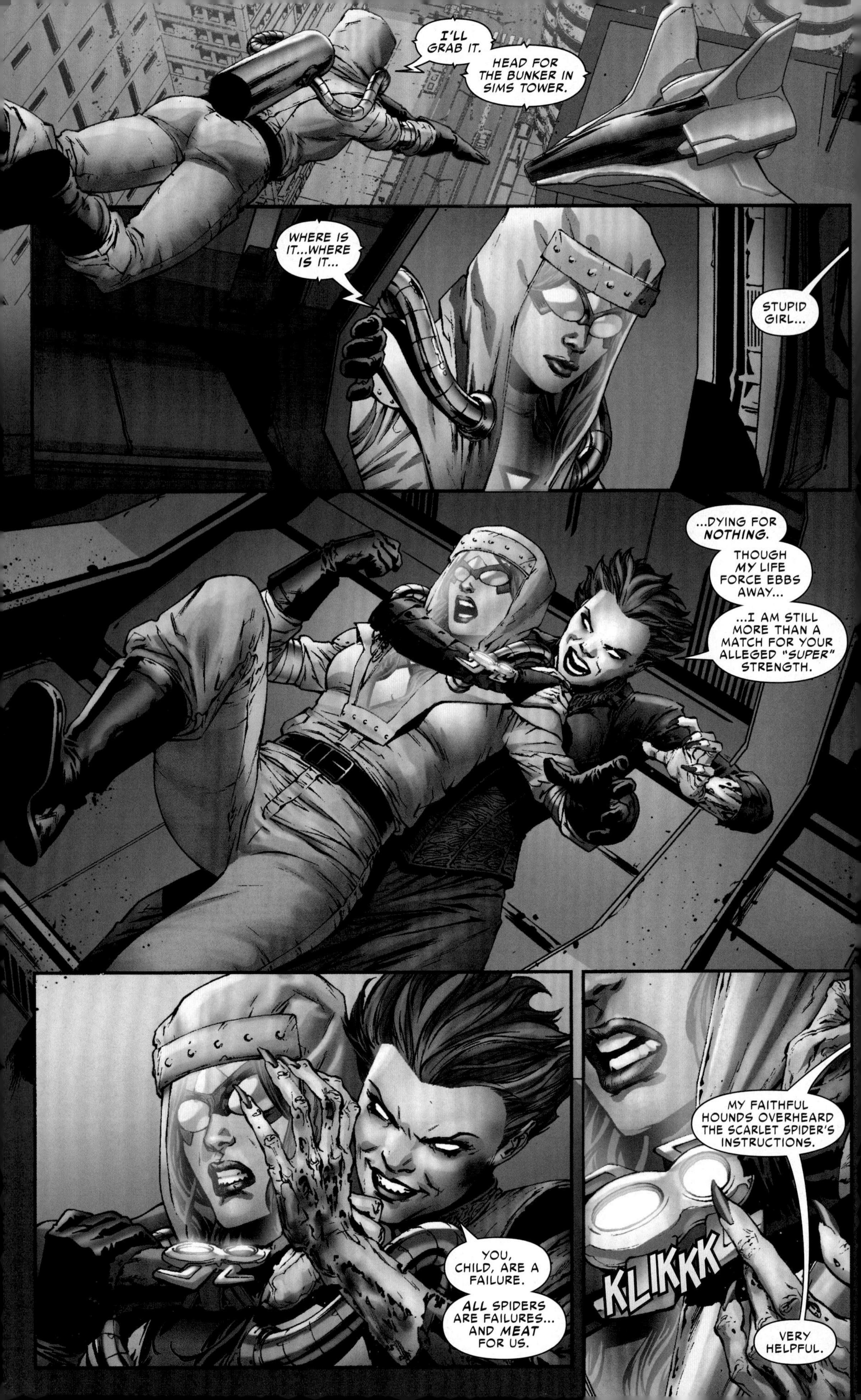
I'LL GRAB IT.
HEAD FOR THE BUNKER IN SIMS TOWER.
WHERE IS IT...WHERE IS IT...
STUPID GIRL...
...DYING FOR NOTHING.
THOUGH MY LIFE FORCE EBBS AWAY...
...I AM STILL MORE THAN A MATCH FOR YOUR ALLEGED "SUPER" STRENGTH.
YOU, CHILD, ARE A FAILURE.
ALL SPIDERS ARE FAILURES... AND MEAT FOR US.
MY FAITHFUL HOUNDS OVERHEARD THE SCARLET SPIDER'S INSTRUCTIONS.
KLIKKK
VERY HELPFUL.

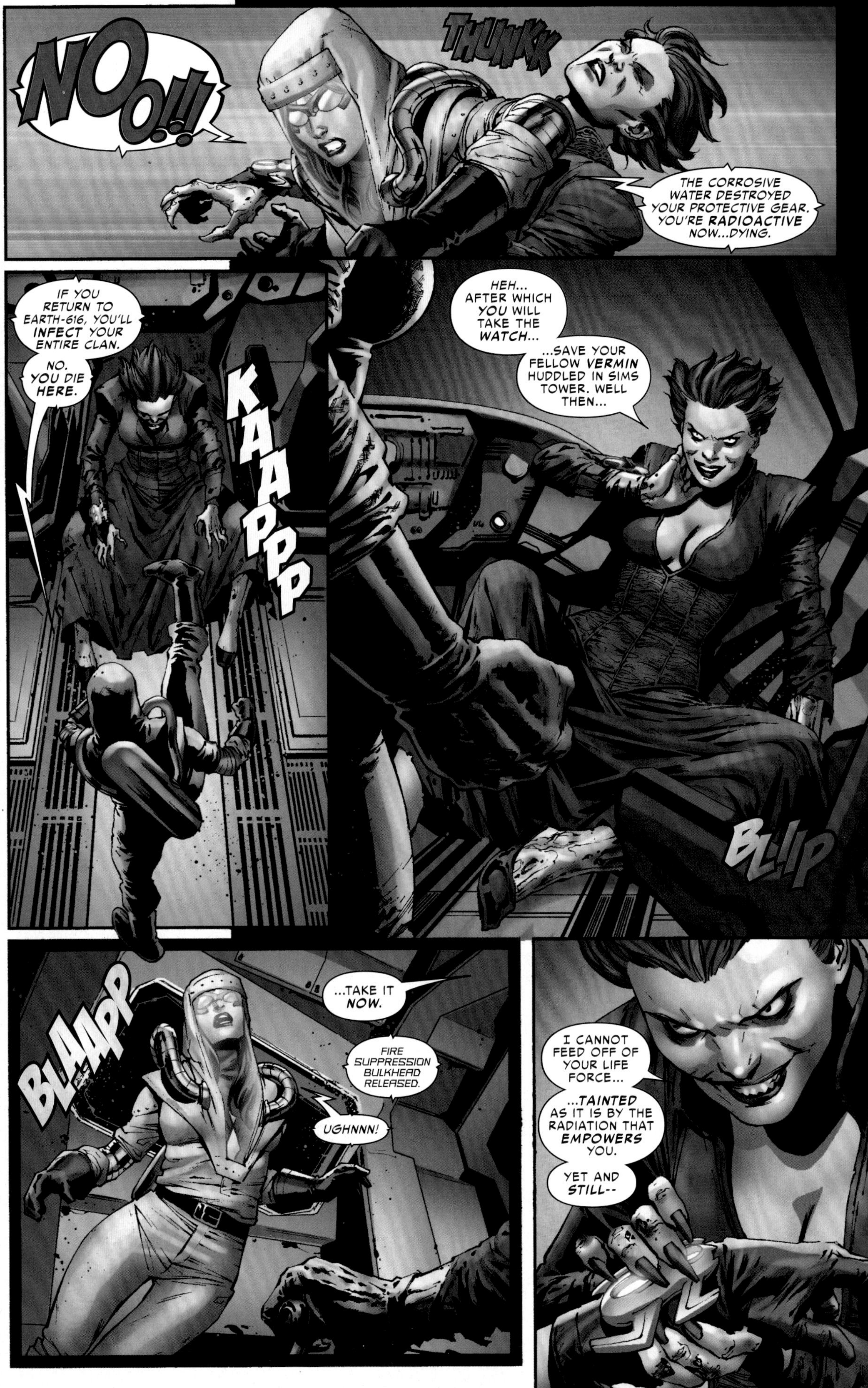
NOOO!!!
THUNKK
THE CORROSIVE WATER DESTROYED YOUR PROTECTIVE GEAR. YOU'RE RADIOACTIVE NOW...DYING.
IF YOU RETURN TO EARTH-616, YOU'LL INFECT YOUR ENTIRE CLAN.
NO. YOU DIE HERE.
KAAPPP
HEH... AFTER WHICH YOU WILL TAKE THE WATCH...
...SAVE YOUR FELLOW VERMIN HUDDLED IN SIMS TOWER. WELL THEN...
BLIP
BLAAPP
...TAKE IT NOW.
FIRE SUPPRESSION BULKHEAD RELEASED.
UGHNNN!
I CANNOT FEED OFF OF YOUR LIFE FORCE...
...TAINTED AS IT IS BY THE RADIATION THAT EMPOWERS YOU.
YET AND STILL--

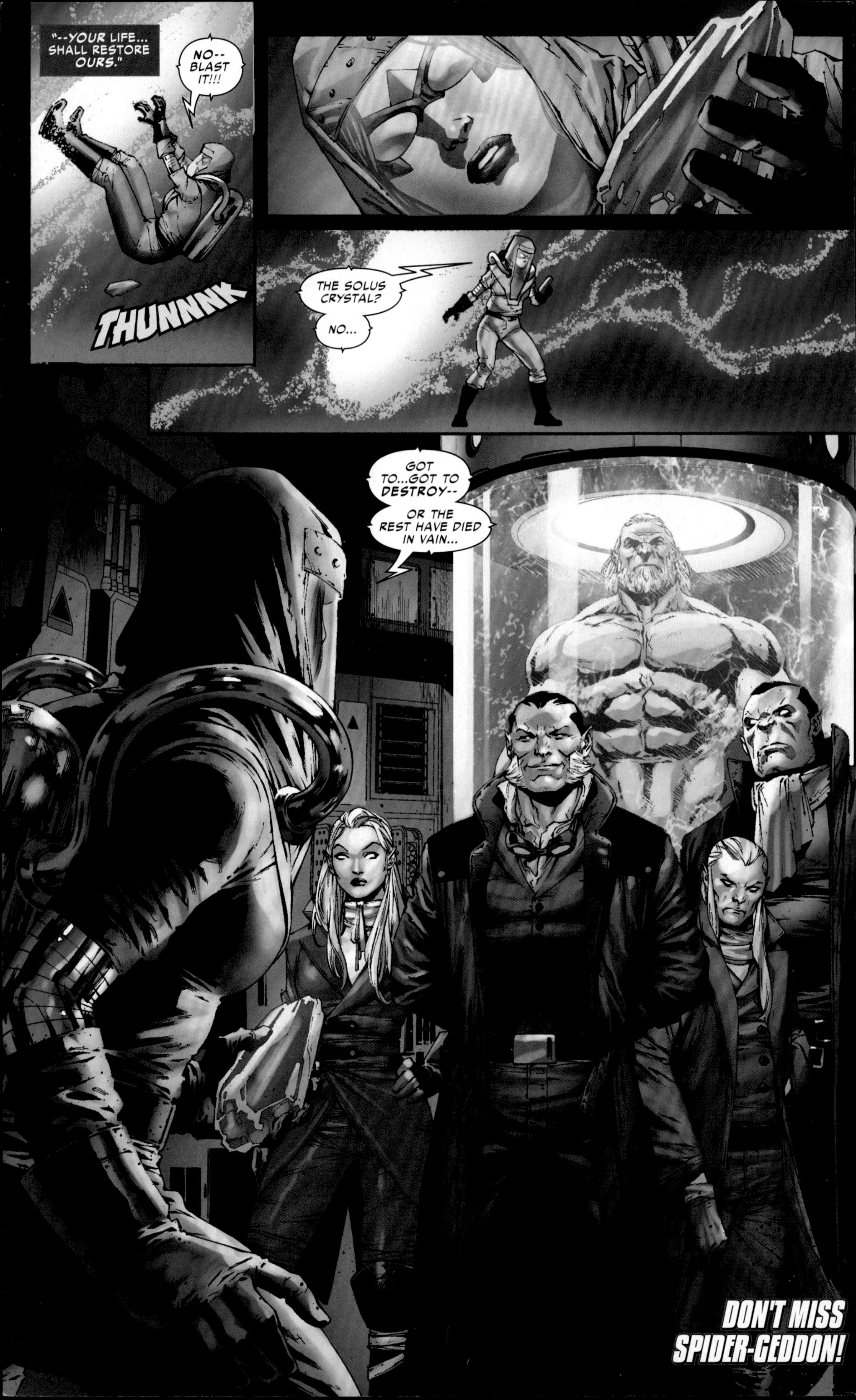
"--YOUR LIFE... SHALL RESTORE OURS."
NO-- BLAST IT!!!
THUNNNK
THE SOLUS CRYSTAL?
NO...
GOT TO...GOT TO DESTROY--
OR THE REST HAVE DIED IN VAIN...
DON'T MISS SPIDER-GEDDON!

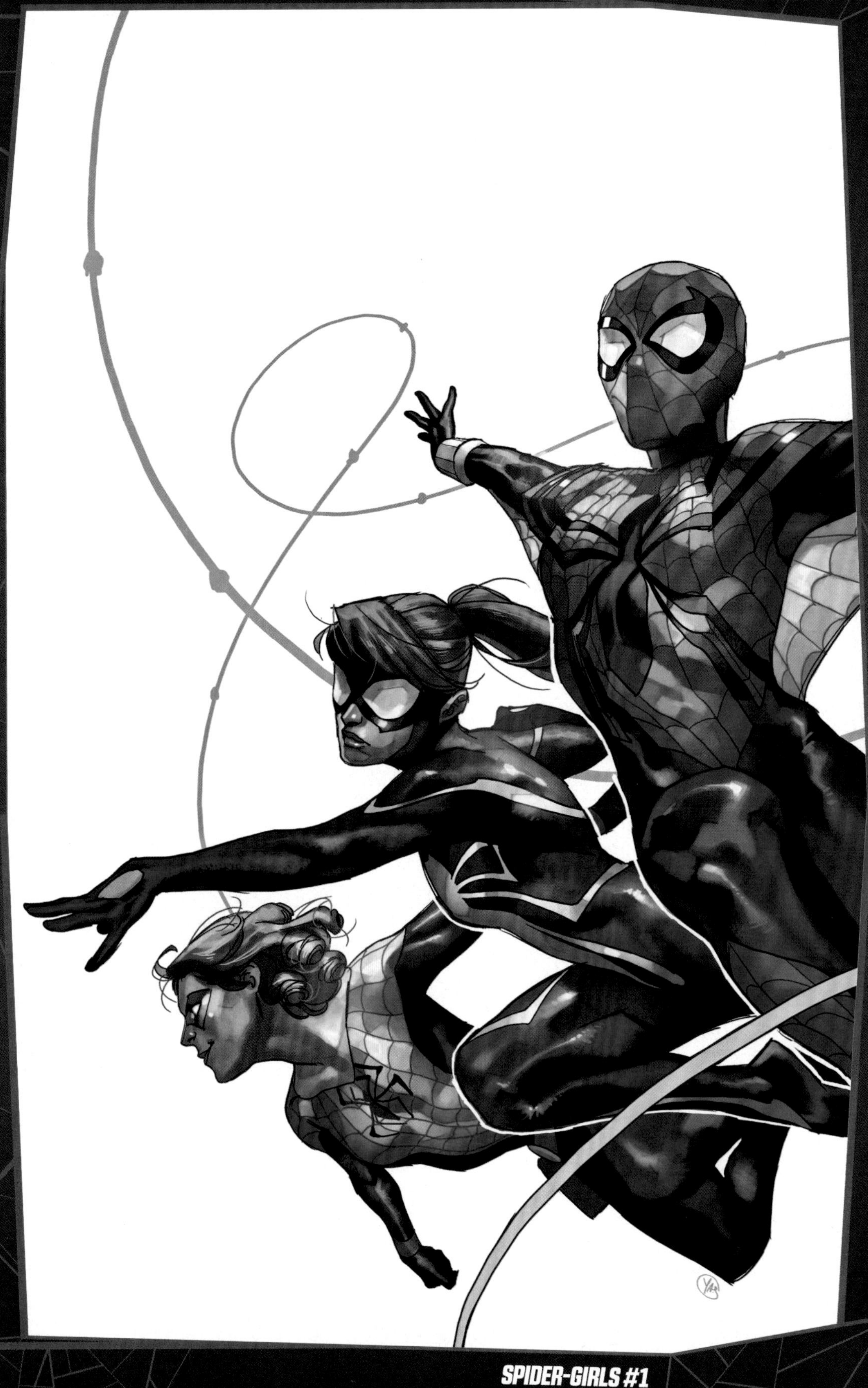

SPIDER-GIRLS #1

SOME TIME AGO, THE SPIDER-POWERED HEROES OF MANY UNIVERSES UNITED IN BATTLE TO DEFEAT THE INHERITORS, A FAMILY OF SUPERHUMAN BEINGS WHO FED ON THE LIFE ESSENCE OF SPIDERS. THE SPIDER-ARMY TRIUMPHED, STRANDING THEIR ENEMY ON A RADIOACTIVE PLANET, AND RETURNED TO THEIR LIVES. THE INHERITORS WAITED.

THEN OTTO OCTAVIUS, ASPIRING TO BECOME THE PREDOMINANT HERO OF SAN FRANCISCO, USED THE INHERITORS' CLONING TECHNOLOGY AND OPENED A DOOR FOR THEIR RETURN. THE WEB-WARRIORS, VETERANS OF THE FIRST WAR FOR THE SPIDER-VERSE, CAME TO WARN HIM--TOO LATE. THREE INHERITORS EMERGED FROM THE CLONING TANKS AND KILLED SPIDER-MAN NOIR AND SPIDER-UK. AS OTTO'S LAB EXPLODED, SPIDER-GWEN FOUGHT THE INHERITORS SO THE SURVIVORS COULD ESCAPE.

WHILE MILES MORALES AND OTTO DISAGREED OVER STRATEGY, MAY "MAYDAY" PARKER (SPIDER-WOMAN OF EARTH-982) REMEMBERED THAT SPIDER-GIRL (A.K.A. ANYA CORAZON)'S INTERPRETATION OF ANCIENT SCROLLS FROM THE INHERITORS' HOMEWORLD TURNED THE TIDE IN THE FIRST WAR. KNOWING THEY'D NEED EVERY POSSIBLE ADVANTAGE, THE TWO HEROES LEFT TO SEE WHERE ANYA'S KNOWLEDGE OF SPIDER-TOTEMS AND THE SPIDER SOCIETY COULD LEAD THEM.

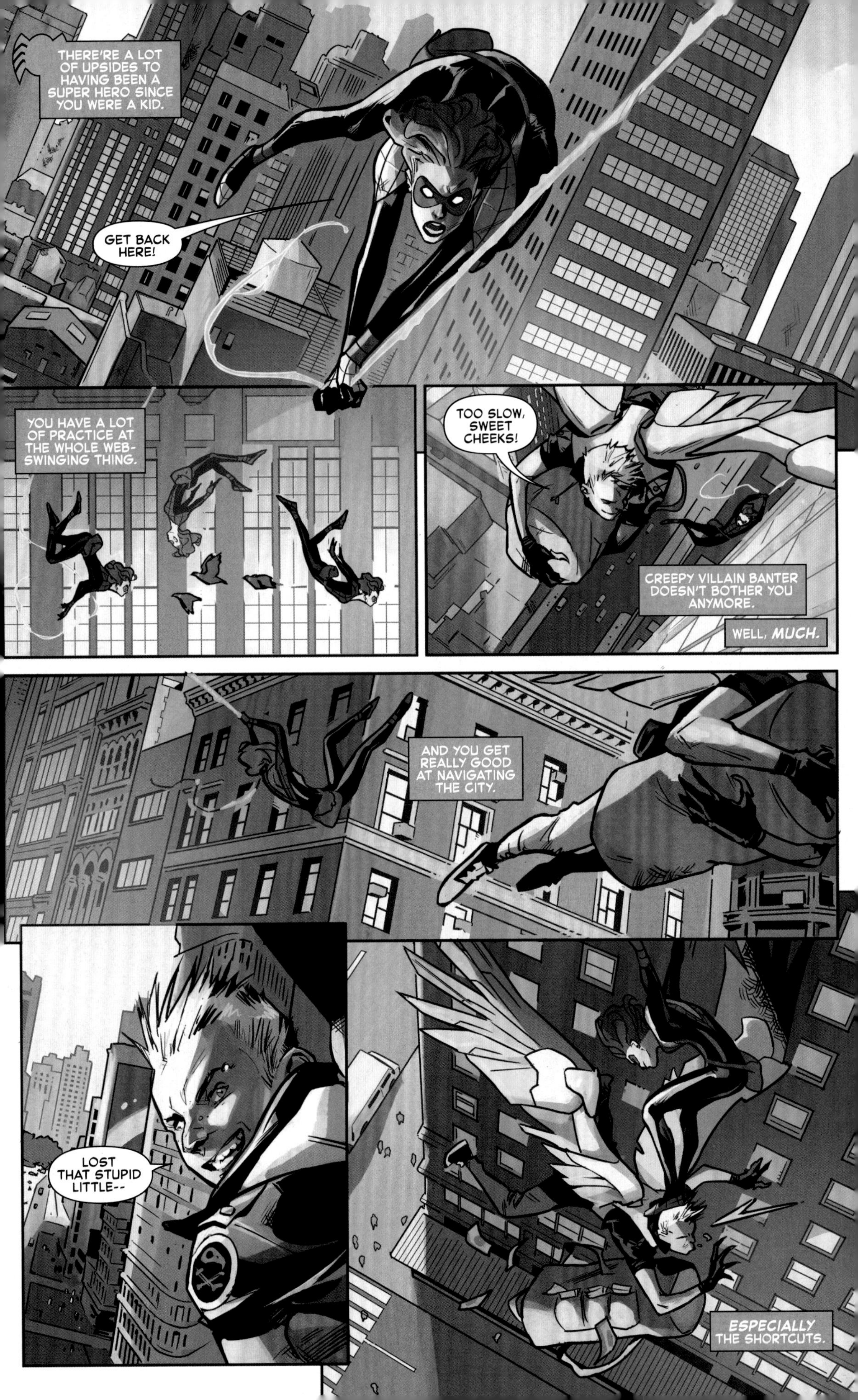

THERE'RE A LOT OF UPSIDES TO HAVING BEEN A SUPER HERO SINCE YOU WERE A KID.
GET BACK HERE!
YOU HAVE A LOT OF PRACTICE AT THE WHOLE WEB-SWINGING THING.
TOO SLOW, SWEET CHEEKS!
CREEPY VILLAIN BANTER DOESN'T BOTHER YOU ANYMORE.
WELL, *MUCH.*
AND YOU GET REALLY GOOD AT NAVIGATING THE CITY.
LOST THAT STUPID LITTLE--
ESPECIALLY THE SHORTCUTS.

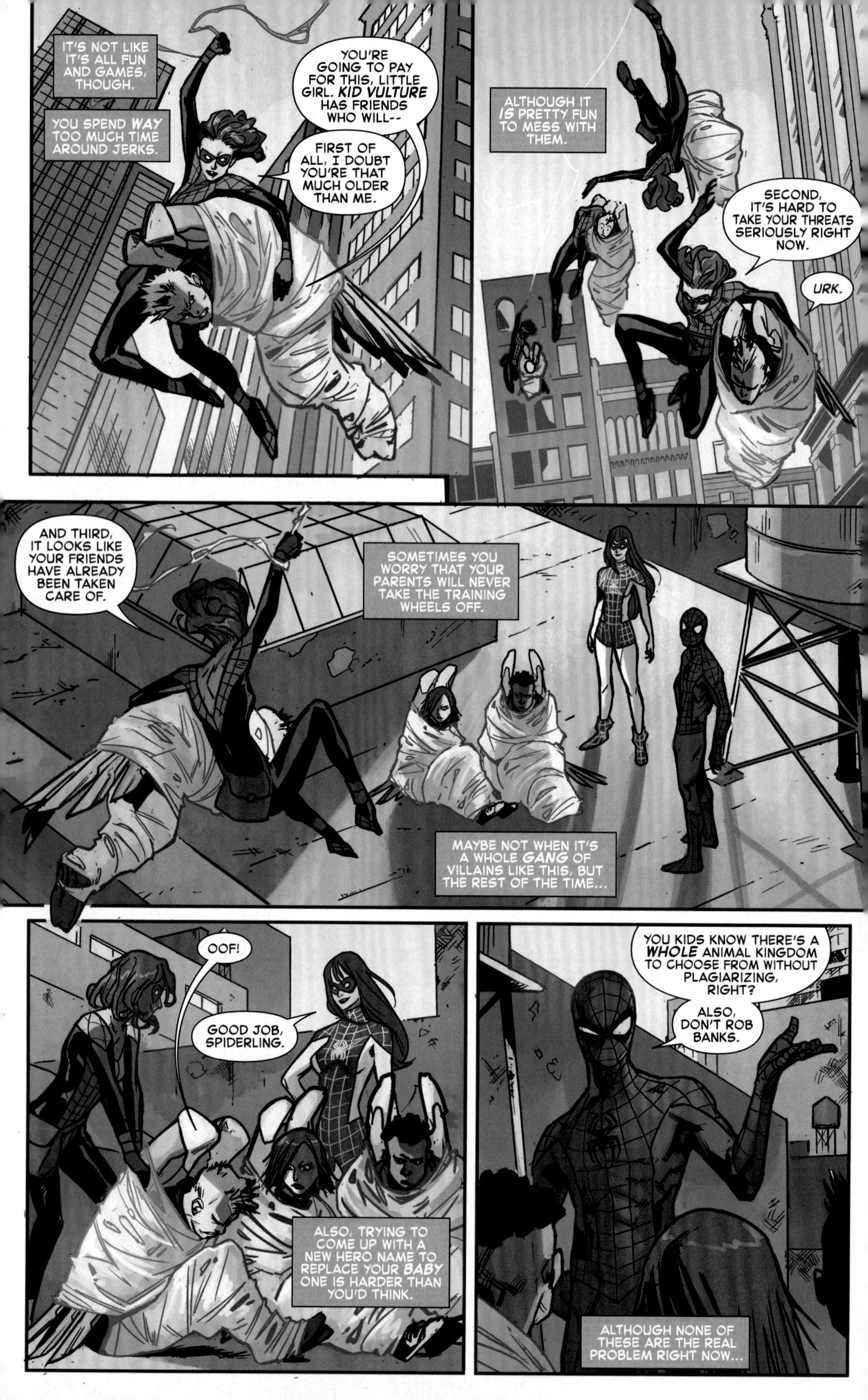
IT'S NOT LIKE IT'S ALL FUN AND GAMES, THOUGH.
YOU SPEND WAY TOO MUCH TIME AROUND JERKS.
YOU'RE GOING TO PAY FOR THIS, LITTLE GIRL. KID VULTURE HAS FRIENDS WHO WILL--
FIRST OF ALL, I DOUBT YOU'RE THAT MUCH OLDER THAN ME.
ALTHOUGH IT IS PRETTY FUN TO MESS WITH THEM.
SECOND, IT'S HARD TO TAKE YOUR THREATS SERIOUSLY RIGHT NOW.
URK.
AND THIRD, IT LOOKS LIKE YOUR FRIENDS HAVE ALREADY BEEN TAKEN CARE OF.
SOMETIMES YOU WORRY THAT YOUR PARENTS WILL NEVER TAKE THE TRAINING WHEELS OFF.
MAYBE NOT WHEN IT'S A WHOLE GANG OF VILLAINS LIKE THIS, BUT THE REST OF THE TIME...
OOF!
GOOD JOB, SPIDERLING.
ALSO, TRYING TO COME UP WITH A NEW HERO NAME TO REPLACE YOUR BABY ONE IS HARDER THAN YOU'D THINK.
YOU KIDS KNOW THERE'S A WHOLE ANIMAL KINGDOM TO CHOOSE FROM WITHOUT PLAGIARIZING, RIGHT?
ALSO, DON'T ROB BANKS.
ALTHOUGH NONE OF THESE ARE THE REAL PROBLEM RIGHT NOW...

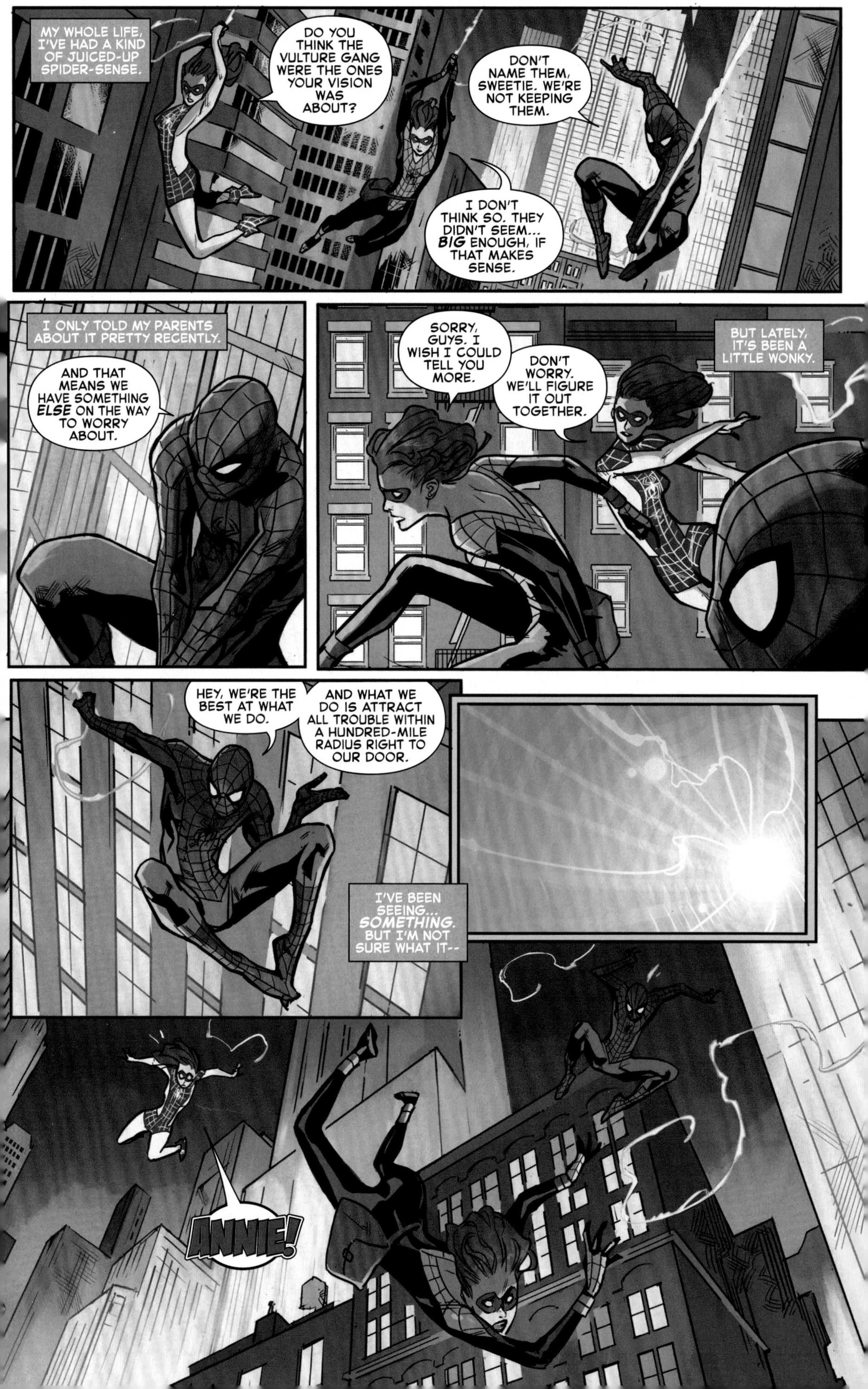
MY WHOLE LIFE, I'VE HAD A KIND OF JUICED-UP SPIDER-SENSE.
DO YOU THINK THE VULTURE GANG WERE THE ONES YOUR VISION WAS ABOUT?
DON'T NAME THEM, SWEETIE. WE'RE NOT KEEPING THEM.
I DON'T THINK SO. THEY DIDN'T SEEM... BIG ENOUGH, IF THAT MAKES SENSE.
I ONLY TOLD MY PARENTS ABOUT IT PRETTY RECENTLY.
AND THAT MEANS WE HAVE SOMETHING ELSE ON THE WAY TO WORRY ABOUT.
SORRY, GUYS. I WISH I COULD TELL YOU MORE.
DON'T WORRY. WE'LL FIGURE IT OUT TOGETHER.
BUT LATELY, IT'S BEEN A LITTLE WONKY.
HEY, WE'RE THE BEST AT WHAT WE DO.
AND WHAT WE DO IS ATTRACT ALL TROUBLE WITHIN A HUNDRED-MILE RADIUS RIGHT TO OUR DOOR.
I'VE BEEN SEEING... SOMETHING. BUT I'M NOT SURE WHAT IT--
ANNIE!

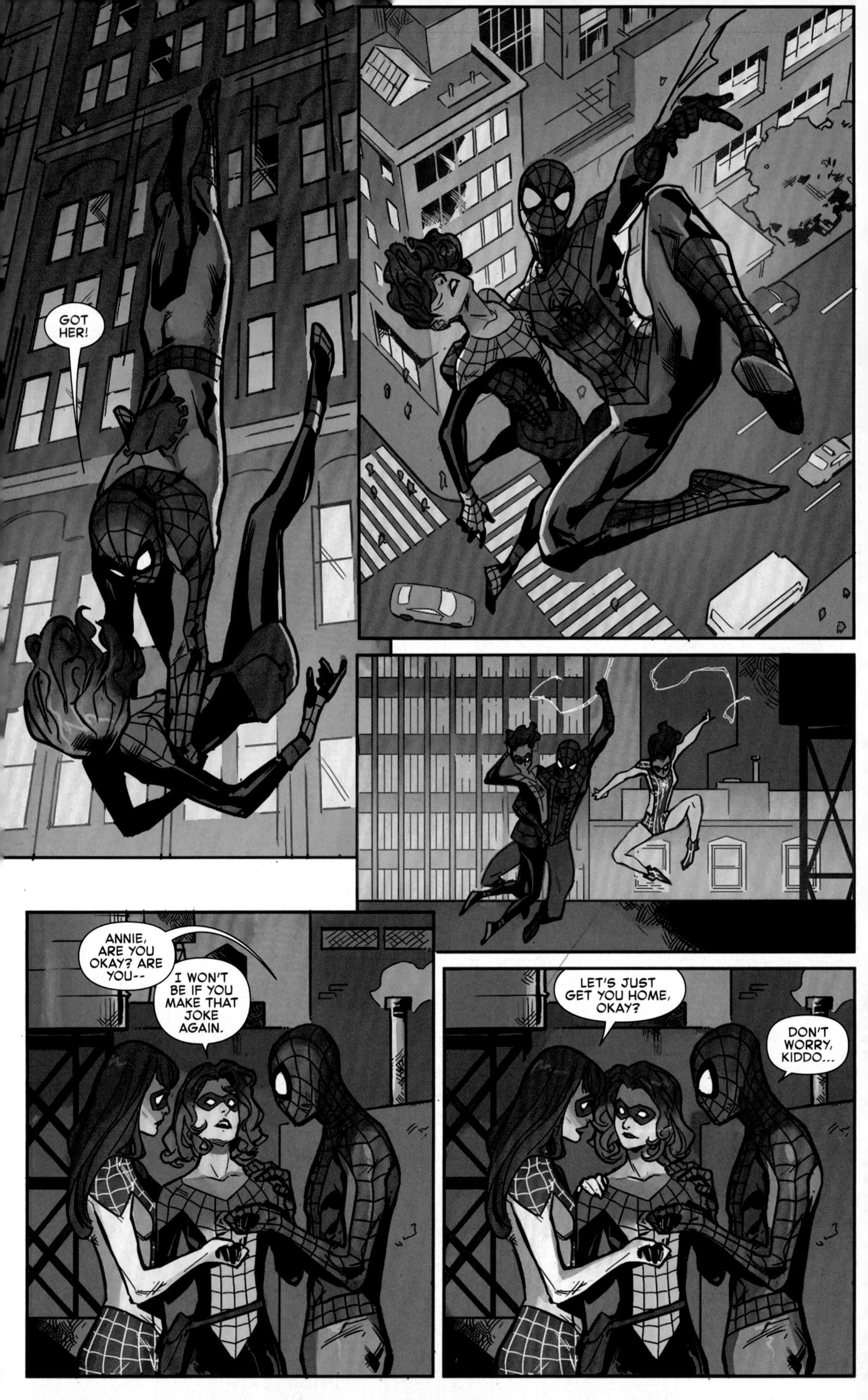
GOT HER!
ANNIE, ARE YOU OKAY? ARE YOU--
I WON'T BE IF YOU MAKE THAT JOKE AGAIN.
LET'S JUST GET YOU HOME, OKAY?
DON'T WORRY, KIDDO...

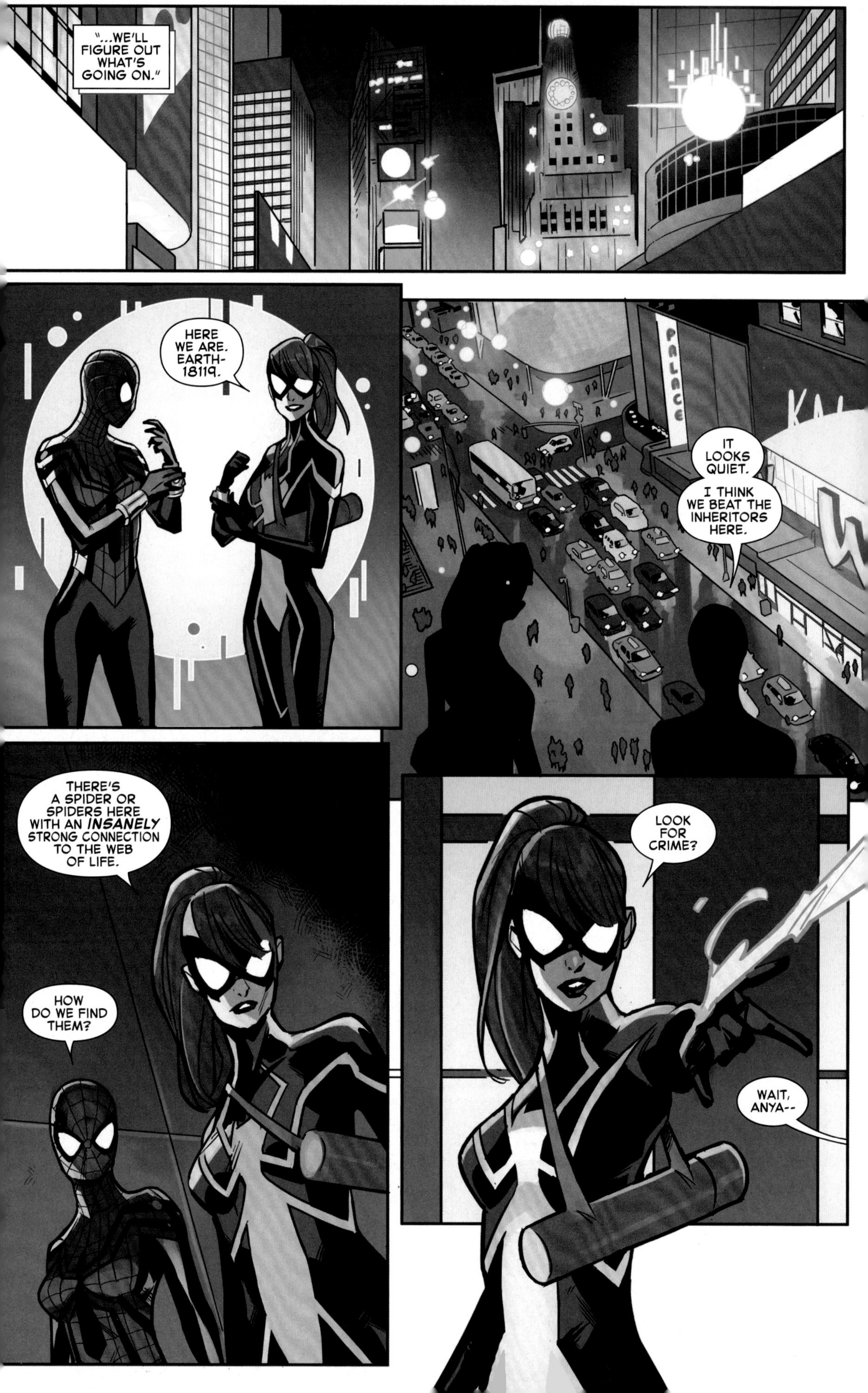
"...WE'LL FIGURE OUT WHAT'S GOING ON."
HERE WE ARE. EARTH-18119.
PALACE
IT LOOKS QUIET.
I THINK WE BEAT THE INHERITORS HERE.
THERE'S A SPIDER OR SPIDERS HERE WITH AN *INSANELY* STRONG CONNECTION TO THE WEB OF LIFE.
HOW DO WE FIND THEM?
LOOK FOR CRIME?
WAIT, ANYA--

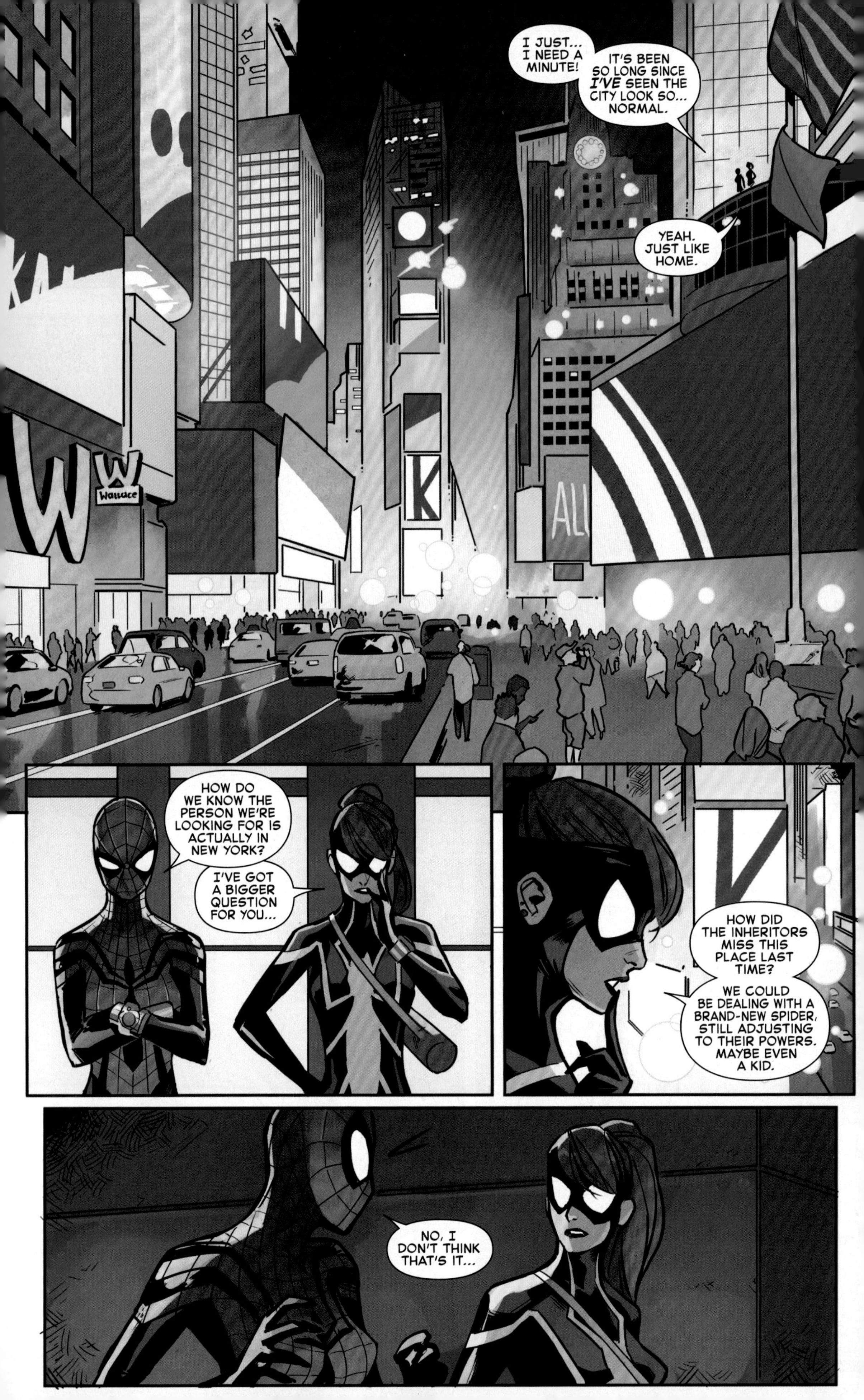

I JUST... I NEED A MINUTE!
IT'S BEEN SO LONG SINCE I'VE SEEN THE CITY LOOK SO... NORMAL.
YEAH. JUST LIKE HOME.
Wallace
HOW DO WE KNOW THE PERSON WE'RE LOOKING FOR IS ACTUALLY IN NEW YORK?
I'VE GOT A BIGGER QUESTION FOR YOU...
HOW DID THE INHERITORS MISS THIS PLACE LAST TIME?
WE COULD BE DEALING WITH A BRAND-NEW SPIDER, STILL ADJUSTING TO THEIR POWERS. MAYBE EVEN A KID.
NO, I DON'T THINK THAT'S IT...

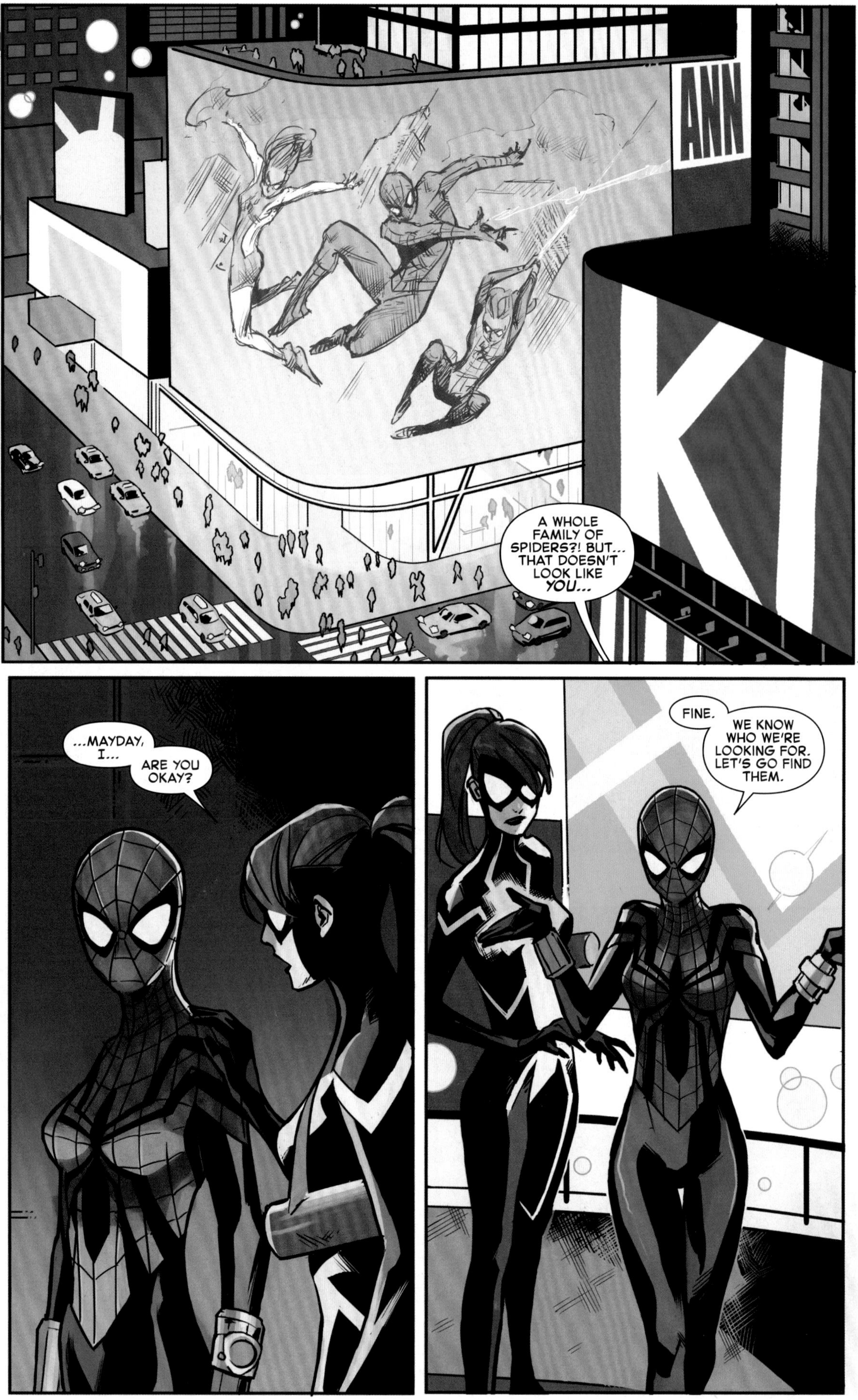
ANN
KI
A WHOLE FAMILY OF SPIDERS?! BUT... THAT DOESN'T LOOK LIKE *YOU*...
...MAYDAY, I...
ARE YOU OKAY?
FINE.
WE KNOW WHO WE'RE LOOKING FOR. LET'S GO FIND THEM.

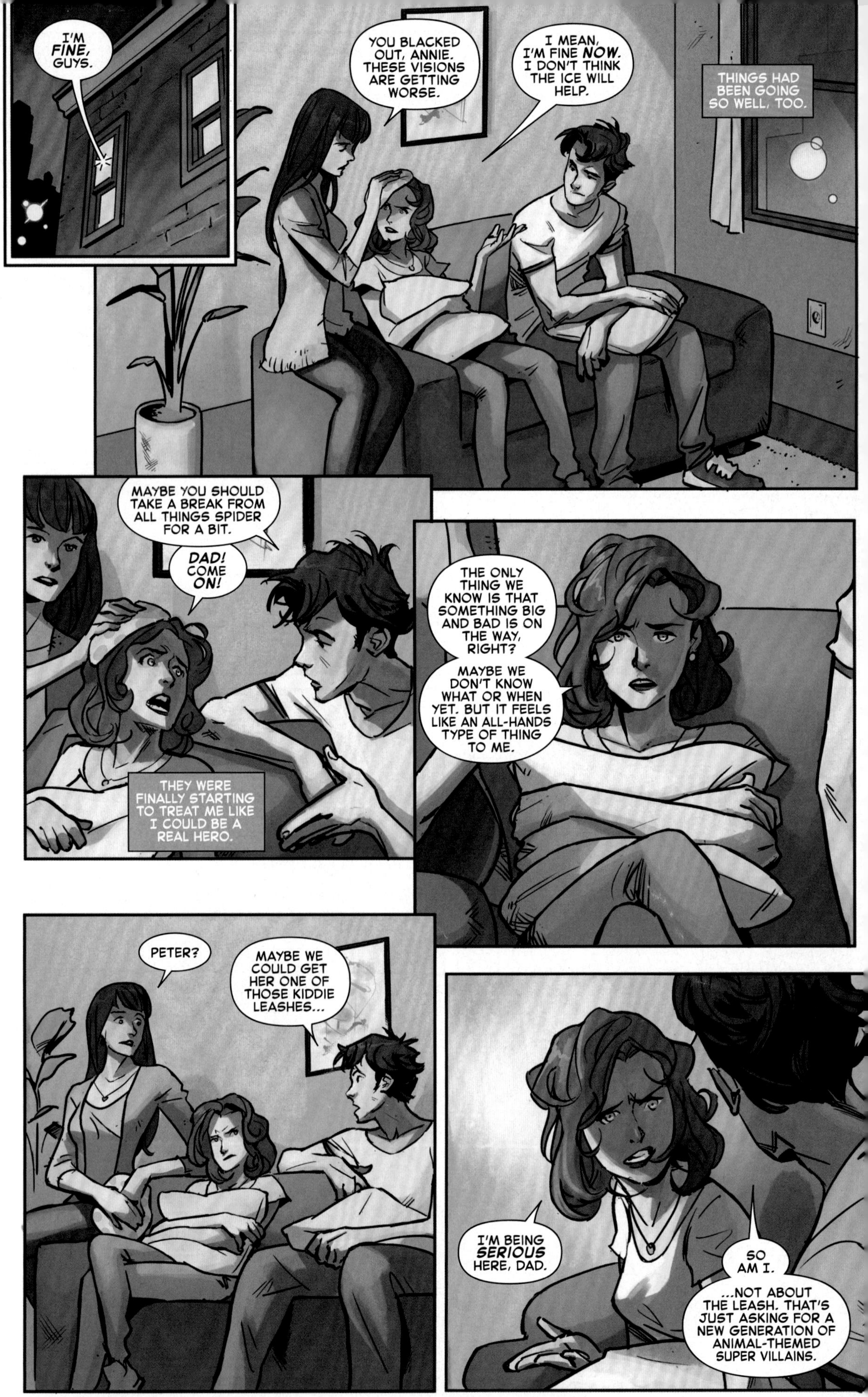

I'M FINE, GUYS.
YOU BLACKED OUT, ANNIE. THESE VISIONS ARE GETTING WORSE.
I MEAN, I'M FINE NOW. I DON'T THINK THE ICE WILL HELP.
THINGS HAD BEEN GOING SO WELL, TOO.
MAYBE YOU SHOULD TAKE A BREAK FROM ALL THINGS SPIDER FOR A BIT.
DAD! COME ON!
THEY WERE FINALLY STARTING TO TREAT ME LIKE I COULD BE A REAL HERO.
THE ONLY THING WE KNOW IS THAT SOMETHING BIG AND BAD IS ON THE WAY, RIGHT?
MAYBE WE DON'T KNOW WHAT OR WHEN YET. BUT IT FEELS LIKE AN ALL-HANDS TYPE OF THING TO ME.
PETER?
MAYBE WE COULD GET HER ONE OF THOSE KIDDIE LEASHES...
I'M BEING SERIOUS HERE, DAD.
SO AM I.
...NOT ABOUT THE LEASH. THAT'S JUST ASKING FOR A NEW GENERATION OF ANIMAL-THEMED SUPER VILLAINS.

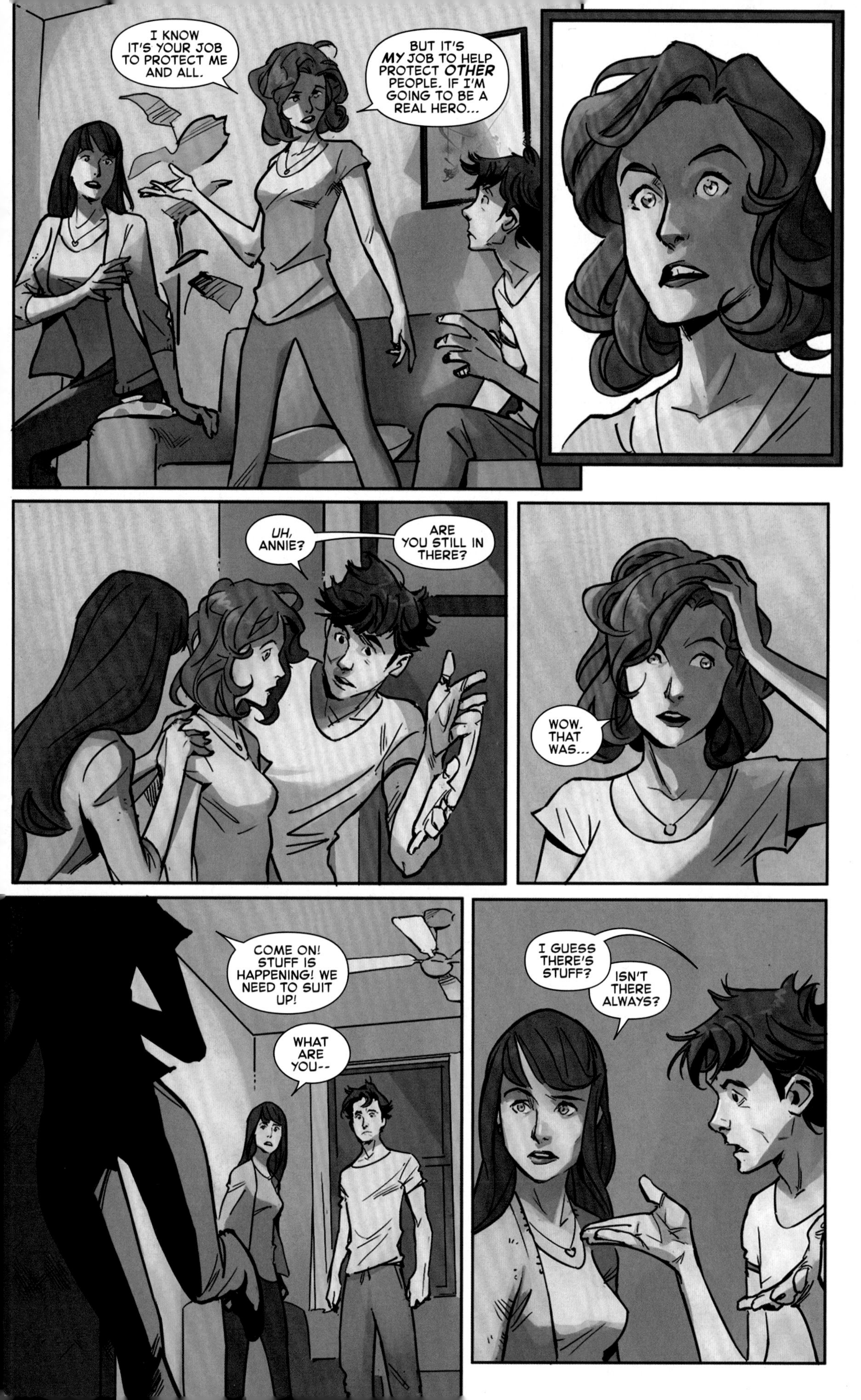
I KNOW IT'S YOUR JOB TO PROTECT ME AND ALL.
BUT IT'S *MY* JOB TO HELP PROTECT *OTHER* PEOPLE. IF I'M GOING TO BE A REAL HERO...
UH, ANNIE?
ARE YOU STILL IN THERE?
WOW. THAT WAS...
COME ON! STUFF IS HAPPENING! WE NEED TO SUIT UP!
WHAT ARE YOU--
I GUESS THERE'S STUFF?
ISN'T THERE ALWAYS?

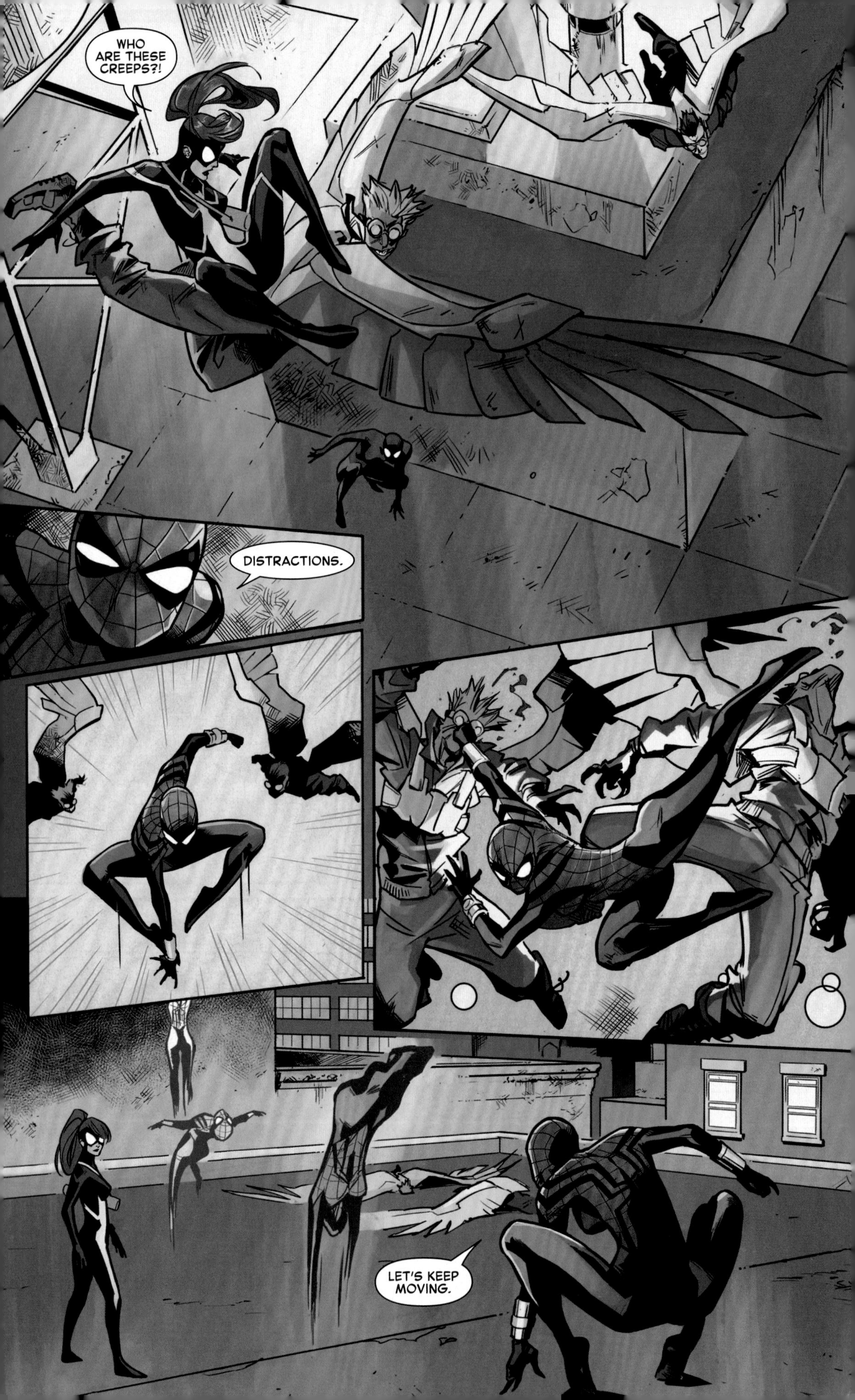
WHO ARE THESE CREEPS?!
DISTRACTIONS.
LET'S KEEP MOVING.

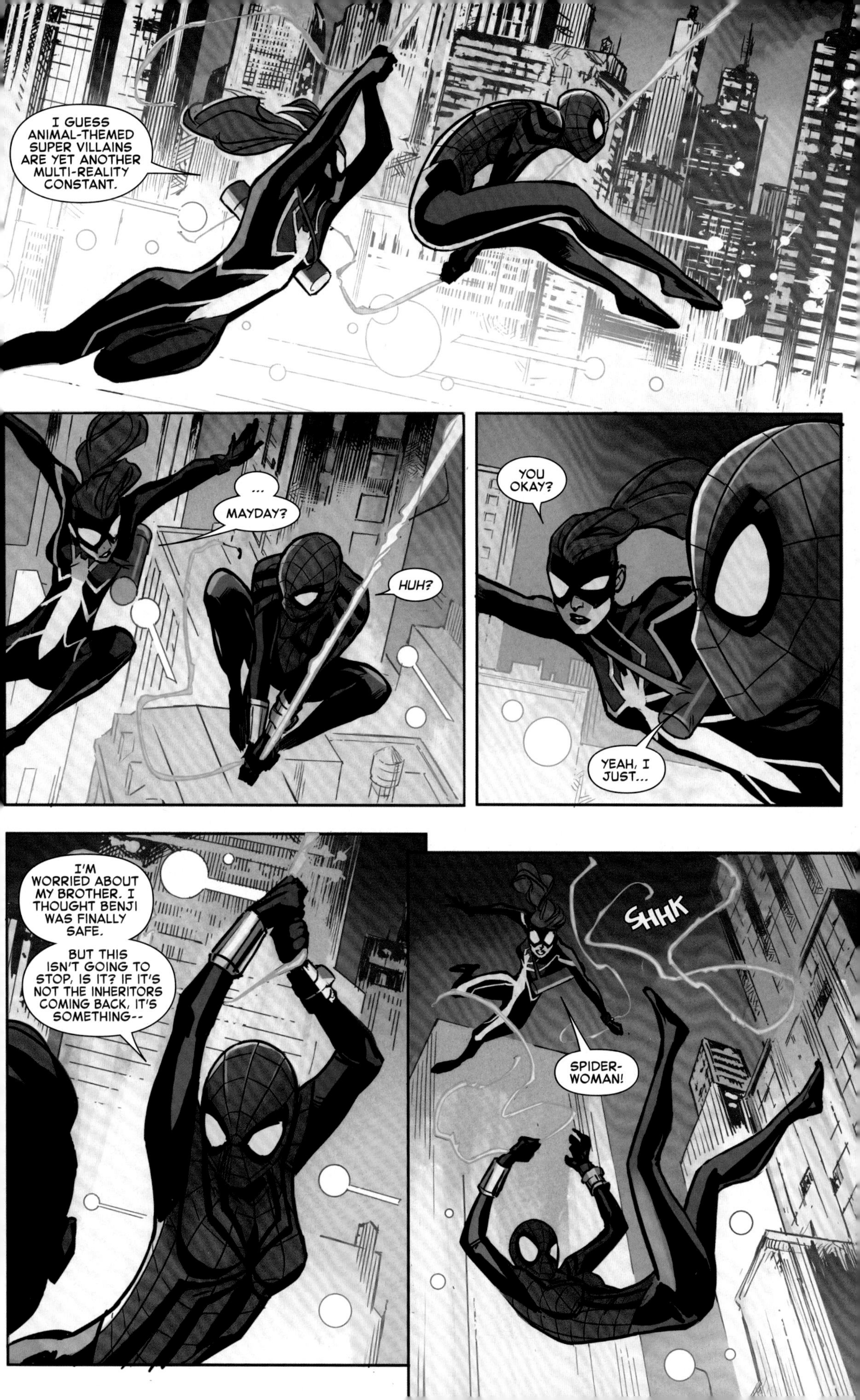
I GUESS ANIMAL-THEMED SUPER VILLAINS ARE YET ANOTHER MULTI-REALITY CONSTANT.
...
MAYDAY?
HUH?
YOU OKAY?
YEAH, I JUST...
I'M WORRIED ABOUT MY BROTHER. I THOUGHT BENJI WAS FINALLY SAFE.
BUT THIS ISN'T GOING TO STOP, IS IT? IF IT'S NOT THE INHERITORS COMING BACK, IT'S SOMETHING--
SHHK
SPIDER-WOMAN!

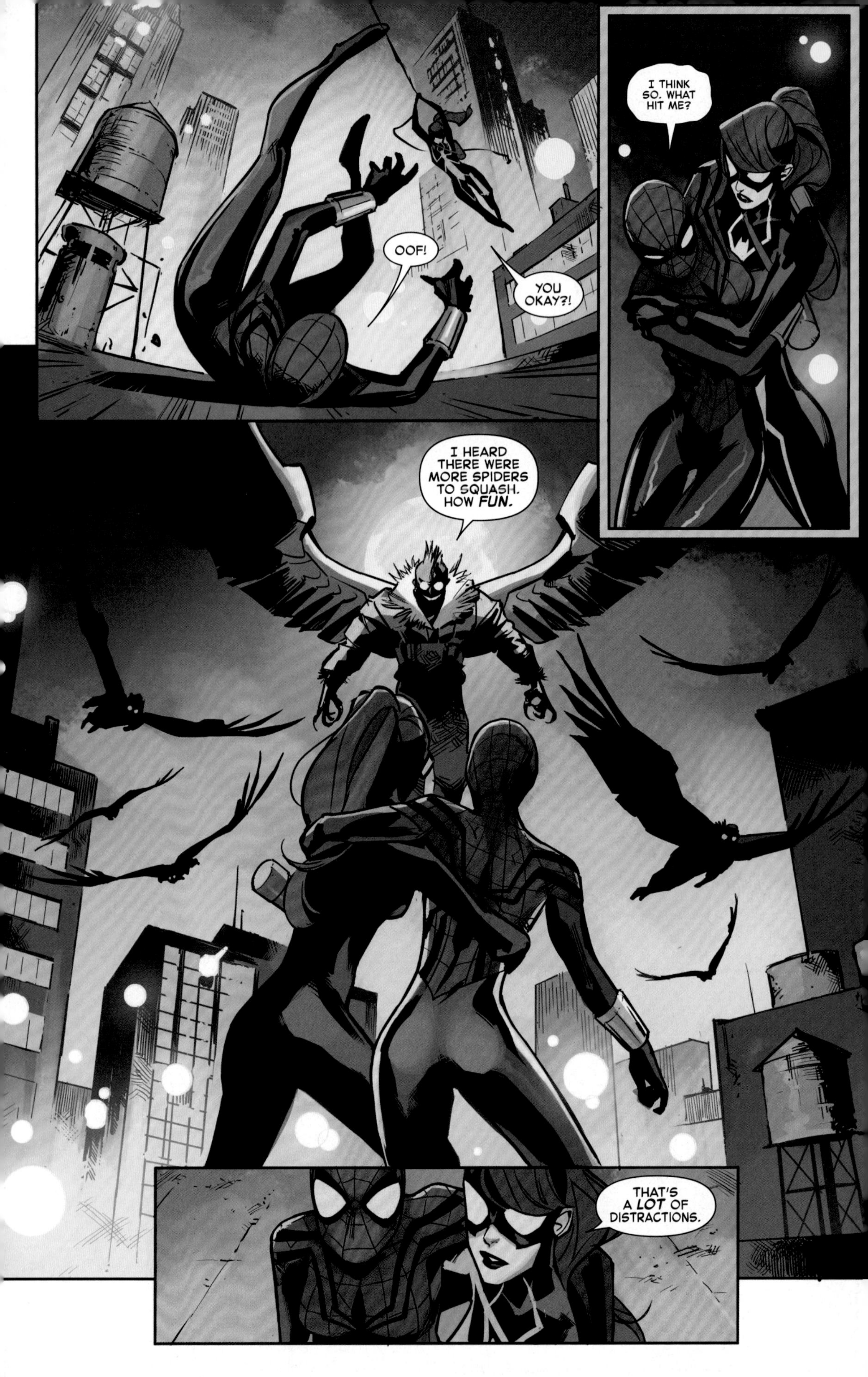
OOF!
YOU OKAY?!
I THINK SO. WHAT HIT ME?
I HEARD THERE WERE MORE SPIDERS TO SQUASH. HOW FUN.
THAT'S A LOT OF DISTRACTIONS.

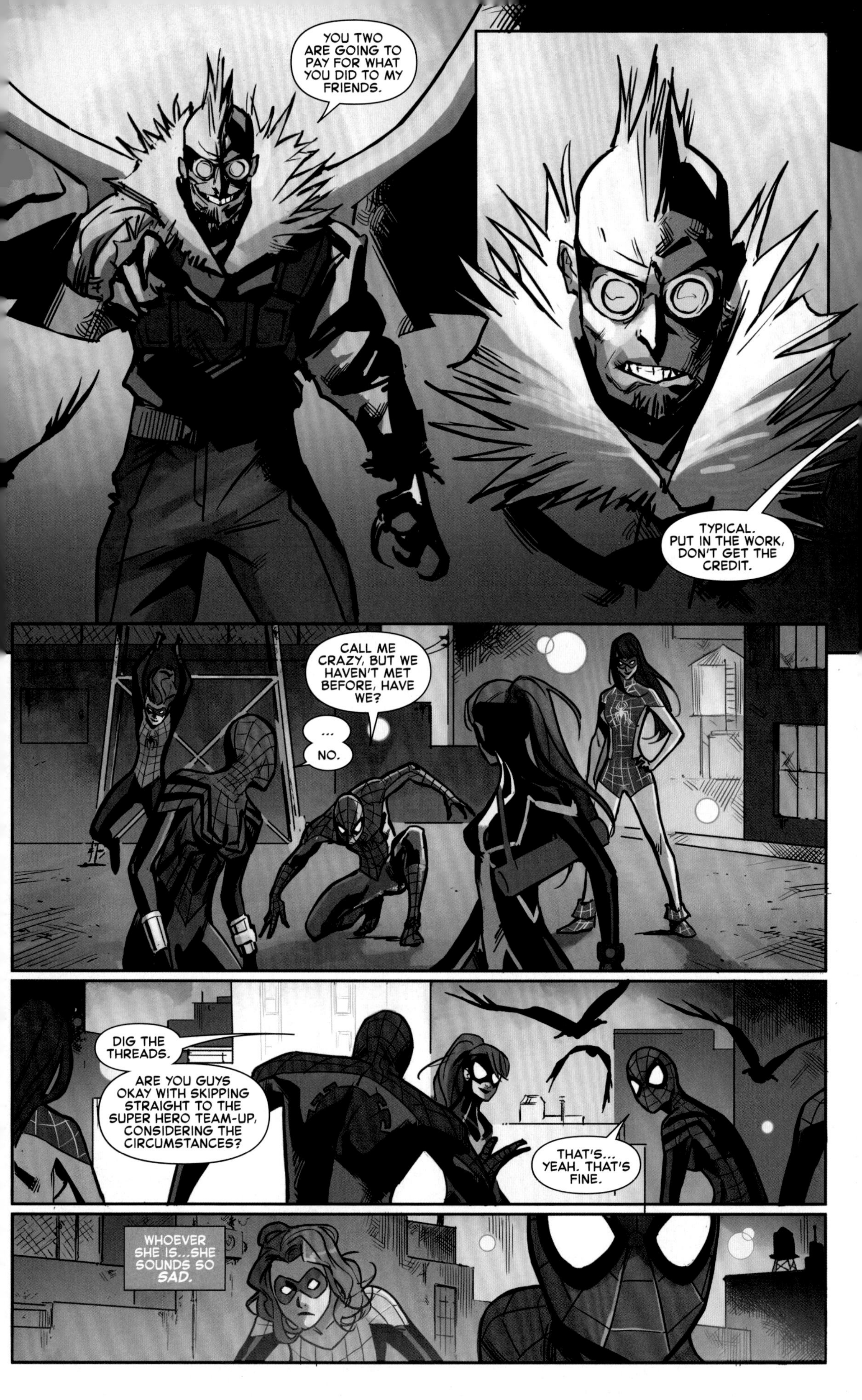
YOU TWO ARE GOING TO PAY FOR WHAT YOU DID TO MY FRIENDS.
TYPICAL. PUT IN THE WORK, DON'T GET THE CREDIT.
CALL ME CRAZY, BUT WE HAVEN'T MET BEFORE, HAVE WE?
...
NO.
DIG THE THREADS.
ARE YOU GUYS OKAY WITH SKIPPING STRAIGHT TO THE SUPER HERO TEAM-UP, CONSIDERING THE CIRCUMSTANCES?
THAT'S... YEAH. THAT'S FINE.
WHOEVER SHE IS...SHE SOUNDS SO SAD.

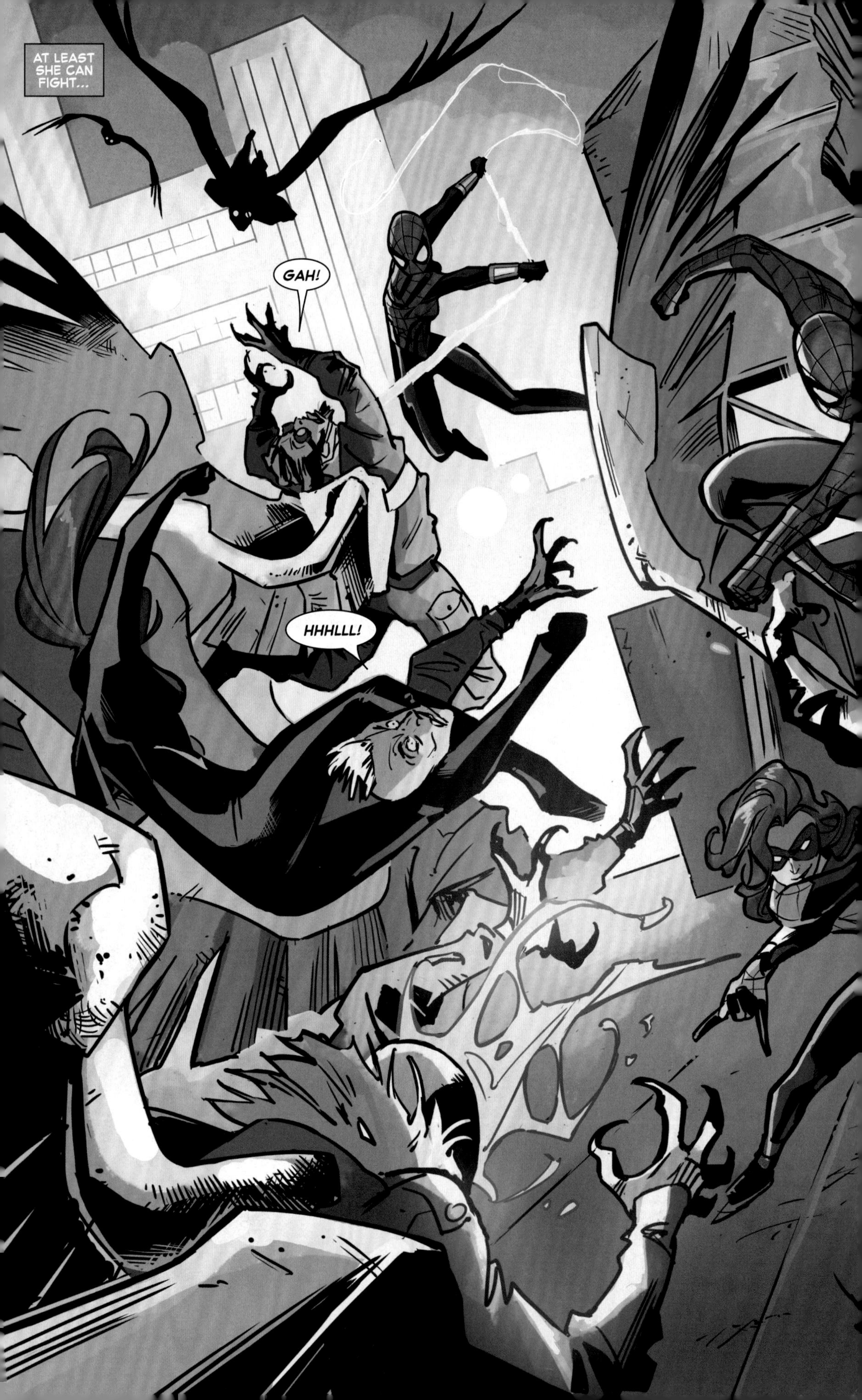
AT LEAST SHE CAN FIGHT...
GAH!
HHHLLL!

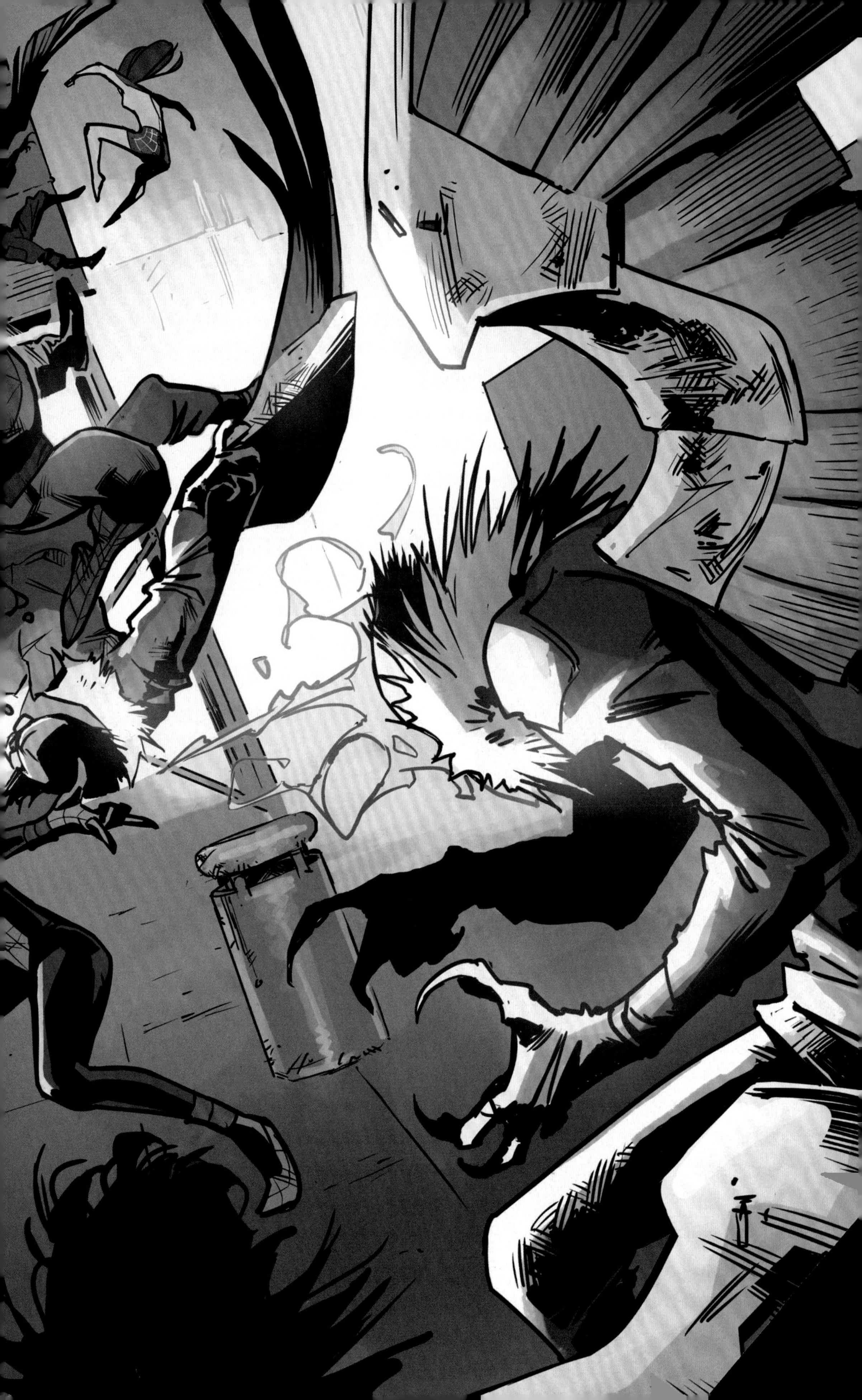

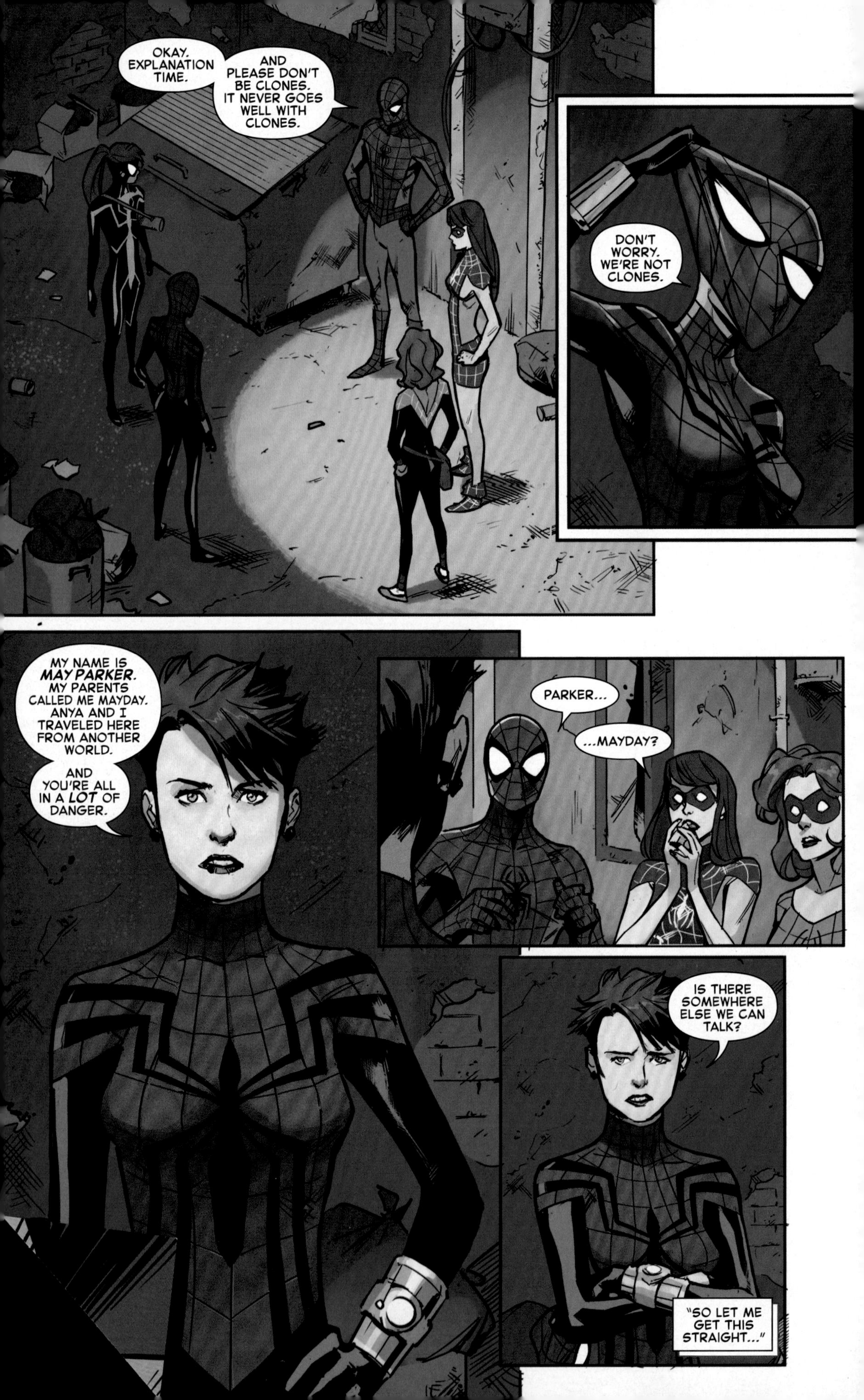
OKAY. EXPLANATION TIME.
AND PLEASE DON'T BE CLONES. IT NEVER GOES WELL WITH CLONES.
DON'T WORRY. WE'RE NOT CLONES.
MY NAME IS MAY PARKER. MY PARENTS CALLED ME MAYDAY. ANYA AND I TRAVELED HERE FROM ANOTHER WORLD.
AND YOU'RE ALL IN A LOT OF DANGER.
PARKER...
...MAYDAY?
IS THERE SOMEWHERE ELSE WE CAN TALK?
"SO LET ME GET THIS STRAIGHT..."

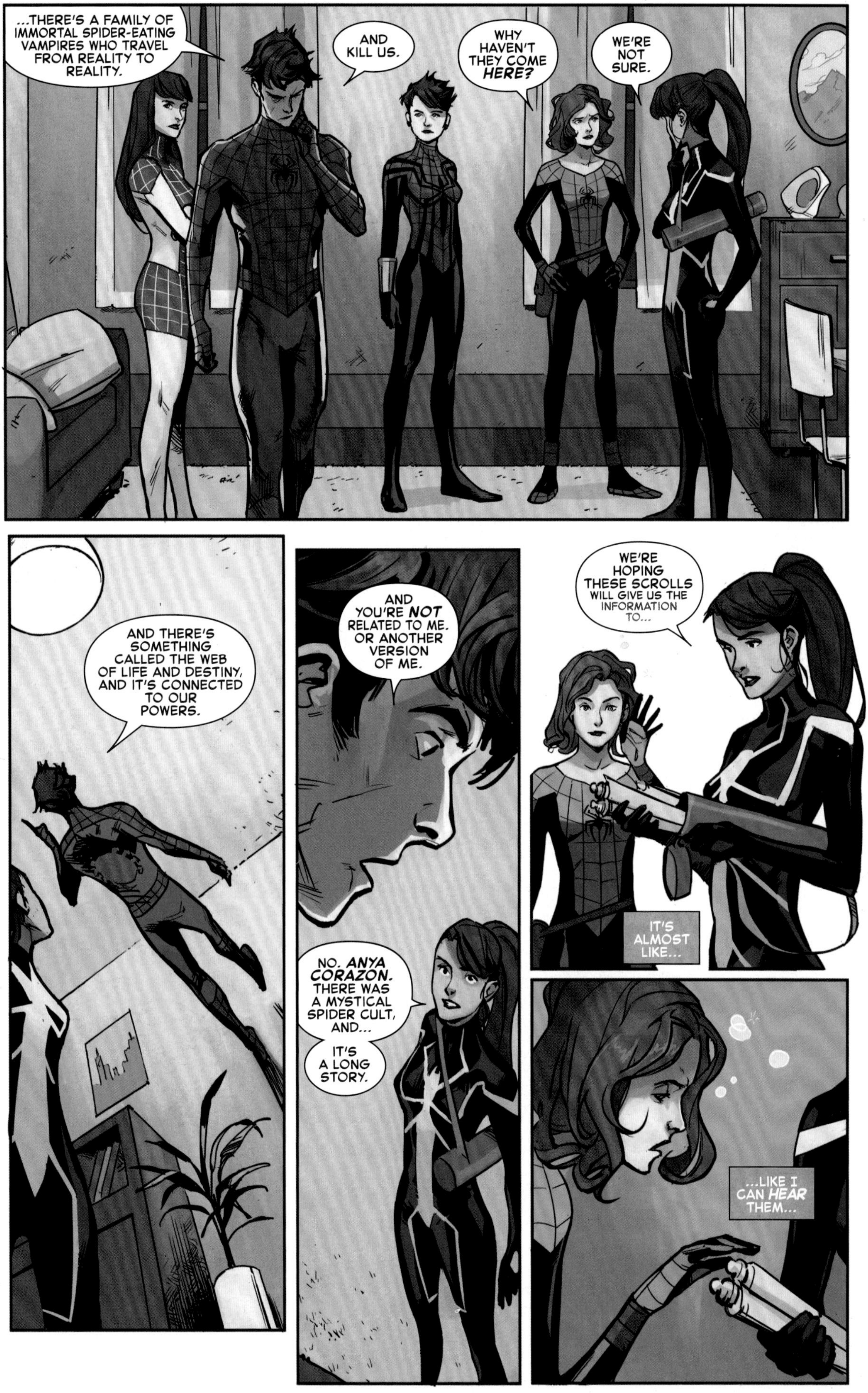

...THERE'S A FAMILY OF IMMORTAL SPIDER-EATING VAMPIRES WHO TRAVEL FROM REALITY TO REALITY.
AND KILL US.
WHY HAVEN'T THEY COME *HERE?*
WE'RE NOT SURE.
AND THERE'S SOMETHING CALLED THE WEB OF LIFE AND DESTINY, AND IT'S CONNECTED TO OUR POWERS.
AND YOU'RE *NOT* RELATED TO ME. OR ANOTHER VERSION OF ME.
NO. *ANYA CORAZON.* THERE WAS A MYSTICAL SPIDER CULT, AND...
IT'S A LONG STORY.
WE'RE HOPING THESE SCROLLS WILL GIVE US THE INFORMATION TO...
IT'S ALMOST LIKE...
...LIKE I CAN *HEAR* THEM...

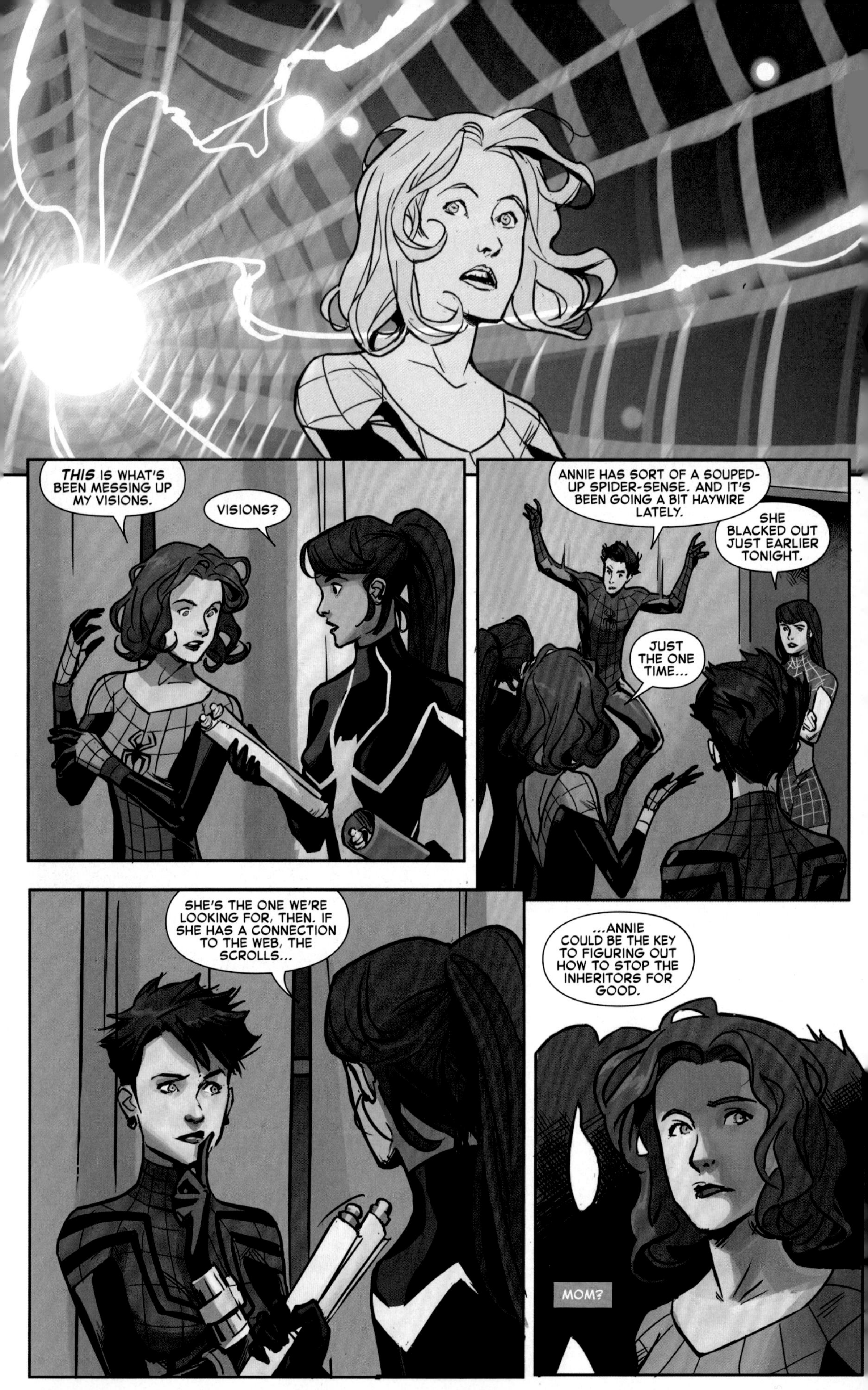
THIS IS WHAT'S BEEN MESSING UP MY VISIONS.
VISIONS?
ANNIE HAS SORT OF A SOUPED-UP SPIDER-SENSE. AND IT'S BEEN GOING A BIT HAYWIRE LATELY.
SHE BLACKED OUT JUST EARLIER TONIGHT.
JUST THE ONE TIME...
SHE'S THE ONE WE'RE LOOKING FOR, THEN. IF SHE HAS A CONNECTION TO THE WEB, THE SCROLLS...
...ANNIE COULD BE THE KEY TO FIGURING OUT HOW TO STOP THE INHERITORS FOR GOOD.
MOM?

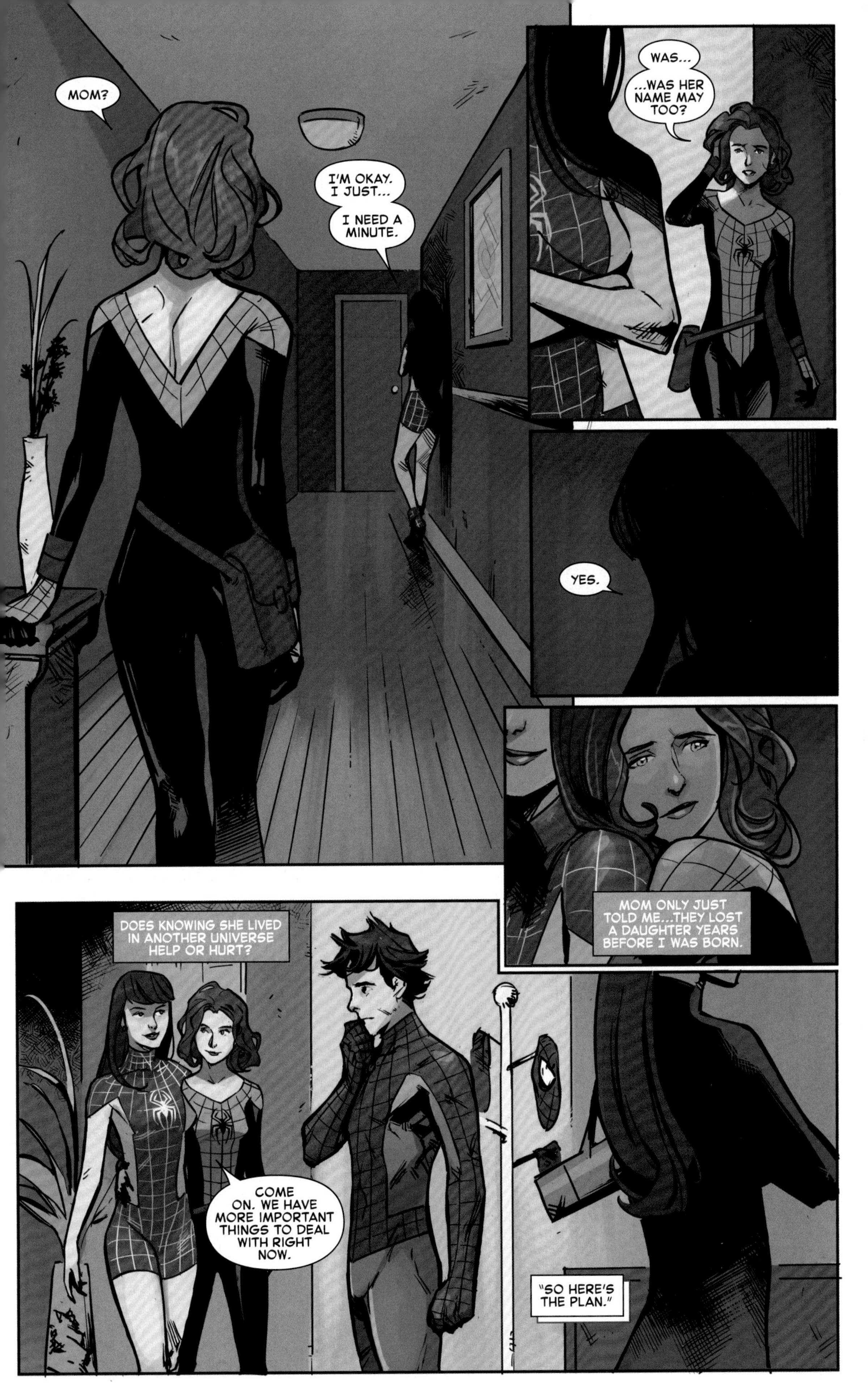
MOM?
I'M OKAY. I JUST...
I NEED A MINUTE.
WAS...
...WAS HER NAME MAY TOO?
YES.
MOM ONLY JUST TOLD ME...THEY LOST A DAUGHTER YEARS BEFORE I WAS BORN.
DOES KNOWING SHE LIVED IN ANOTHER UNIVERSE HELP OR HURT?
COME ON. WE HAVE MORE IMPORTANT THINGS TO DEAL WITH RIGHT NOW.
"SO HERE'S THE PLAN."

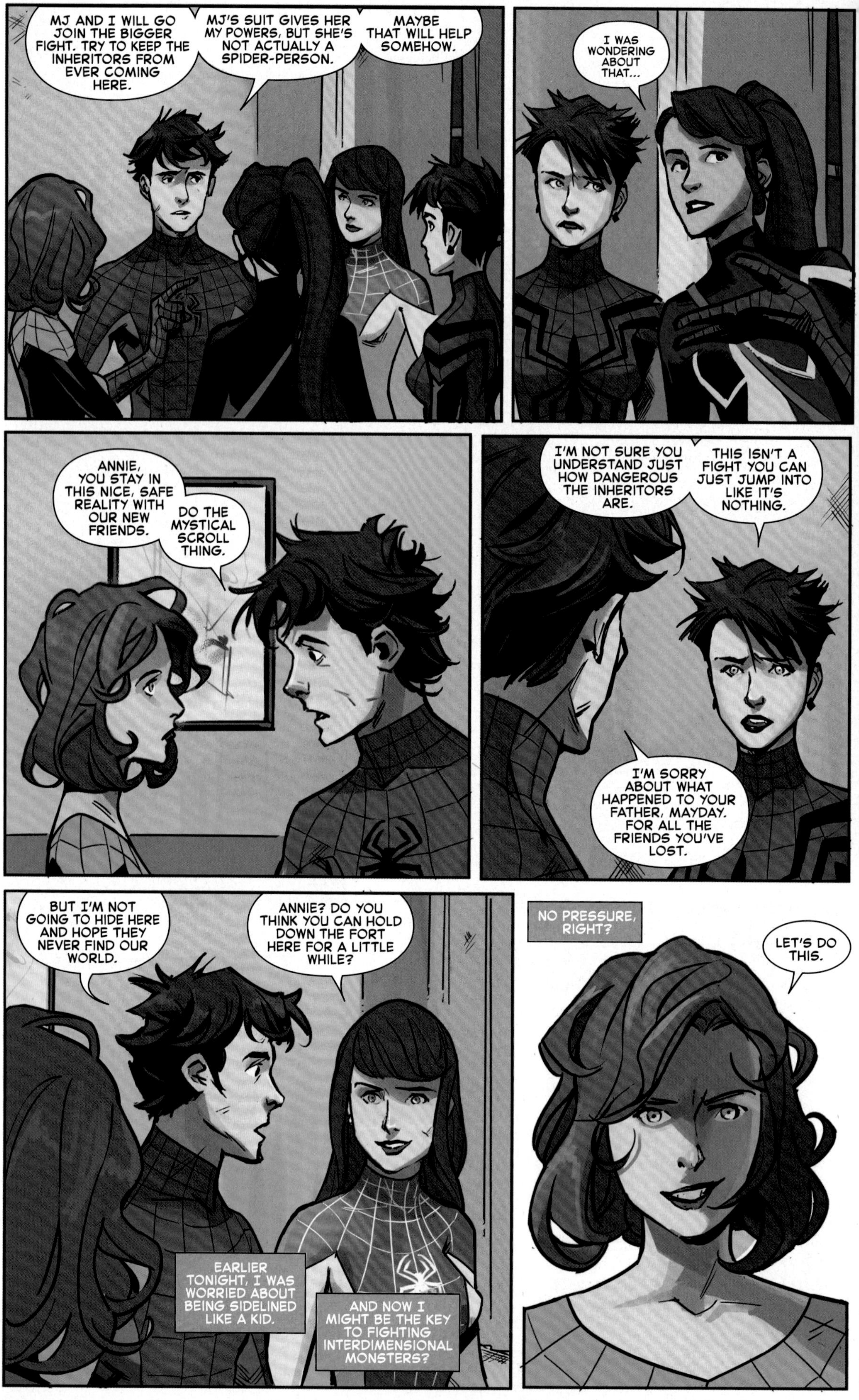
MJ AND I WILL GO JOIN THE BIGGER FIGHT. TRY TO KEEP THE INHERITORS FROM EVER COMING HERE.
MJ'S SUIT GIVES HER MY POWERS, BUT SHE'S NOT ACTUALLY A SPIDER-PERSON.
MAYBE THAT WILL HELP SOMEHOW.
I WAS WONDERING ABOUT THAT...
ANNIE, YOU STAY IN THIS NICE, SAFE REALITY WITH OUR NEW FRIENDS.
DO THE MYSTICAL SCROLL THING.
I'M NOT SURE YOU UNDERSTAND JUST HOW DANGEROUS THE INHERITORS ARE.
THIS ISN'T A FIGHT YOU CAN JUST JUMP INTO LIKE IT'S NOTHING.
I'M SORRY ABOUT WHAT HAPPENED TO YOUR FATHER, MAYDAY. FOR ALL THE FRIENDS YOU'VE LOST.
BUT I'M NOT GOING TO HIDE HERE AND HOPE THEY NEVER FIND OUR WORLD.
ANNIE? DO YOU THINK YOU CAN HOLD DOWN THE FORT HERE FOR A LITTLE WHILE?
EARLIER TONIGHT, I WAS WORRIED ABOUT BEING SIDELINED LIKE A KID.
AND NOW I MIGHT BE THE KEY TO FIGHTING INTERDIMENSIONAL MONSTERS?
NO PRESSURE, RIGHT?
LET'S DO THIS.

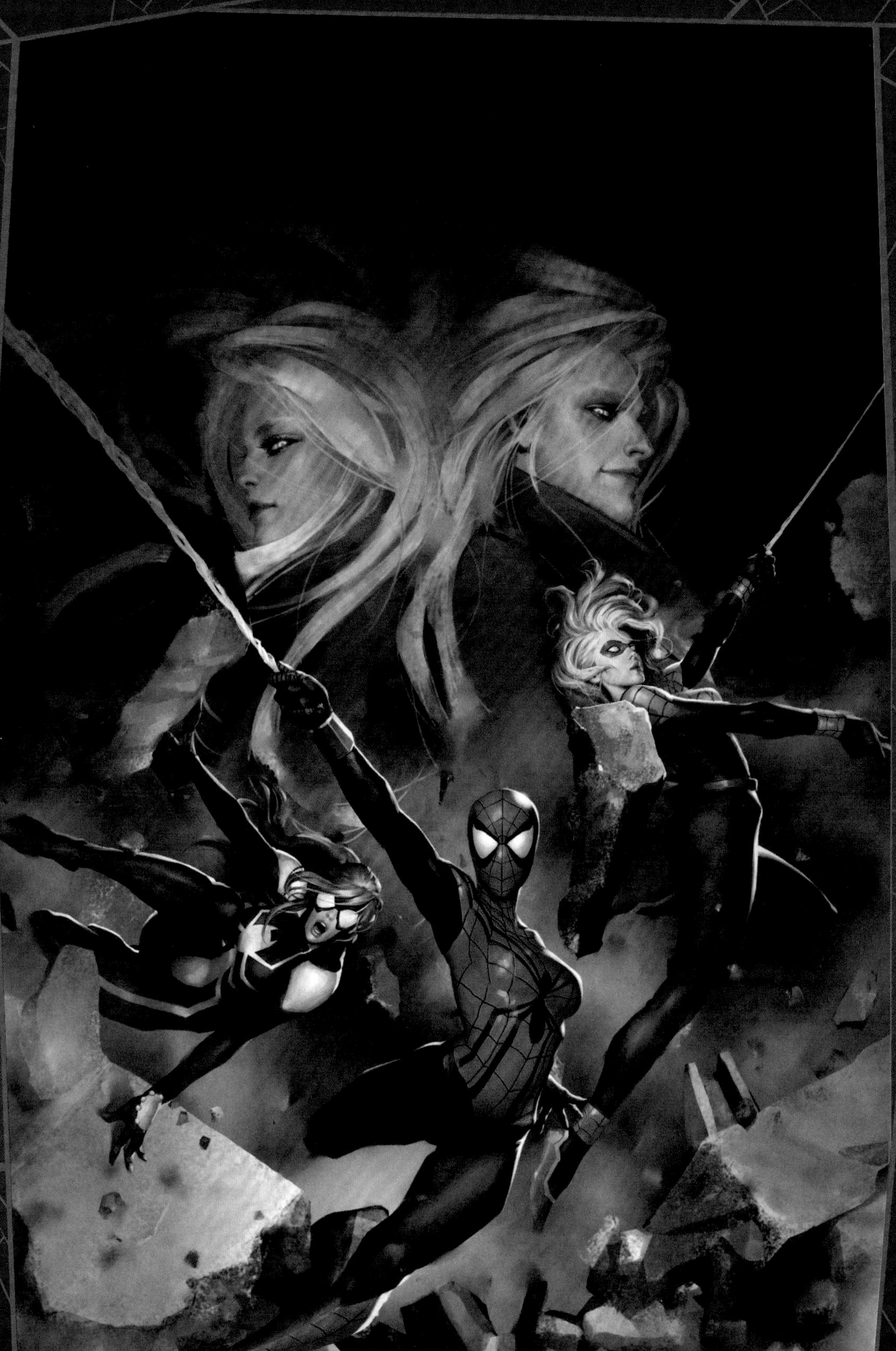

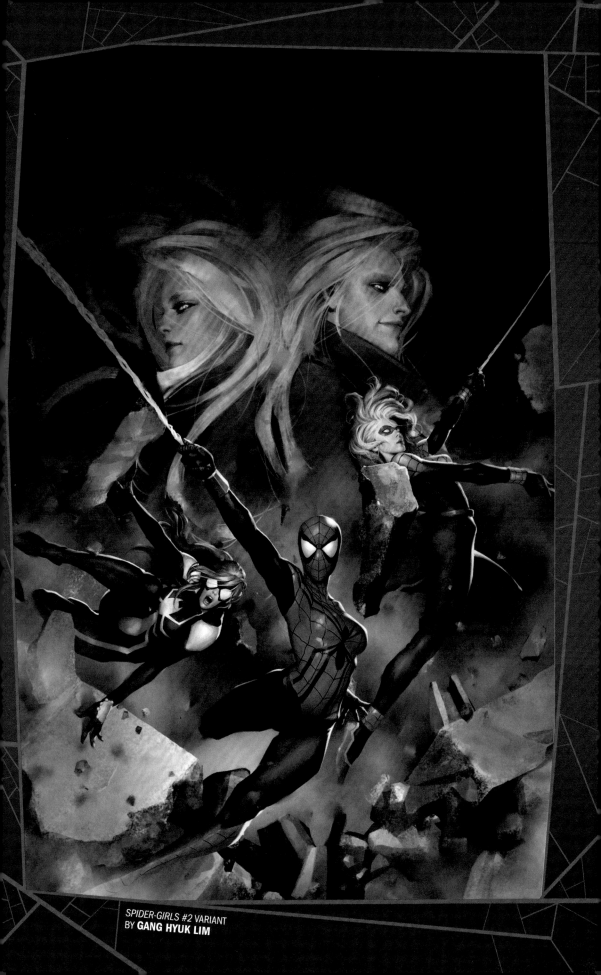

SPIDER-GIRLS #2 VARIANT
BY **GANG HYUK LIM**

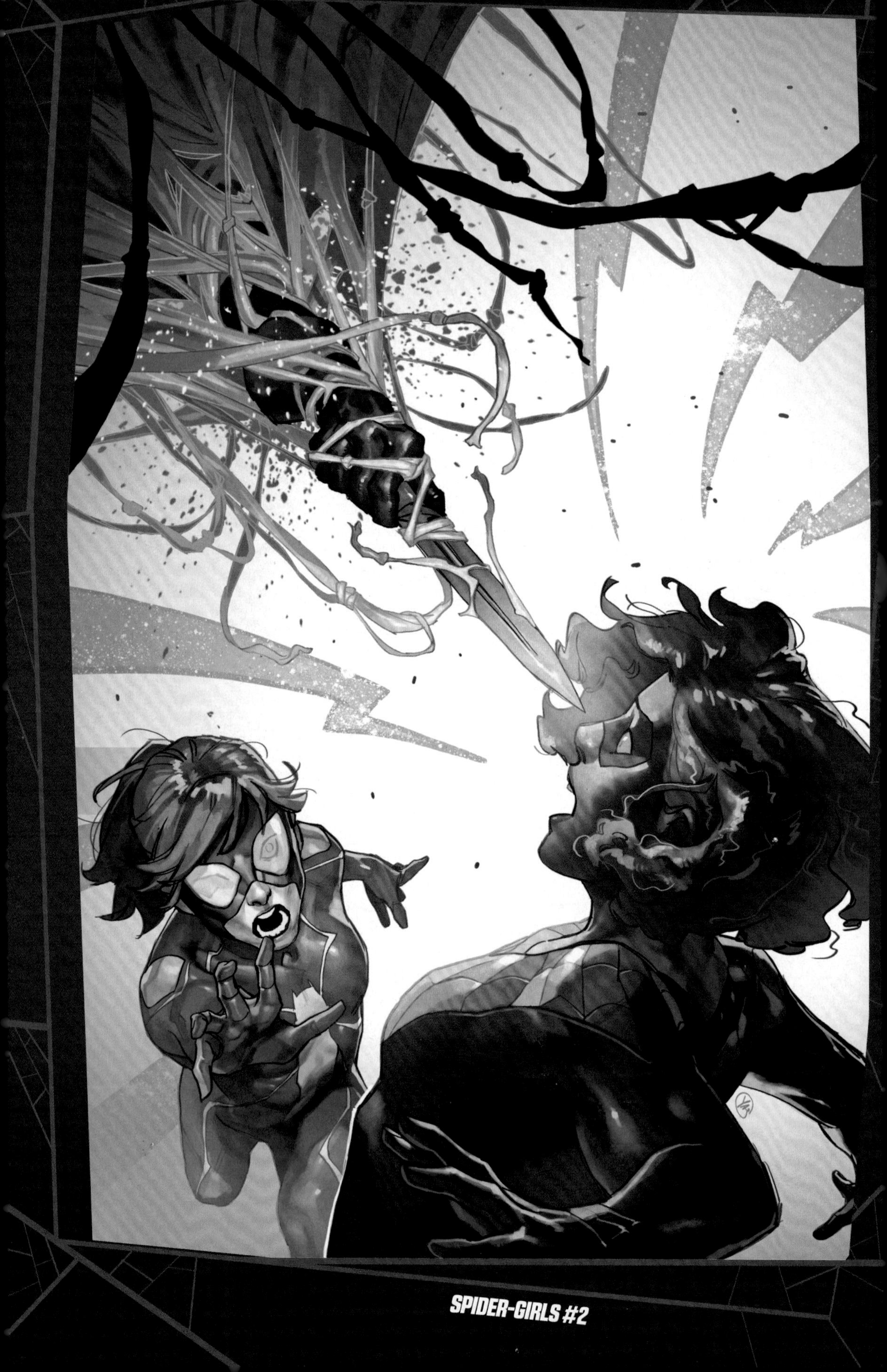

SPIDER-GIRLS #2

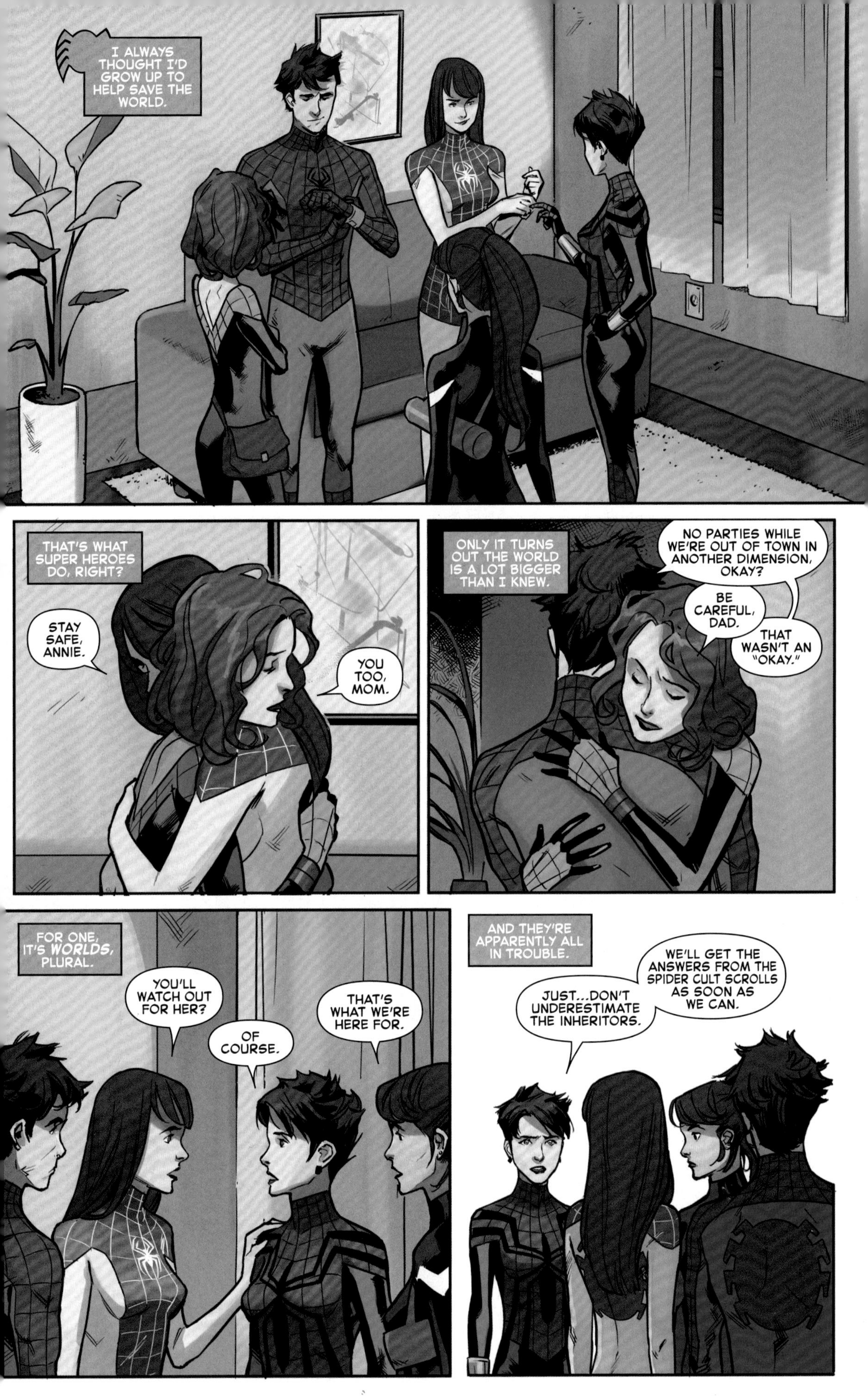
I ALWAYS THOUGHT I'D GROW UP TO HELP SAVE THE WORLD.
THAT'S WHAT SUPER HEROES DO, RIGHT?
STAY SAFE, ANNIE.
YOU TOO, MOM.
ONLY IT TURNS OUT THE WORLD IS A LOT BIGGER THAN I KNEW.
NO PARTIES WHILE WE'RE OUT OF TOWN IN ANOTHER DIMENSION, OKAY?
BE CAREFUL, DAD.
THAT WASN'T AN "OKAY."
FOR ONE, IT'S *WORLDS*, PLURAL.
YOU'LL WATCH OUT FOR HER?
OF COURSE.
THAT'S WHAT WE'RE HERE FOR.
AND THEY'RE APPARENTLY ALL IN TROUBLE.
JUST...DON'T UNDERESTIMATE THE INHERITORS.
WE'LL GET THE ANSWERS FROM THE SPIDER CULT SCROLLS AS SOON AS WE CAN.

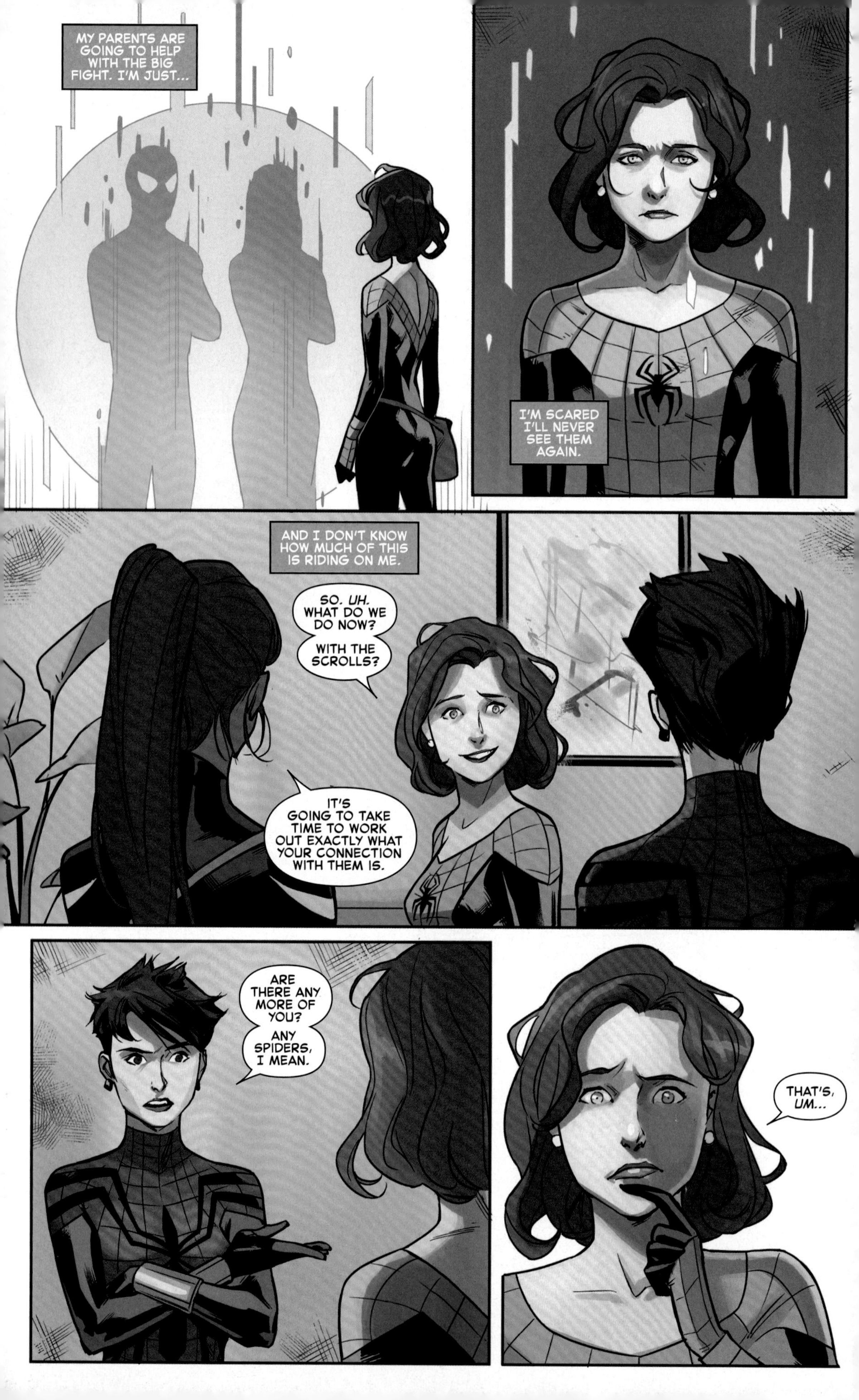
MY PARENTS ARE GOING TO HELP WITH THE BIG FIGHT. I'M JUST...
I'M SCARED I'LL NEVER SEE THEM AGAIN.
AND I DON'T KNOW HOW MUCH OF THIS IS RIDING ON ME.
SO. *UH.* WHAT DO WE DO NOW?
WITH THE SCROLLS?
IT'S GOING TO TAKE TIME TO WORK OUT EXACTLY WHAT YOUR CONNECTION WITH THEM IS.
ARE THERE ANY MORE OF YOU?
ANY SPIDERS, I MEAN.
THAT'S, UM...

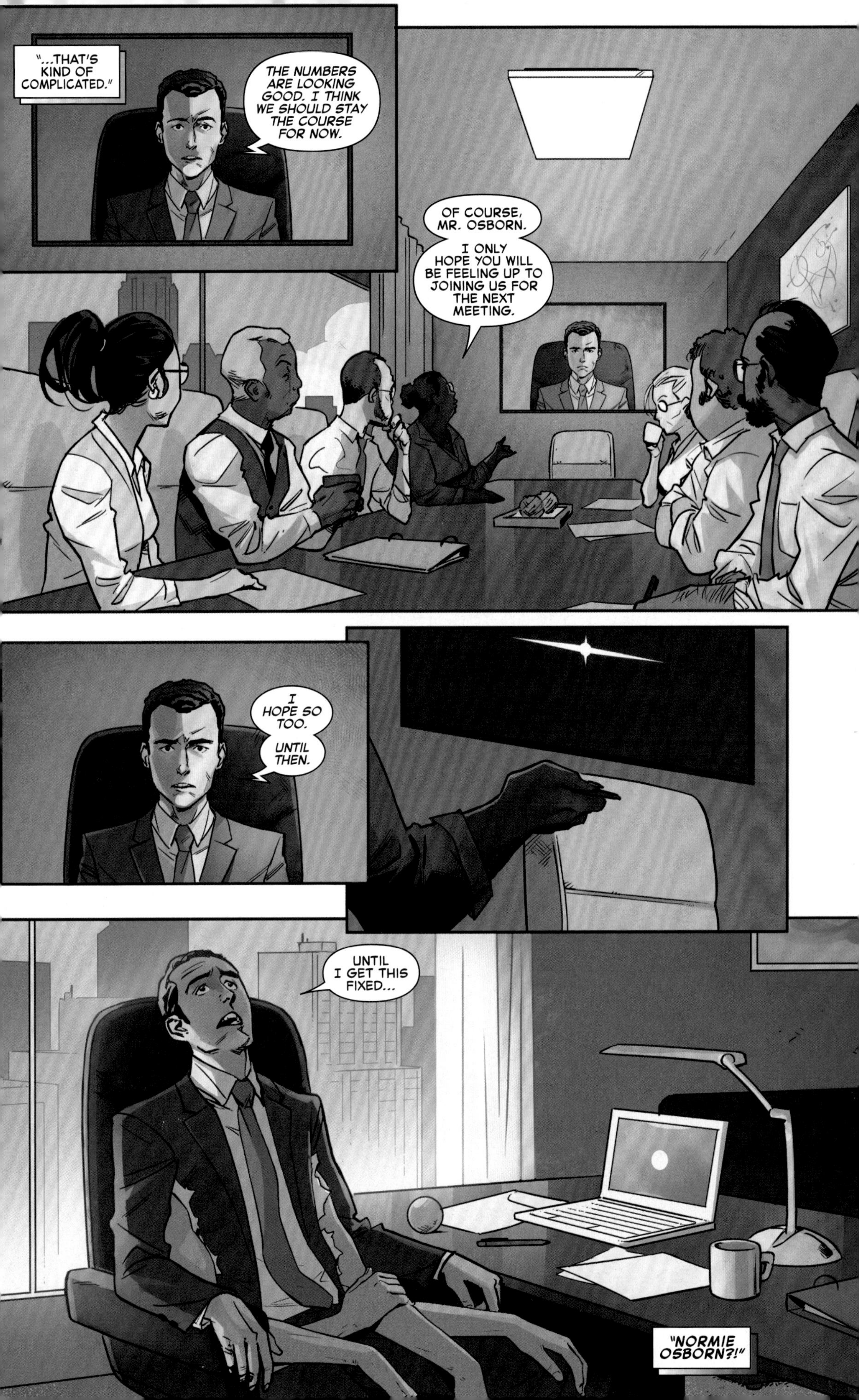
"...THAT'S KIND OF COMPLICATED."
THE NUMBERS ARE LOOKING GOOD. I THINK WE SHOULD STAY THE COURSE FOR NOW.
OF COURSE, MR. OSBORN.
I ONLY HOPE YOU WILL BE FEELING UP TO JOINING US FOR THE NEXT MEETING.
I HOPE SO TOO.
UNTIL THEN.
UNTIL I GET THIS FIXED...
"NORMIE OSBORN?!"

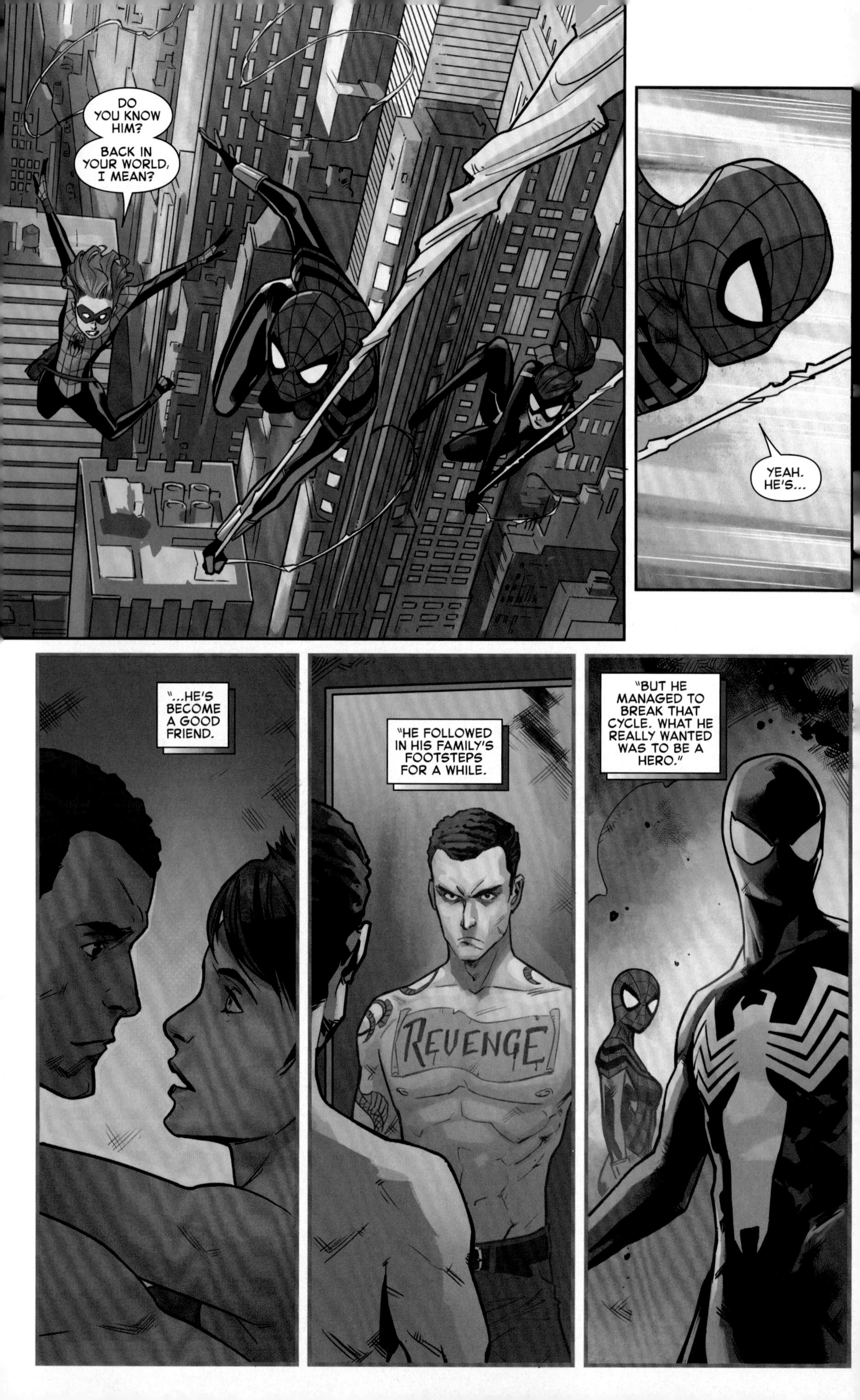
DO YOU KNOW HIM?
BACK IN YOUR WORLD, I MEAN?
YEAH. HE'S...
"...HE'S BECOME A GOOD FRIEND.
"HE FOLLOWED IN HIS FAMILY'S FOOTSTEPS FOR A WHILE.
REVENGE
"BUT HE MANAGED TO BREAK THAT CYCLE. WHAT HE REALLY WANTED WAS TO BE A HERO."

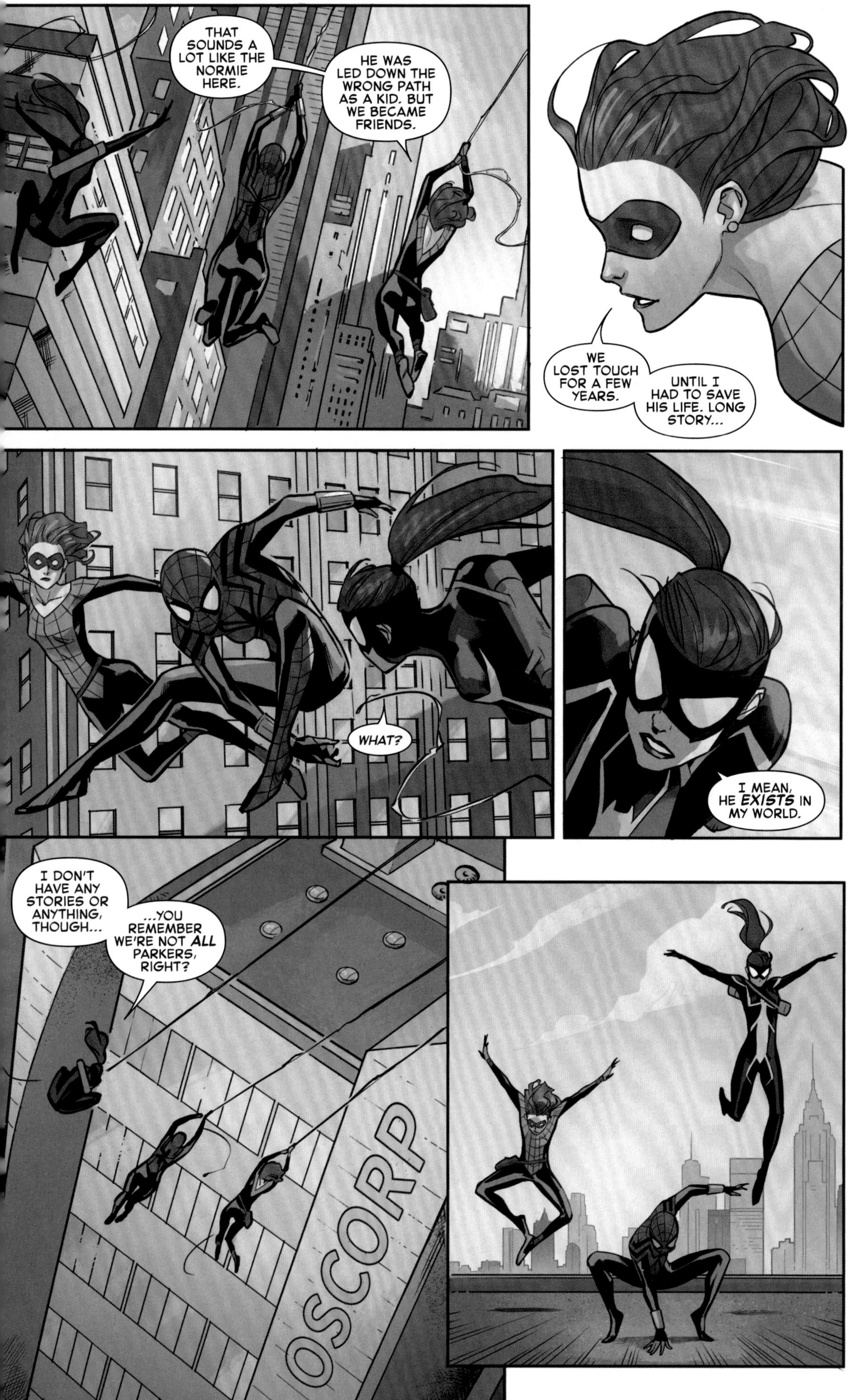
THAT SOUNDS A LOT LIKE THE NORMIE HERE.
HE WAS LED DOWN THE WRONG PATH AS A KID. BUT WE BECAME FRIENDS.
WE LOST TOUCH FOR A FEW YEARS.
UNTIL I HAD TO SAVE HIS LIFE. LONG STORY...
WHAT?
I MEAN, HE EXISTS IN MY WORLD.
I DON'T HAVE ANY STORIES OR ANYTHING, THOUGH...
...YOU REMEMBER WE'RE NOT ALL PARKERS, RIGHT?
OSCORP

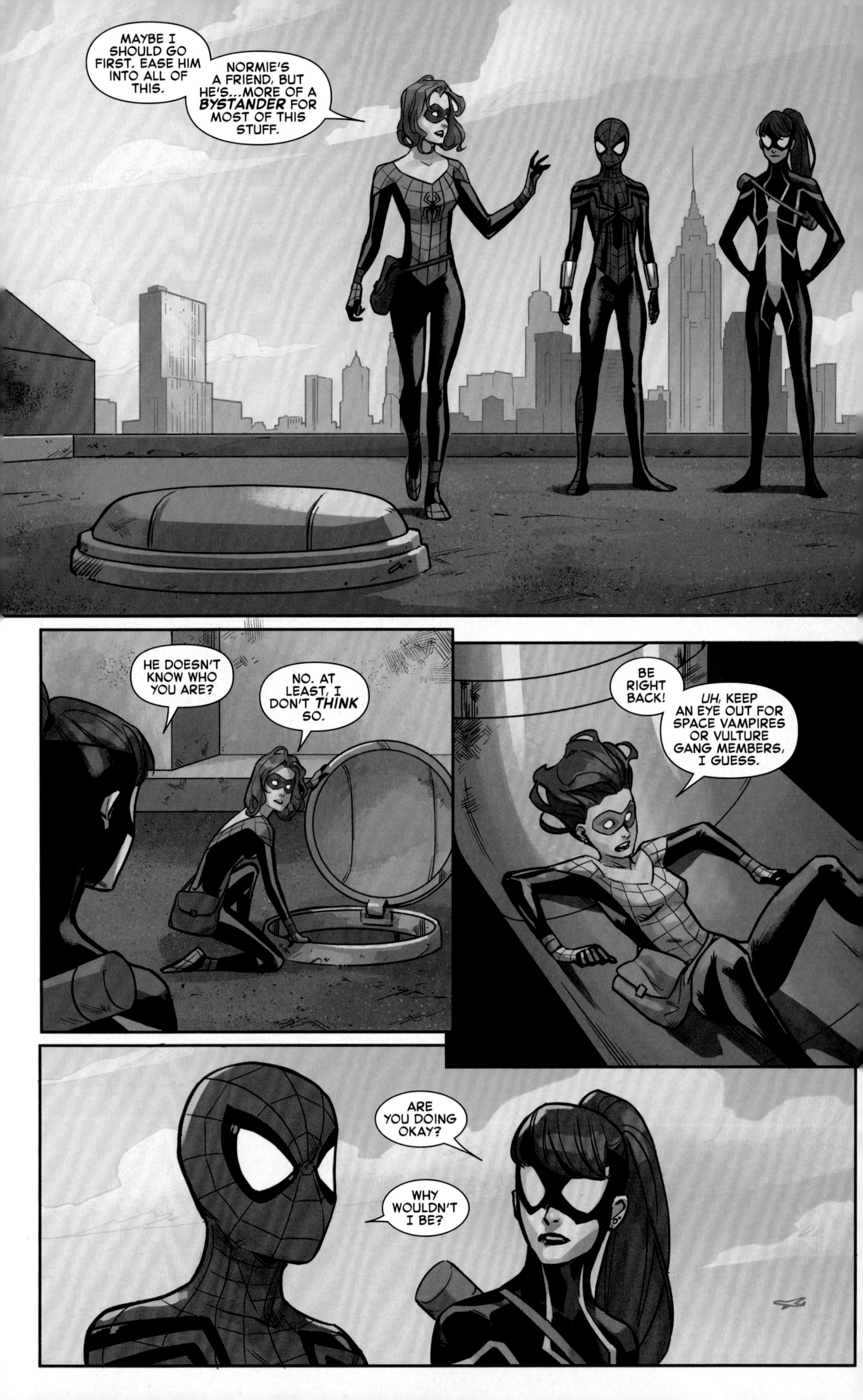
MAYBE I SHOULD GO FIRST. EASE HIM INTO ALL OF THIS.
NORMIE'S A FRIEND, BUT HE'S...MORE OF A BYSTANDER FOR MOST OF THIS STUFF.
HE DOESN'T KNOW WHO YOU ARE?
NO. AT LEAST, I DON'T THINK SO.
BE RIGHT BACK!
UH, KEEP AN EYE OUT FOR SPACE VAMPIRES OR VULTURE GANG MEMBERS, I GUESS.
ARE YOU DOING OKAY?
WHY WOULDN'T I BE?

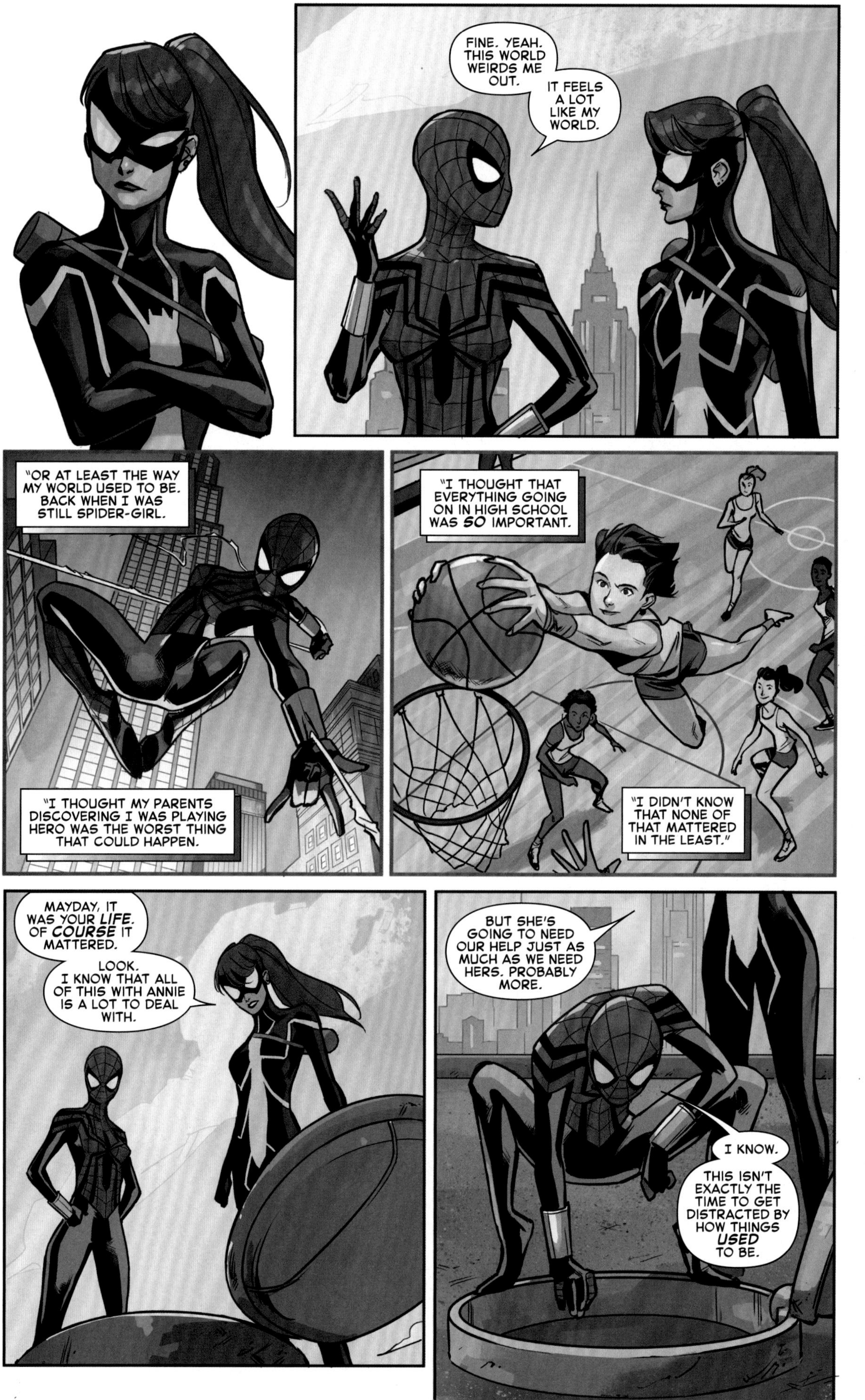
FINE. YEAH. THIS WORLD WEIRDS ME OUT.
IT FEELS A LOT LIKE MY WORLD.
"OR AT LEAST THE WAY MY WORLD USED TO BE. BACK WHEN I WAS STILL SPIDER-GIRL.
"I THOUGHT MY PARENTS DISCOVERING I WAS PLAYING HERO WAS THE WORST THING THAT COULD HAPPEN.
"I THOUGHT THAT EVERYTHING GOING ON IN HIGH SCHOOL WAS SO IMPORTANT.
"I DIDN'T KNOW THAT NONE OF THAT MATTERED IN THE LEAST."
MAYDAY, IT WAS YOUR LIFE. OF COURSE IT MATTERED.
LOOK. I KNOW THAT ALL OF THIS WITH ANNIE IS A LOT TO DEAL WITH.
BUT SHE'S GOING TO NEED OUR HELP JUST AS MUCH AS WE NEED HERS. PROBABLY MORE.
I KNOW.
THIS ISN'T EXACTLY THE TIME TO GET DISTRACTED BY HOW THINGS USED TO BE.

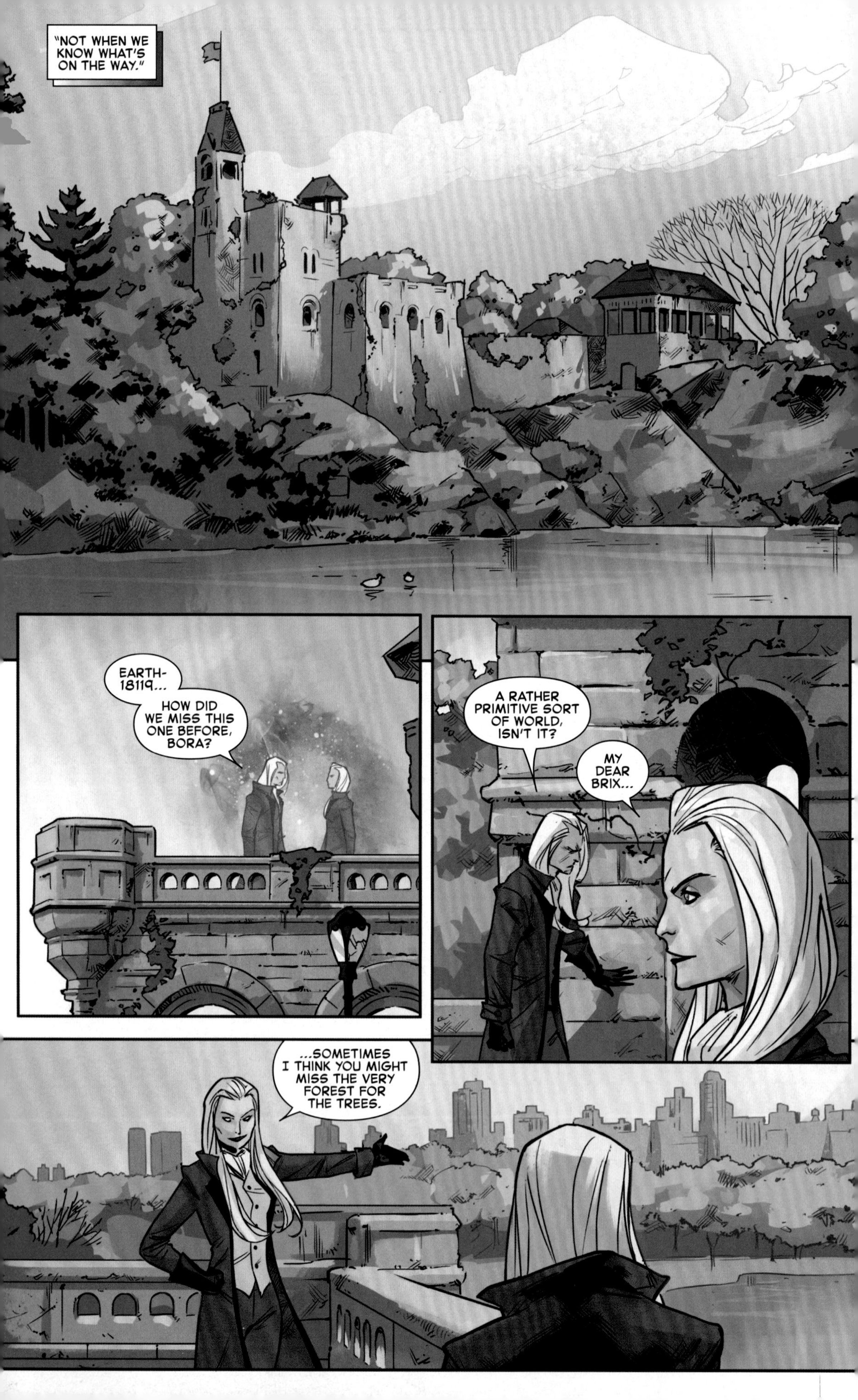
"NOT WHEN WE KNOW WHAT'S ON THE WAY."
EARTH-18119...
HOW DID WE MISS THIS ONE BEFORE, BORA?
A RATHER PRIMITIVE SORT OF WORLD, ISN'T IT?
MY DEAR BRIX...
...SOMETIMES I THINK YOU MIGHT MISS THE VERY FOREST FOR THE TREES.

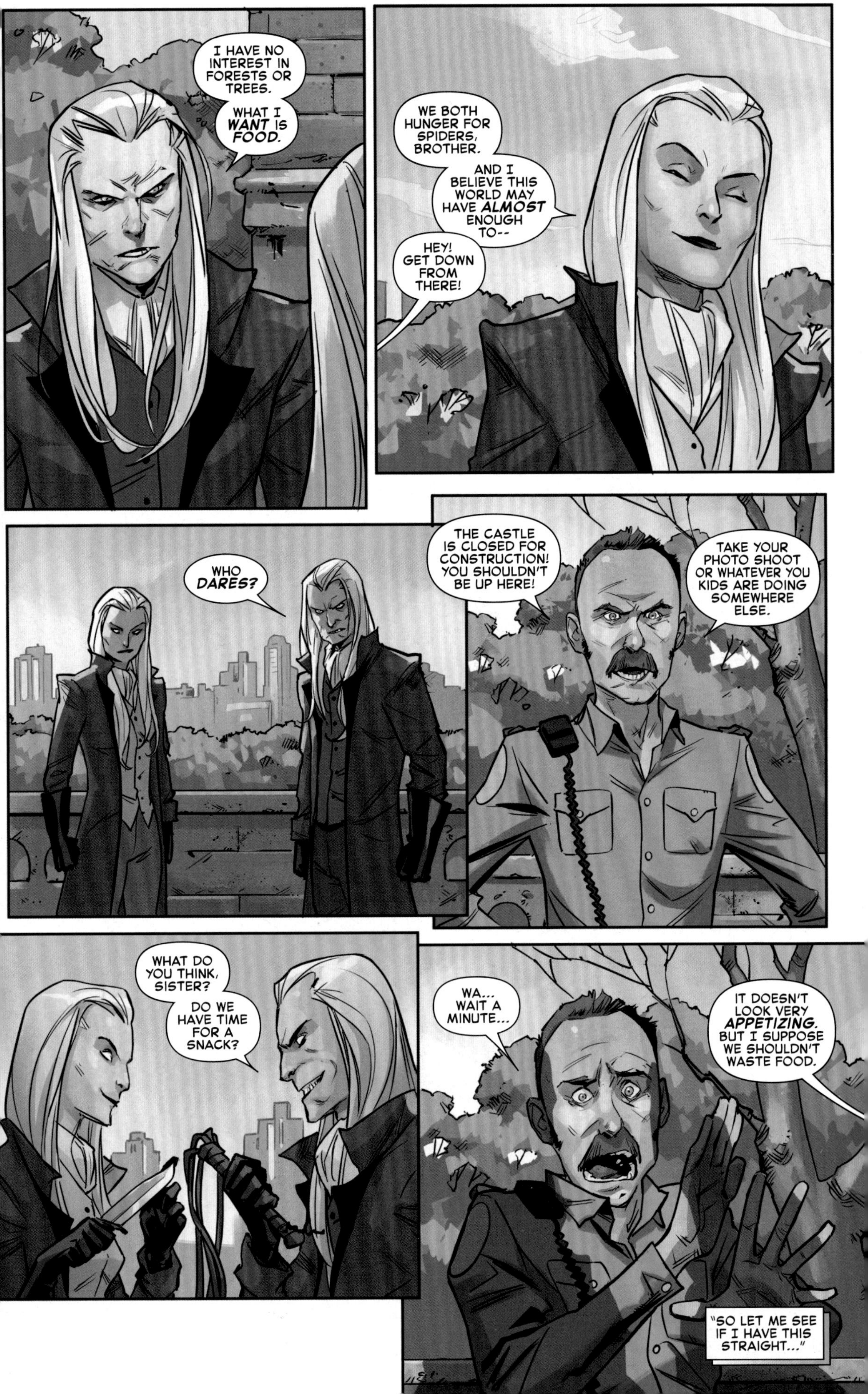
I HAVE NO INTEREST IN FORESTS OR TREES.
WHAT I WANT IS FOOD.
WE BOTH HUNGER FOR SPIDERS, BROTHER.
AND I BELIEVE THIS WORLD MAY HAVE ALMOST ENOUGH TO--
HEY! GET DOWN FROM THERE!
WHO DARES?
THE CASTLE IS CLOSED FOR CONSTRUCTION! YOU SHOULDN'T BE UP HERE!
TAKE YOUR PHOTO SHOOT OR WHATEVER YOU KIDS ARE DOING SOMEWHERE ELSE.
WHAT DO YOU THINK, SISTER?
DO WE HAVE TIME FOR A SNACK?
WA... WAIT A MINUTE...
IT DOESN'T LOOK VERY APPETIZING. BUT I SUPPOSE WE SHOULDN'T WASTE FOOD.
"SO LET ME SEE IF I HAVE THIS STRAIGHT..."

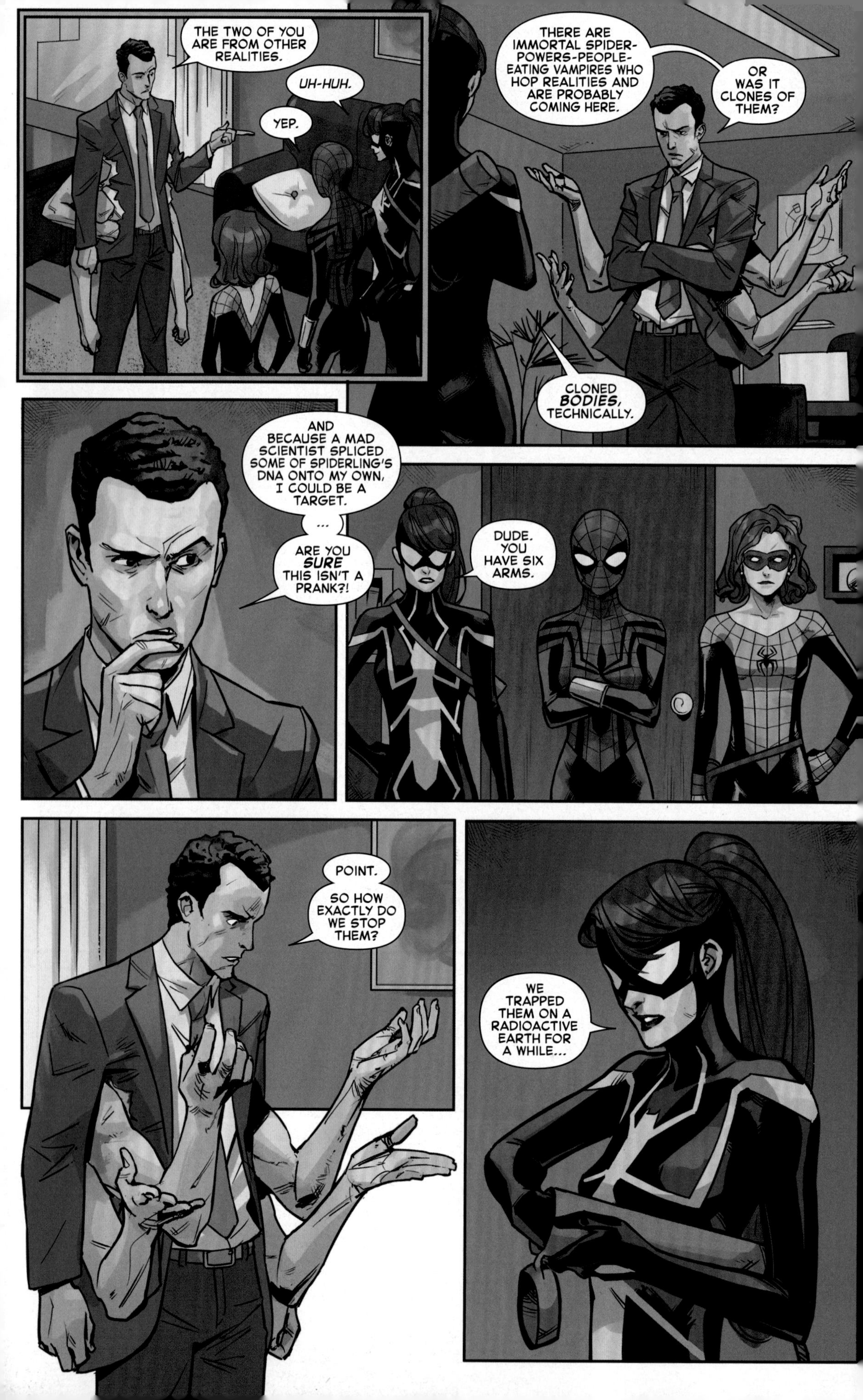
THE TWO OF YOU ARE FROM OTHER REALITIES.
UH-HUH.
YEP.
THERE ARE IMMORTAL SPIDER-POWERS-PEOPLE-EATING VAMPIRES WHO HOP REALITIES AND ARE PROBABLY COMING HERE.
OR WAS IT CLONES OF THEM?
CLONED BODIES, TECHNICALLY.
AND BECAUSE A MAD SCIENTIST SPLICED SOME OF SPIDERLING'S DNA ONTO MY OWN, I COULD BE A TARGET.
...
ARE YOU SURE THIS ISN'T A PRANK?!
DUDE. YOU HAVE SIX ARMS.
POINT.
SO HOW EXACTLY DO WE STOP THEM?
WE TRAPPED THEM ON A RADIOACTIVE EARTH FOR A WHILE...

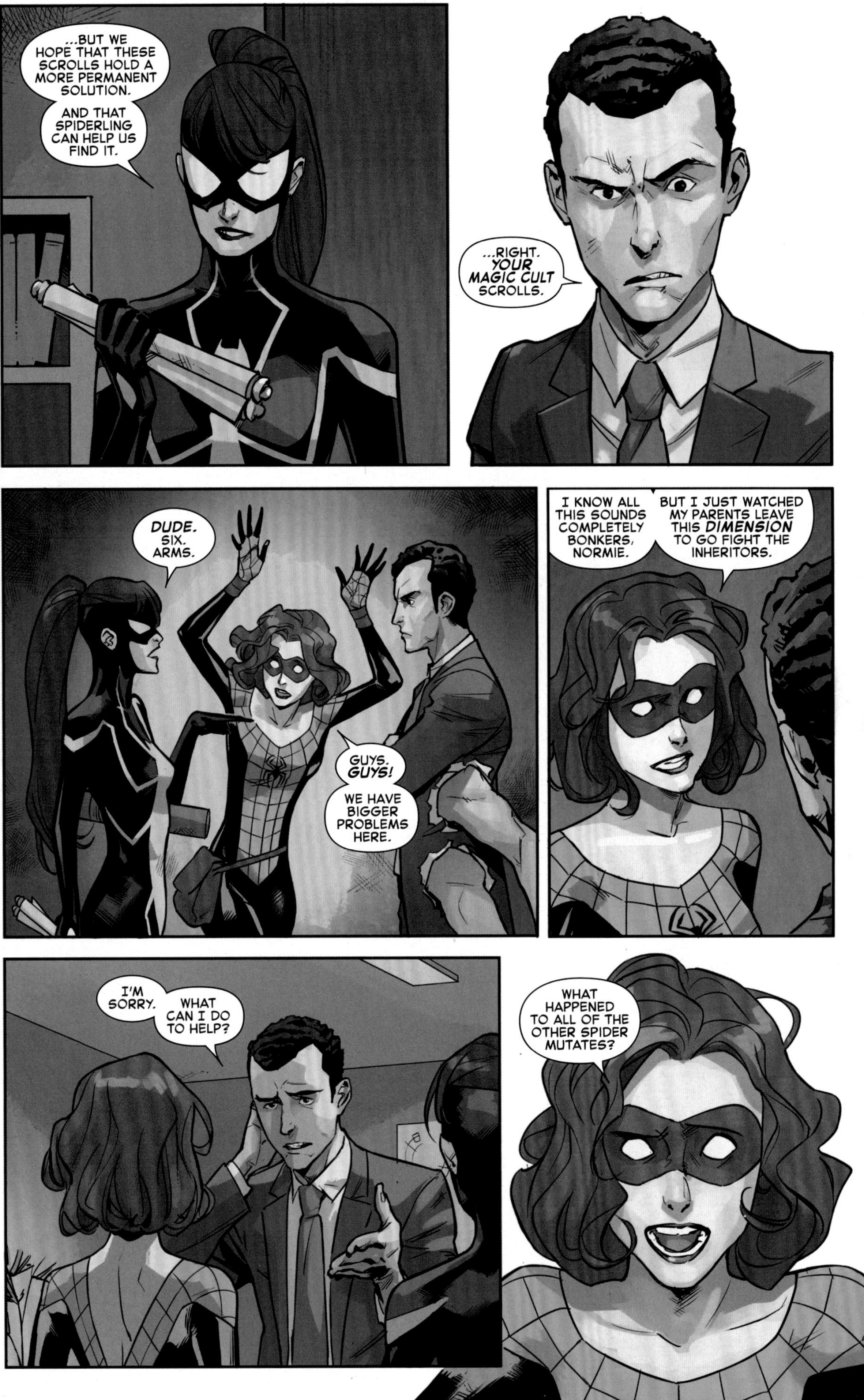
...BUT WE HOPE THAT THESE SCROLLS HOLD A MORE PERMANENT SOLUTION.
AND THAT SPIDERLING CAN HELP US FIND IT.
...RIGHT. YOUR MAGIC CULT SCROLLS.
DUDE. SIX. ARMS.
GUYS. GUYS!
WE HAVE BIGGER PROBLEMS HERE.
I KNOW ALL THIS SOUNDS COMPLETELY BONKERS, NORMIE.
BUT I JUST WATCHED MY PARENTS LEAVE THIS DIMENSION TO GO FIGHT THE INHERITORS.
I'M SORRY.
WHAT CAN I DO TO HELP?
WHAT HAPPENED TO ALL OF THE OTHER SPIDER MUTATES?

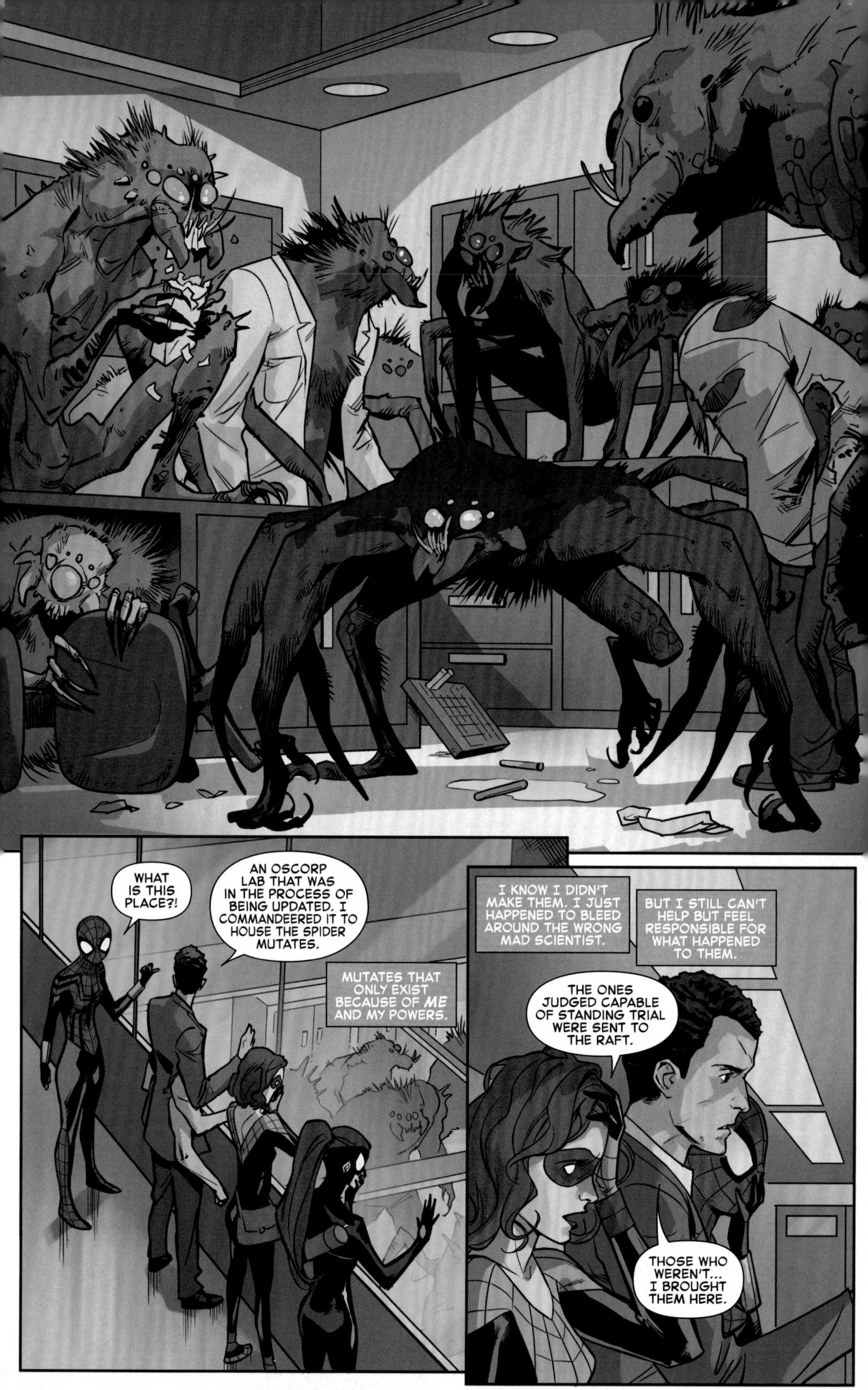
WHAT IS THIS PLACE?!
AN OSCORP LAB THAT WAS IN THE PROCESS OF BEING UPDATED. I COMMANDEERED IT TO HOUSE THE SPIDER MUTATES.
MUTATES THAT ONLY EXIST BECAUSE OF *ME* AND MY POWERS.
I KNOW I DIDN'T MAKE THEM. I JUST HAPPENED TO BLEED AROUND THE WRONG MAD SCIENTIST.
BUT I STILL CAN'T HELP BUT FEEL RESPONSIBLE FOR WHAT HAPPENED TO THEM.
THE ONES JUDGED CAPABLE OF STANDING TRIAL WERE SENT TO THE RAFT.
THOSE WHO WEREN'T... I BROUGHT THEM HERE.

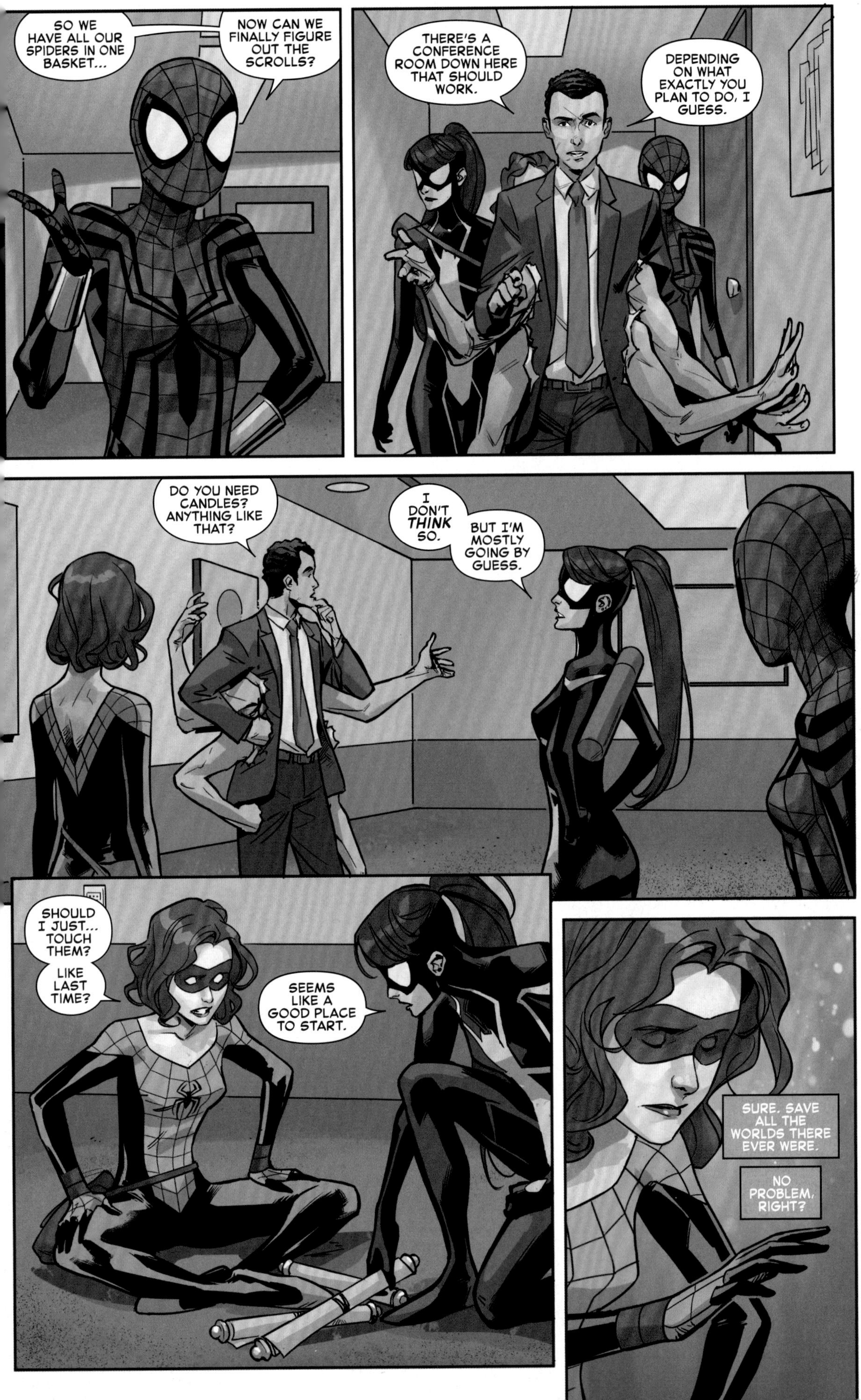
SO WE HAVE ALL OUR SPIDERS IN ONE BASKET...
NOW CAN WE FINALLY FIGURE OUT THE SCROLLS?
THERE'S A CONFERENCE ROOM DOWN HERE THAT SHOULD WORK.
DEPENDING ON WHAT EXACTLY YOU PLAN TO DO, I GUESS.
DO YOU NEED CANDLES? ANYTHING LIKE THAT?
I DON'T *THINK* SO.
BUT I'M MOSTLY GOING BY GUESS.
SHOULD I JUST... TOUCH THEM?
LIKE LAST TIME?
SEEMS LIKE A GOOD PLACE TO START.
SURE. SAVE ALL THE WORLDS THERE EVER WERE.
NO PROBLEM, RIGHT?

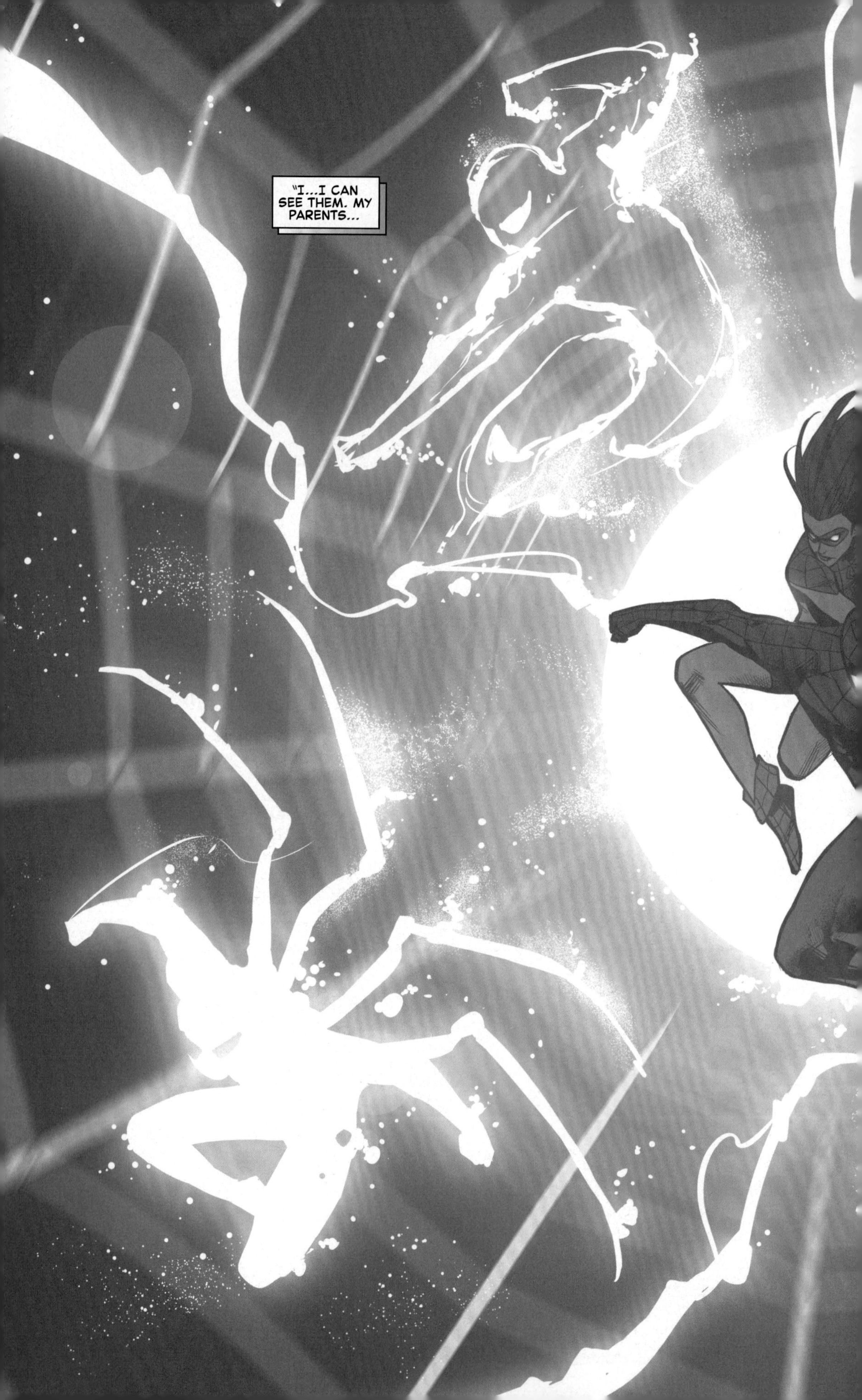
"I...I CAN SEE THEM. MY PARENTS...

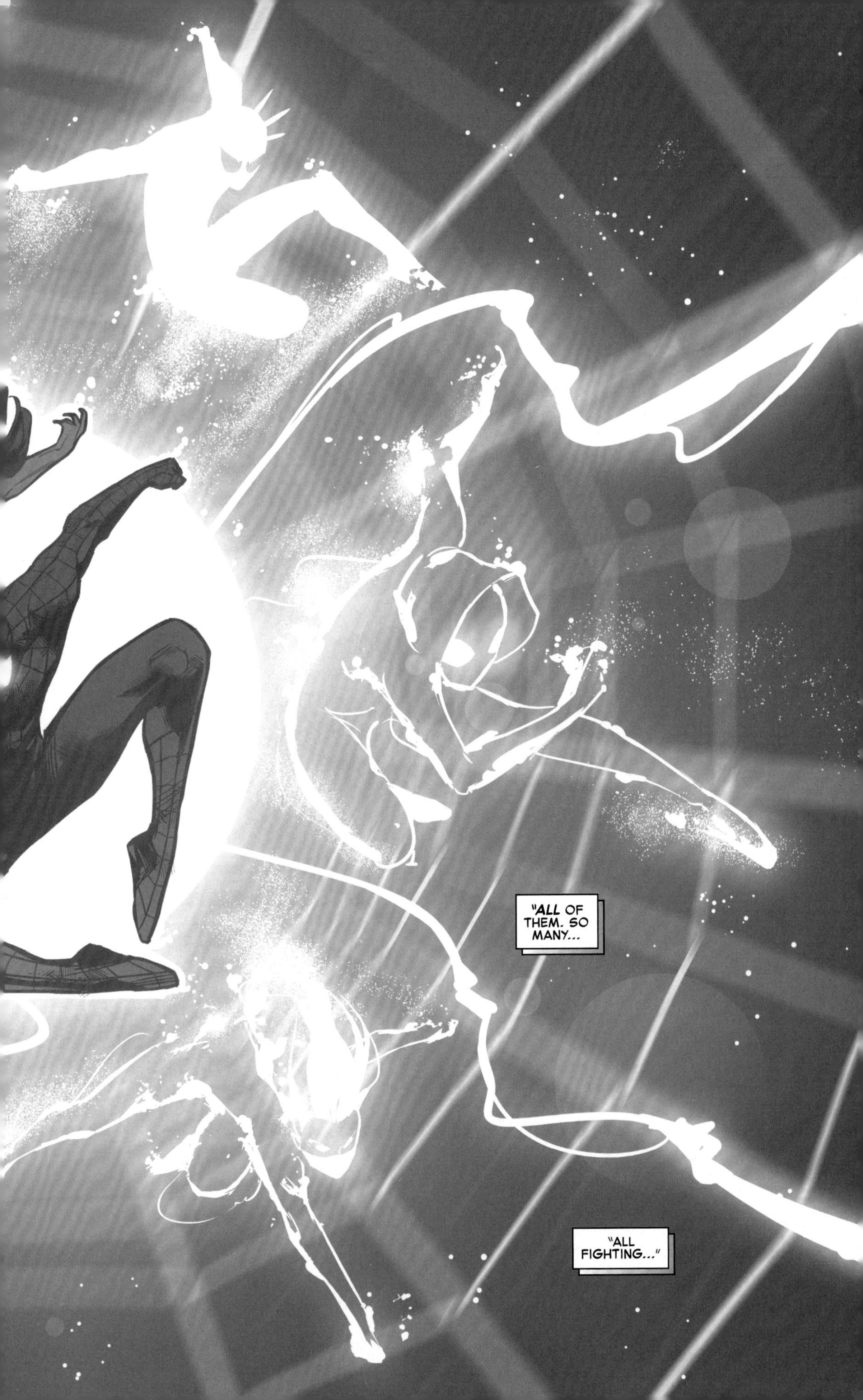
"ALL OF THEM. SO MANY...
"ALL FIGHTING..."

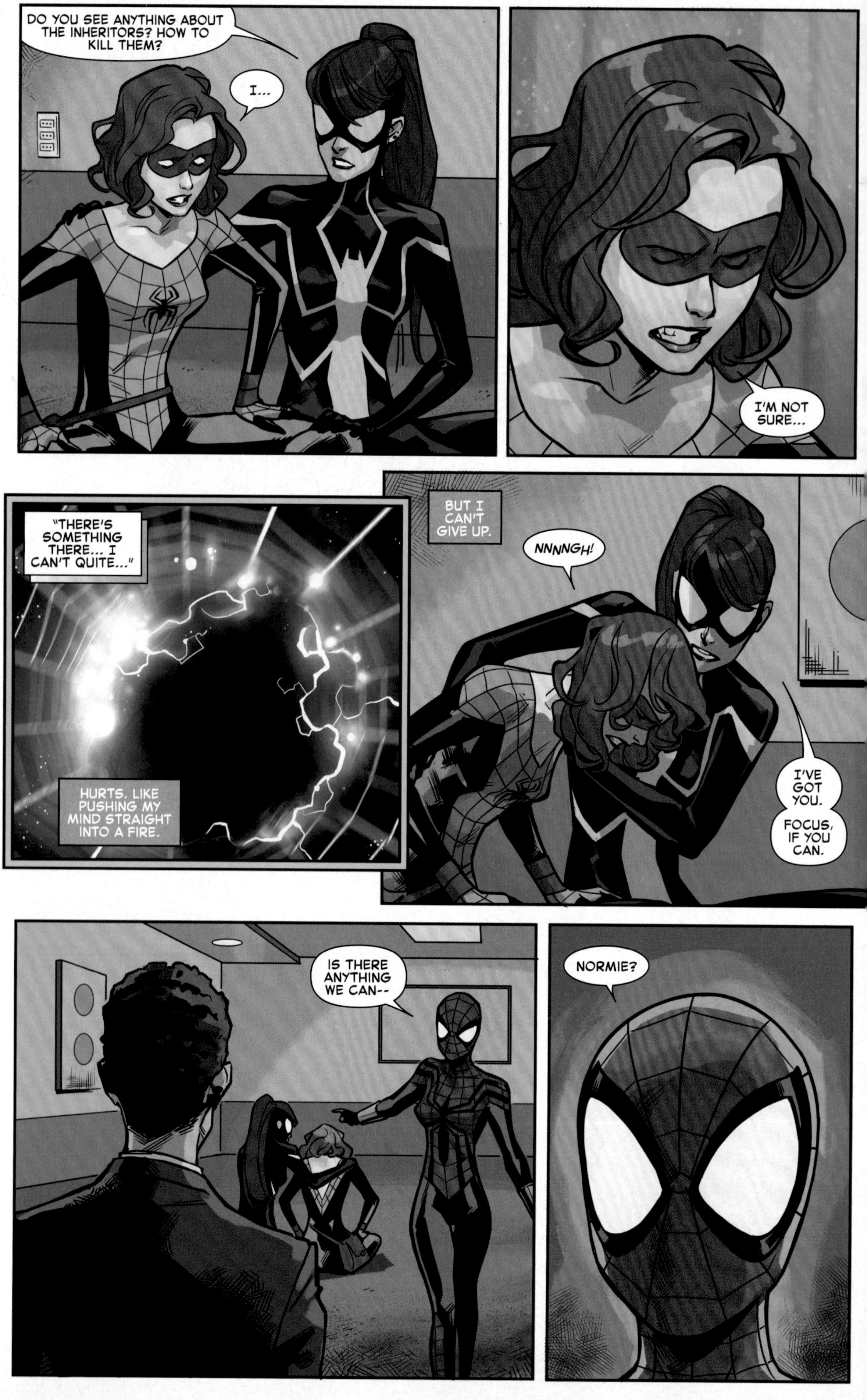
DO YOU SEE ANYTHING ABOUT THE INHERITORS? HOW TO KILL THEM?
I...
I'M NOT SURE...
"THERE'S SOMETHING THERE... I CAN'T QUITE..."
HURTS. LIKE PUSHING MY MIND STRAIGHT INTO A FIRE.
BUT I CAN'T GIVE UP.
NNNNGH!
I'VE GOT YOU.
FOCUS, IF YOU CAN.
IS THERE ANYTHING WE CAN--
NORMIE?

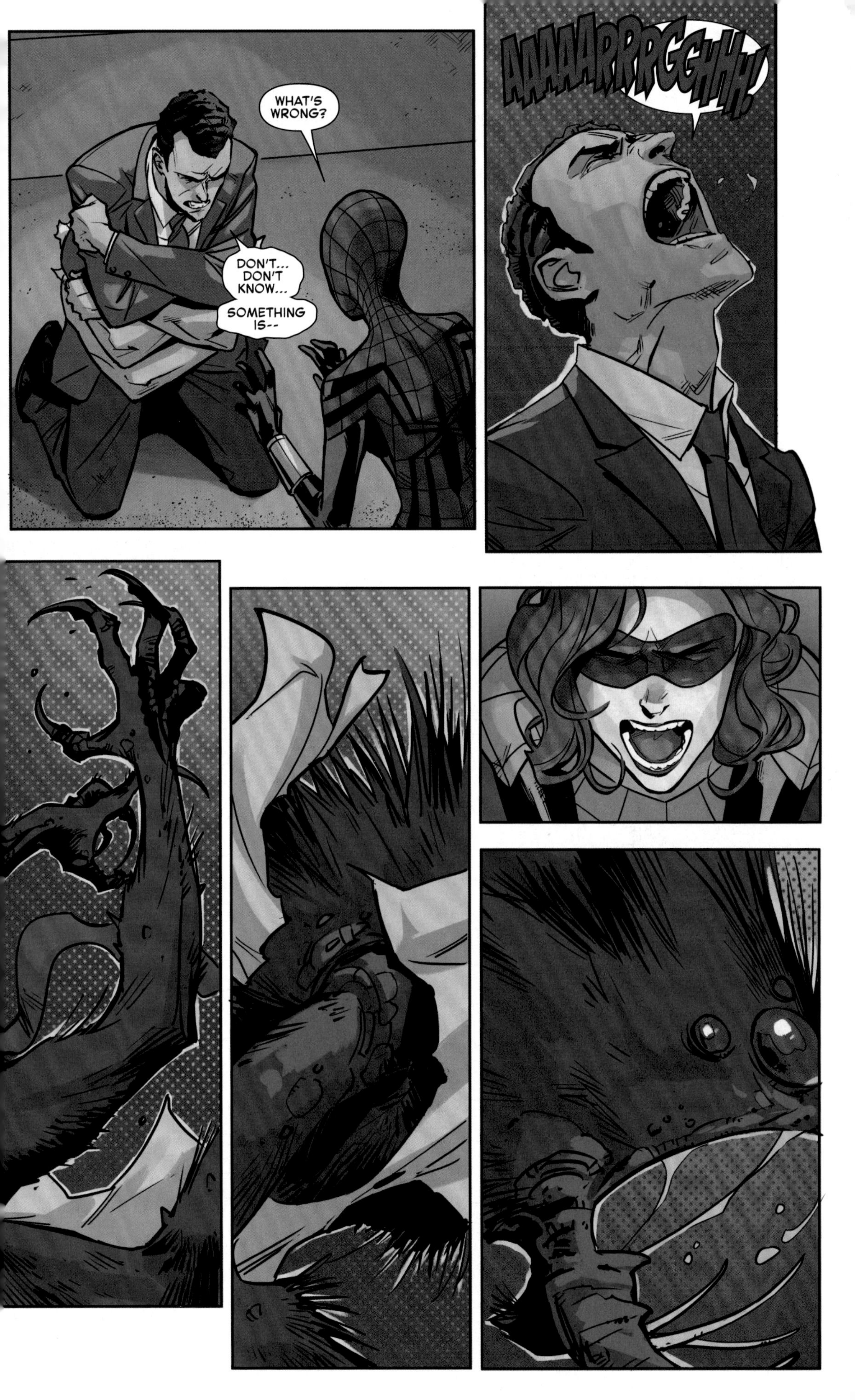
WHAT'S WRONG?
DON'T... DON'T KNOW...
SOMETHING IS--
AAAAARRRGGHH!

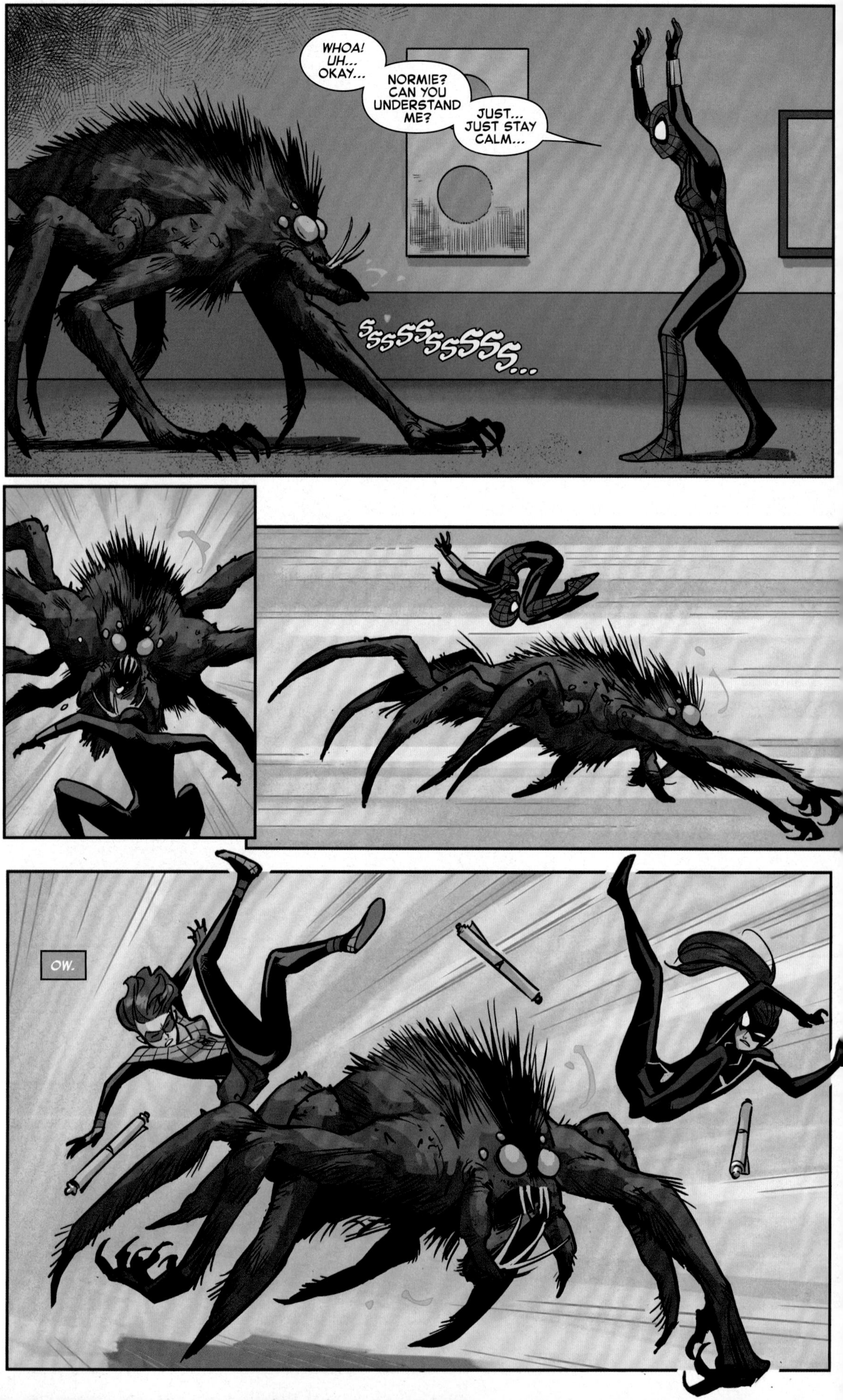
WHOA! UH... OKAY...
NORMIE? CAN YOU UNDERSTAND ME?
JUST... JUST STAY CALM...
SSSSSSSSSSS...
OW.

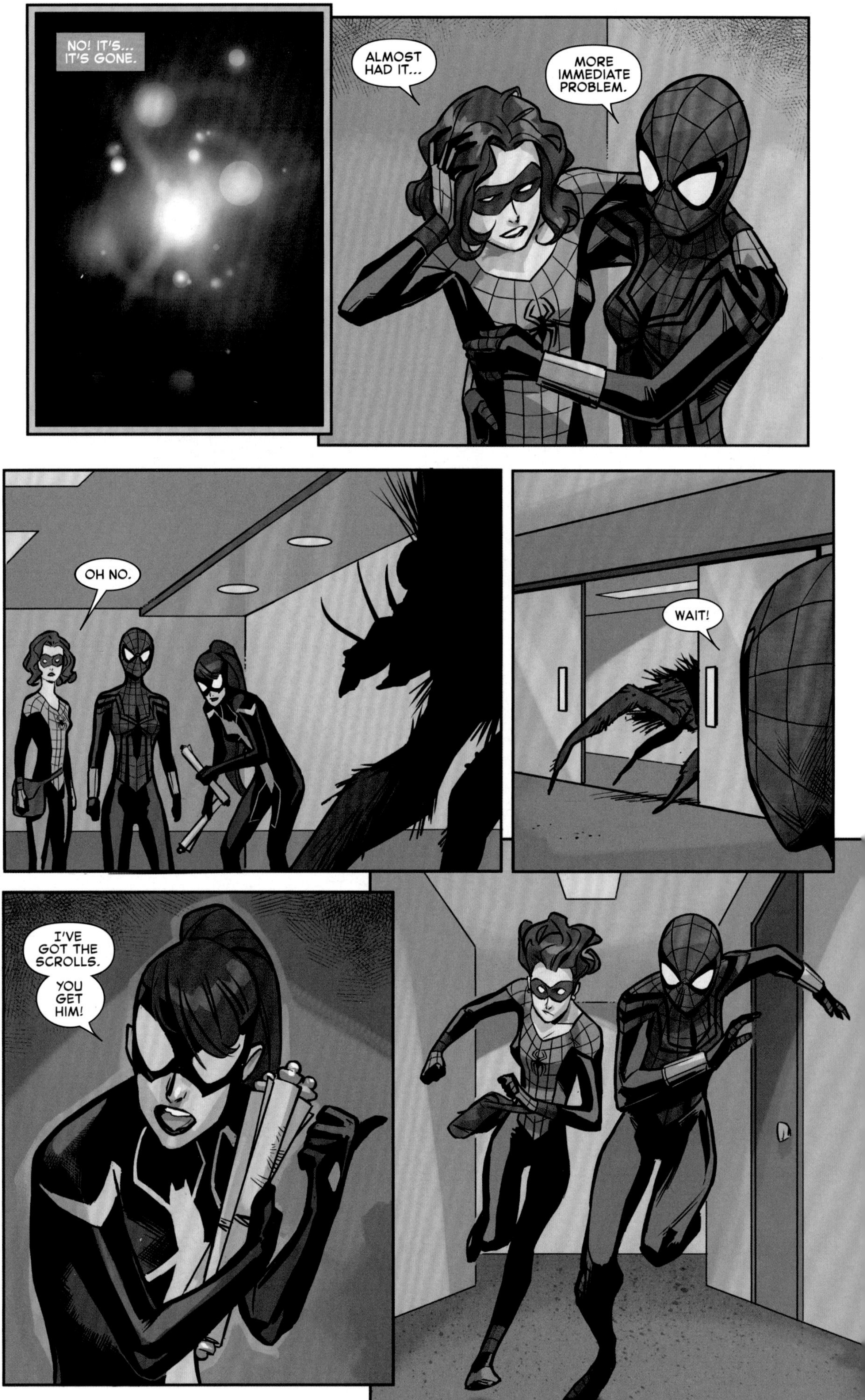
NO! IT'S... IT'S GONE.
ALMOST HAD IT...
MORE IMMEDIATE PROBLEM.
OH NO.
WAIT!
I'VE GOT THE SCROLLS.
YOU GET HIM!

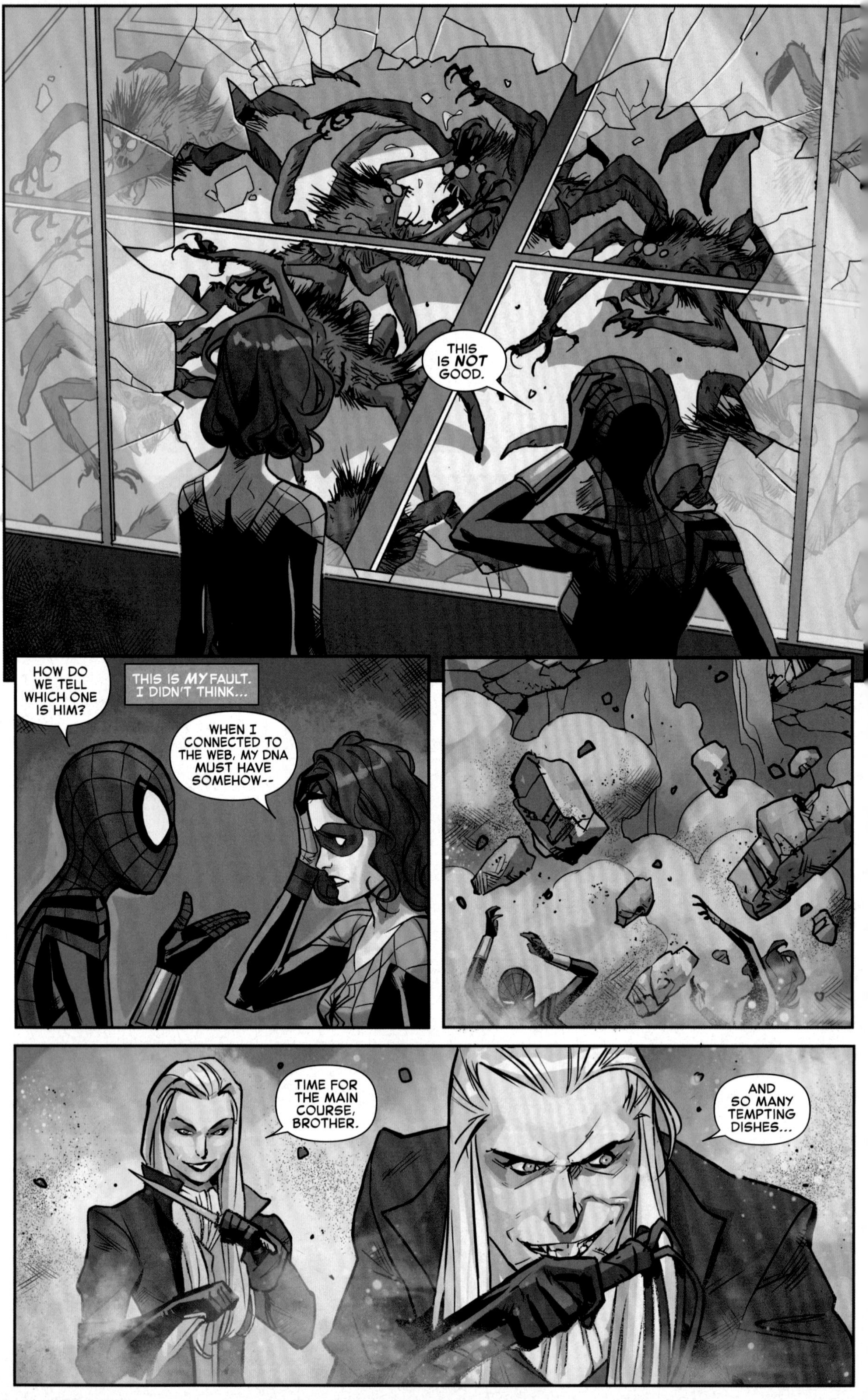
THIS IS NOT GOOD.
HOW DO WE TELL WHICH ONE IS HIM?
THIS IS MY FAULT. I DIDN'T THINK...
WHEN I CONNECTED TO THE WEB, MY DNA MUST HAVE SOMEHOW--
TIME FOR THE MAIN COURSE, BROTHER.
AND SO MANY TEMPTING DISHES...

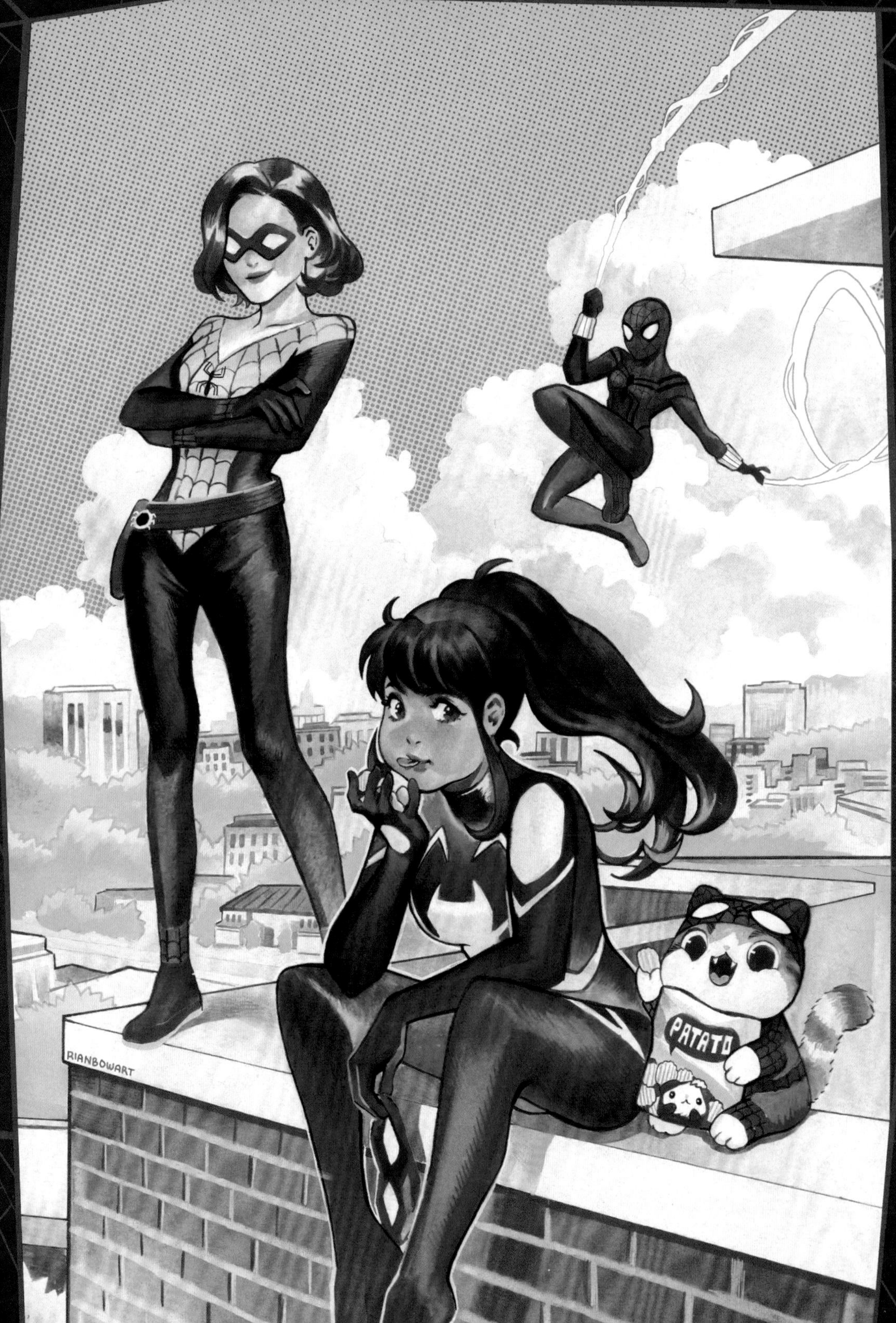
RIANBOWART
PATATO

SPIDER-GIRLS #3 VARIANT
BY **RIAN GONZALES**

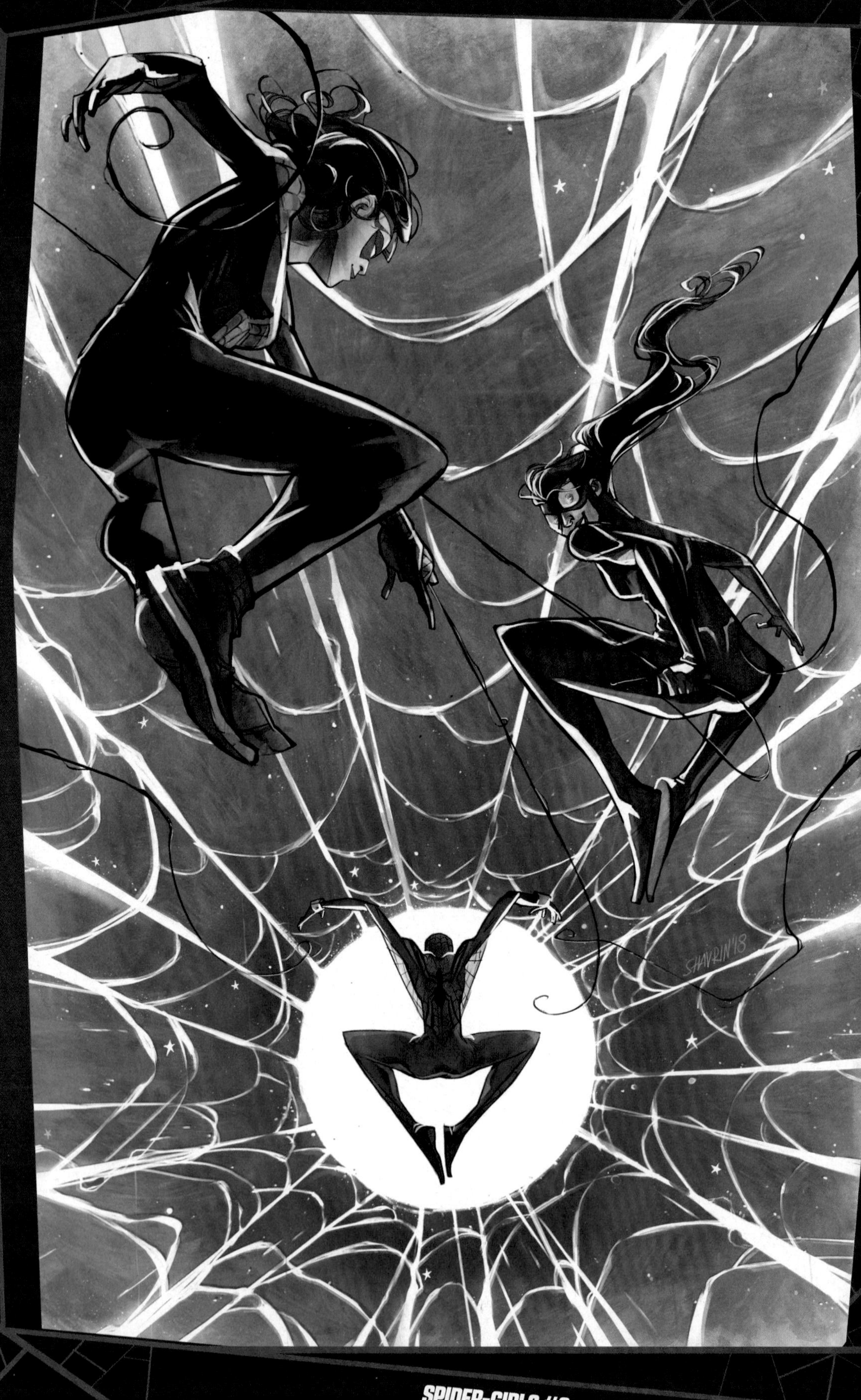
SHAVRIN '18

SPIDER-GIRLS #3

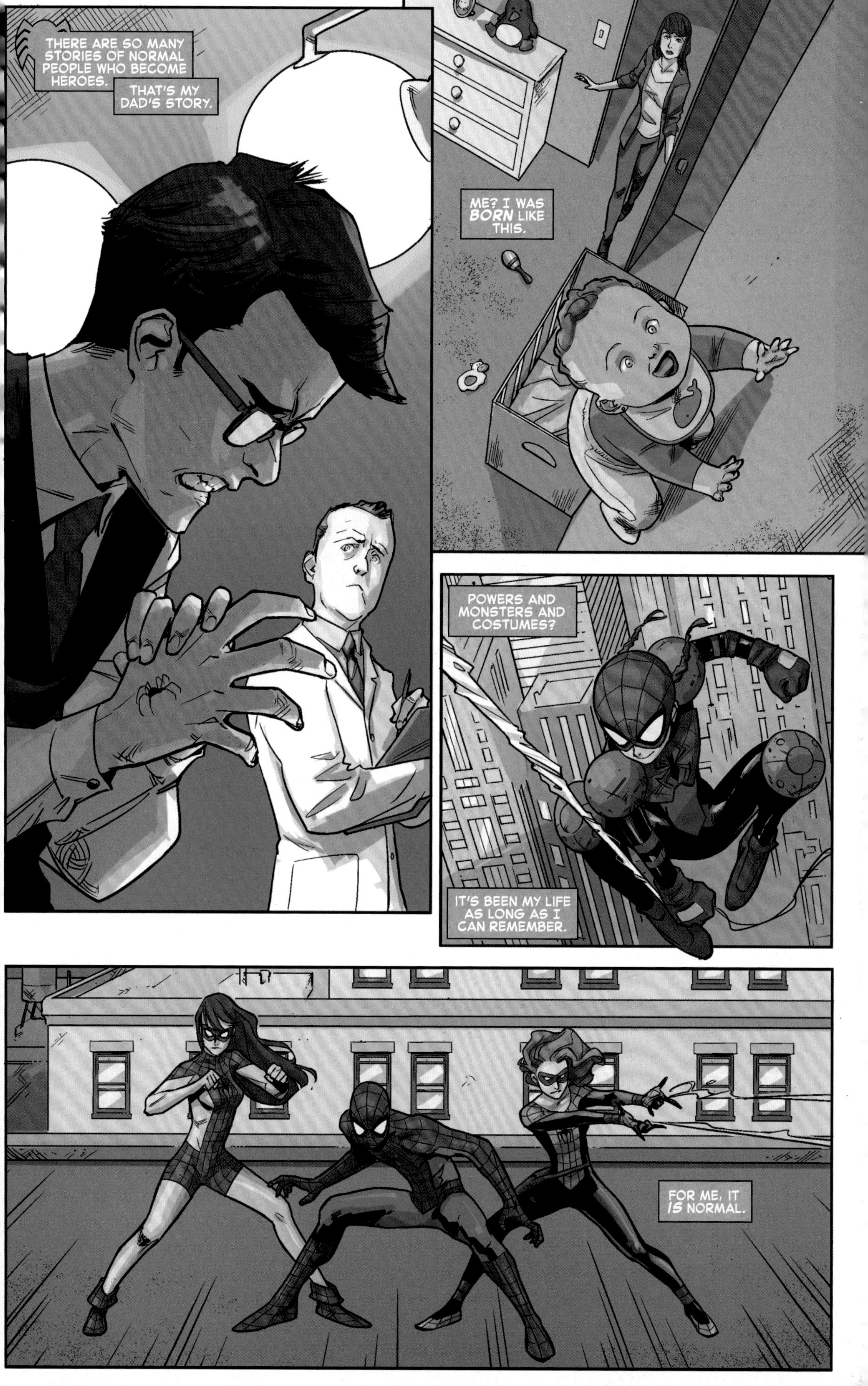
THERE ARE SO MANY STORIES OF NORMAL PEOPLE WHO BECOME HEROES.
THAT'S MY DAD'S STORY.
ME? I WAS *BORN* LIKE THIS.
POWERS AND MONSTERS AND COSTUMES?
IT'S BEEN MY LIFE AS LONG AS I CAN REMEMBER.
FOR ME, IT *IS* NORMAL.

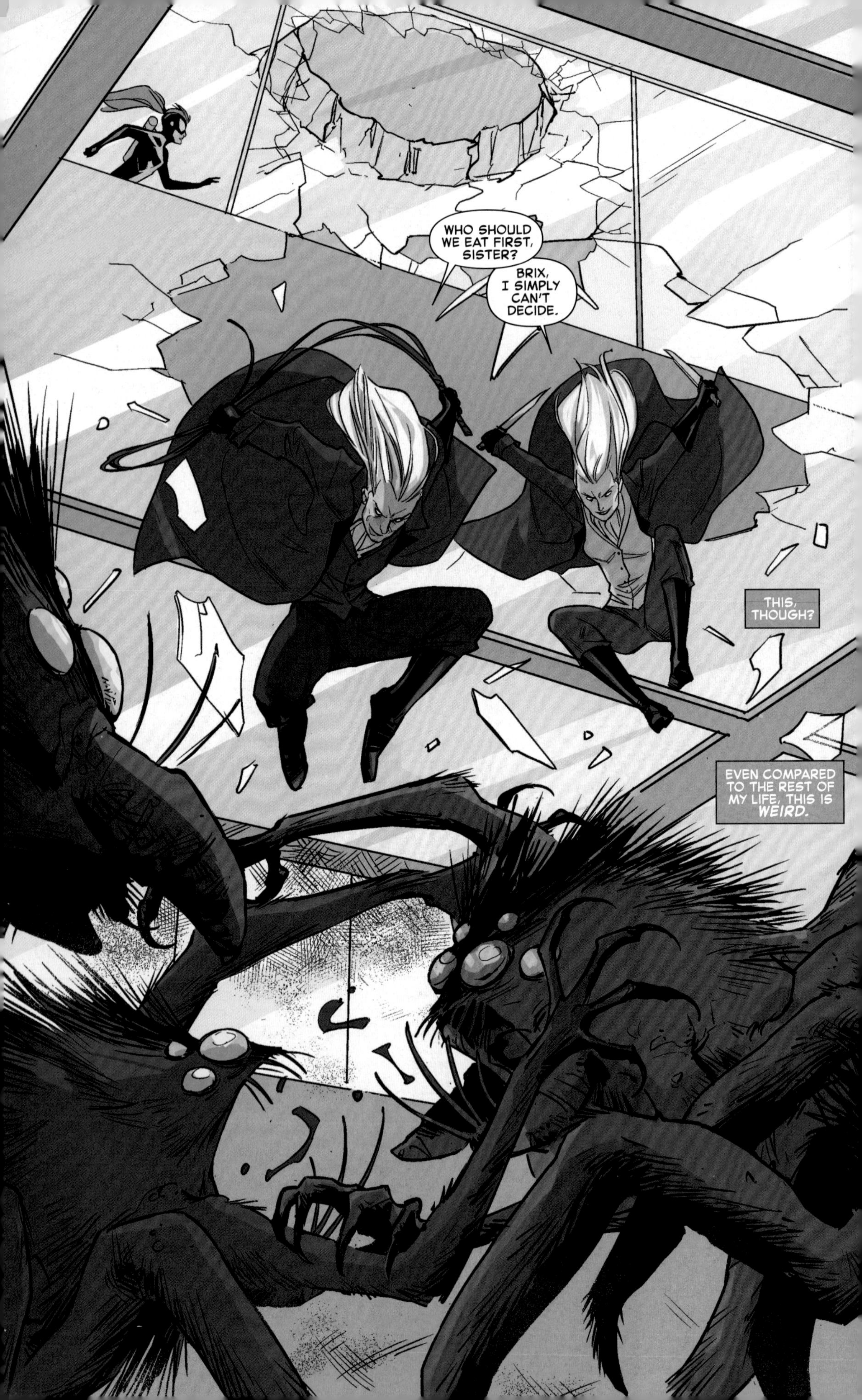
WHO SHOULD WE EAT FIRST, SISTER?
BRIX, I SIMPLY CAN'T DECIDE.
THIS, THOUGH?
EVEN COMPARED TO THE REST OF MY LIFE, THIS IS WEIRD.

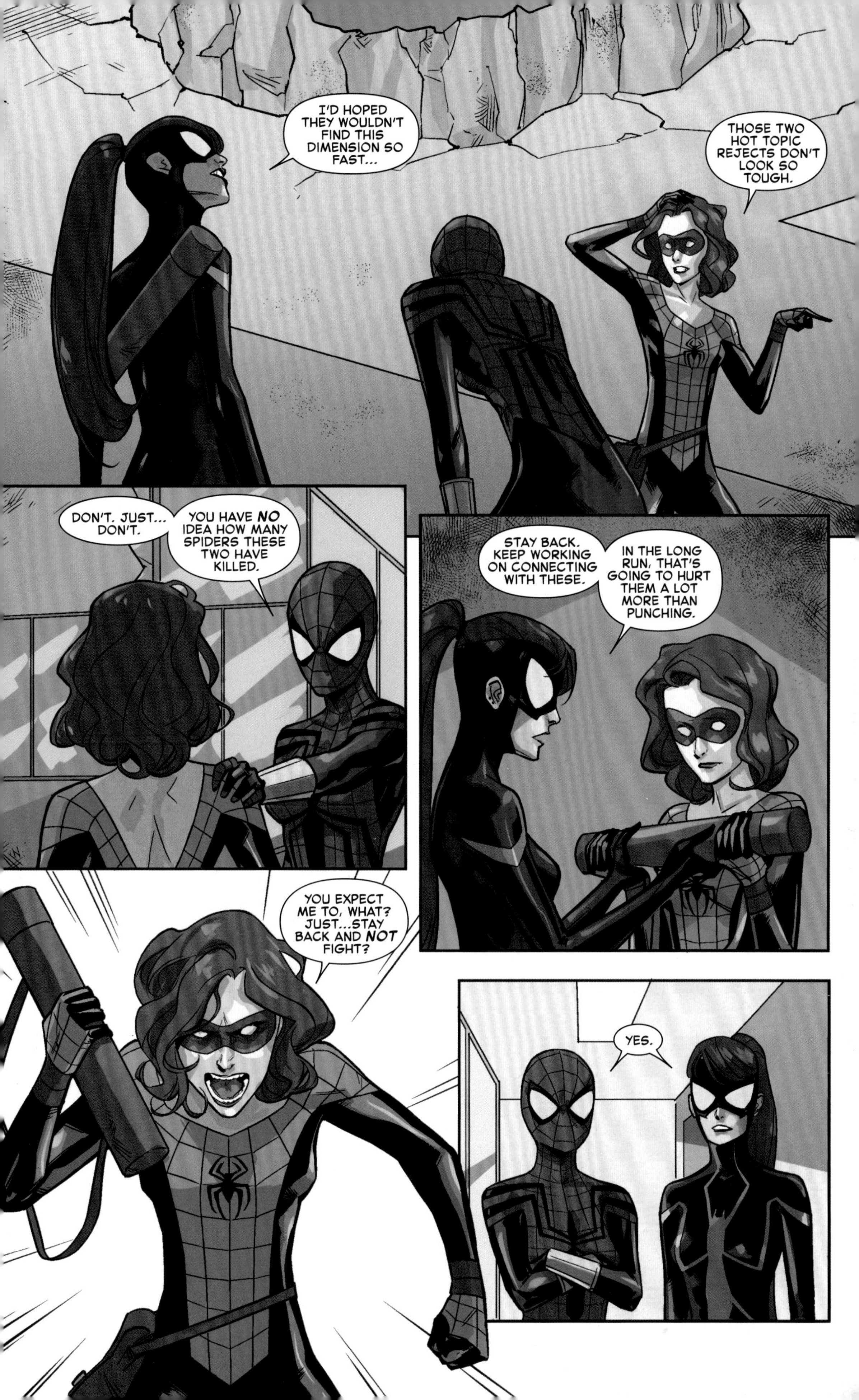
I'D HOPED THEY WOULDN'T FIND THIS DIMENSION SO FAST...
THOSE TWO HOT TOPIC REJECTS DON'T LOOK SO TOUGH.
DON'T. JUST... DON'T.
YOU HAVE NO IDEA HOW MANY SPIDERS THESE TWO HAVE KILLED.
STAY BACK. KEEP WORKING ON CONNECTING WITH THESE.
IN THE LONG RUN, THAT'S GOING TO HURT THEM A LOT MORE THAN PUNCHING.
YOU EXPECT ME TO, WHAT? JUST...STAY BACK AND NOT FIGHT?
YES.

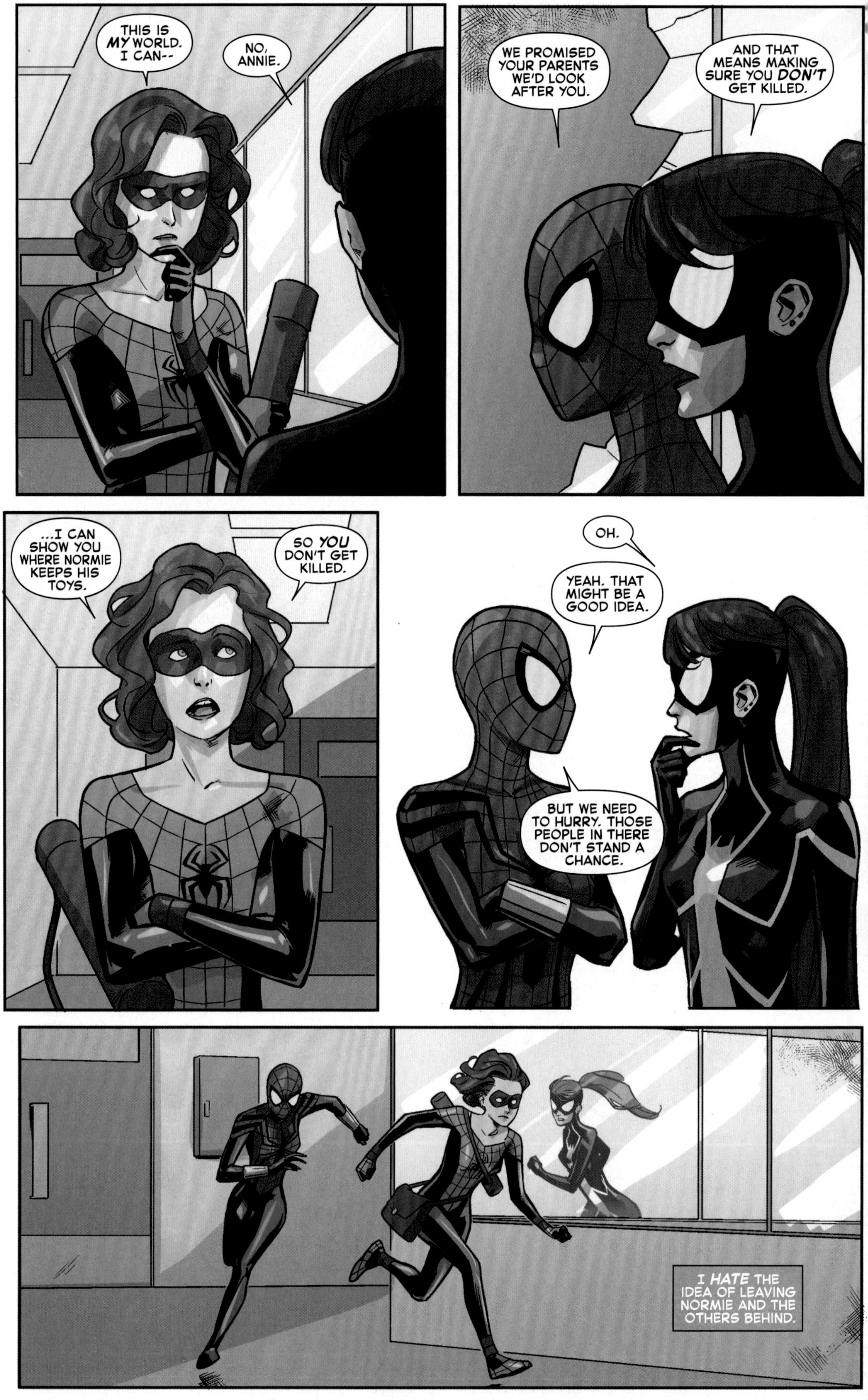

THIS IS MY WORLD. I CAN--
NO, ANNIE.
WE PROMISED YOUR PARENTS WE'D LOOK AFTER YOU.
AND THAT MEANS MAKING SURE YOU DON'T GET KILLED.
...I CAN SHOW YOU WHERE NORMIE KEEPS HIS TOYS.
SO YOU DON'T GET KILLED.
OH.
YEAH. THAT MIGHT BE A GOOD IDEA.
BUT WE NEED TO HURRY. THOSE PEOPLE IN THERE DON'T STAND A CHANCE.
I HATE THE IDEA OF LEAVING NORMIE AND THE OTHERS BEHIND.

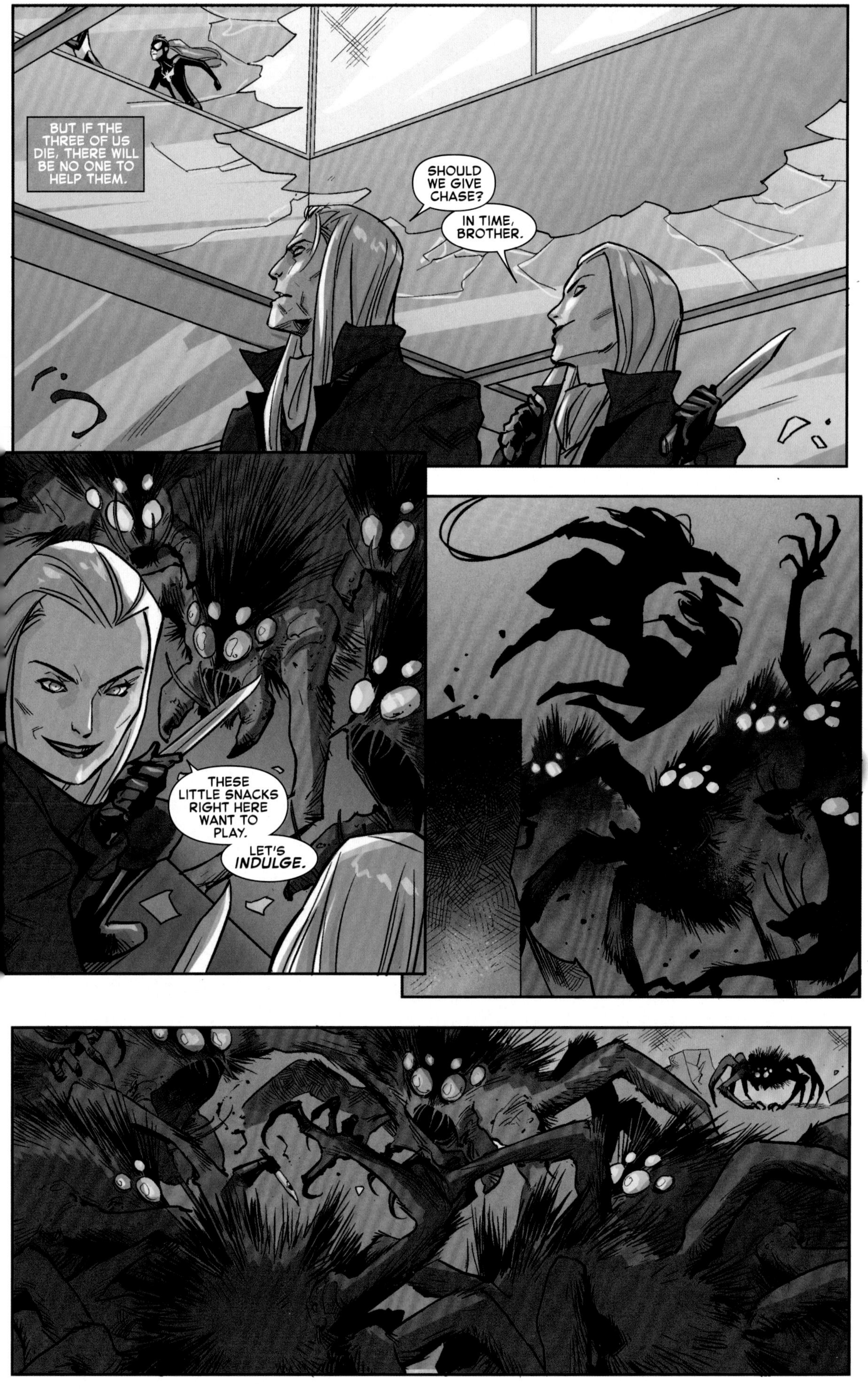
BUT IF THE THREE OF US DIE, THERE WILL BE NO ONE TO HELP THEM.
SHOULD WE GIVE CHASE?
IN TIME, BROTHER.
THESE LITTLE SNACKS RIGHT HERE WANT TO PLAY.
LET'S *INDULGE.*

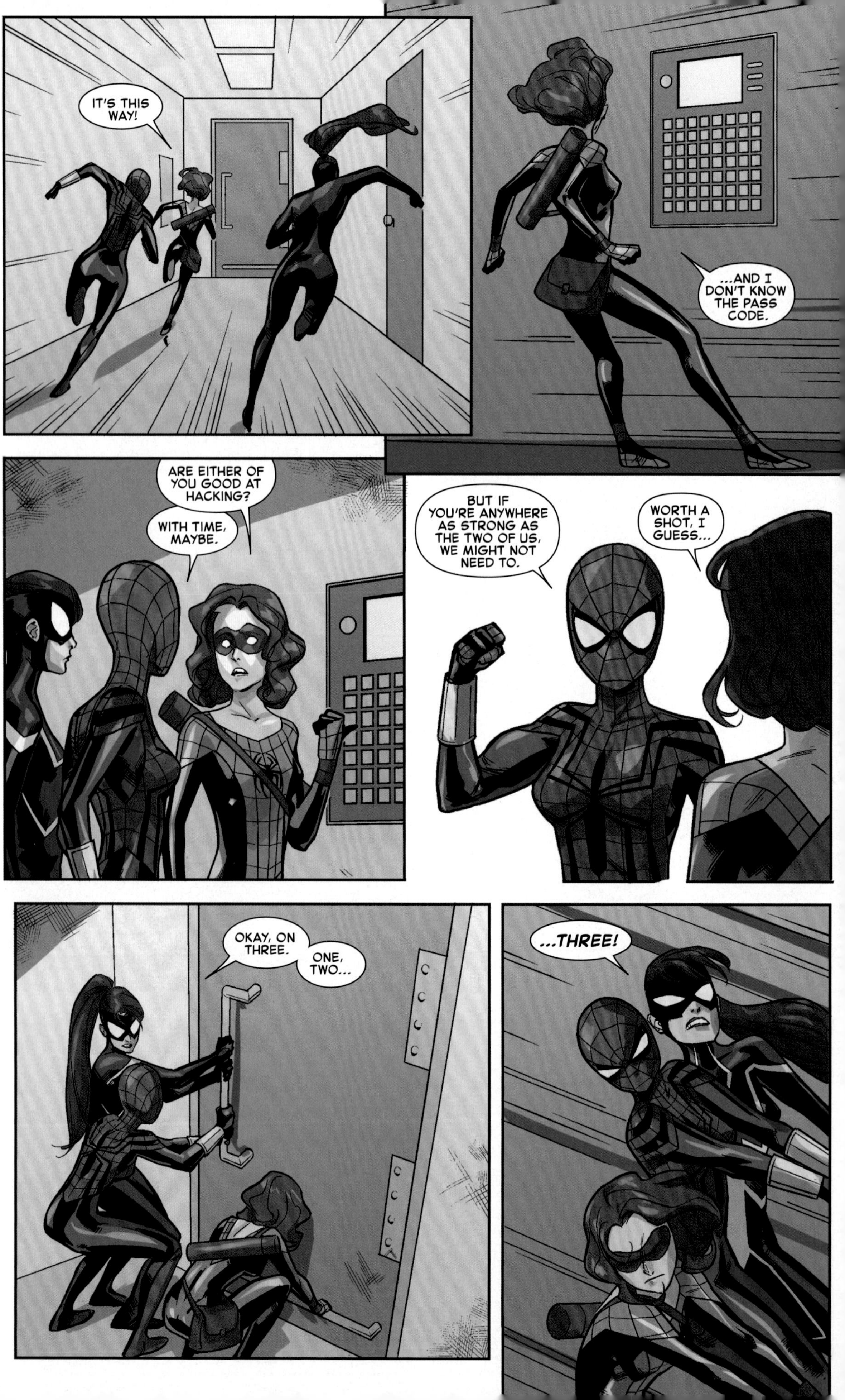
IT'S THIS WAY!
...AND I DON'T KNOW THE PASS CODE.
ARE EITHER OF YOU GOOD AT HACKING?
WITH TIME, MAYBE.
BUT IF YOU'RE ANYWHERE AS STRONG AS THE TWO OF US, WE MIGHT NOT NEED TO.
WORTH A SHOT, I GUESS...
OKAY, ON THREE.
ONE, TWO...
...THREE!

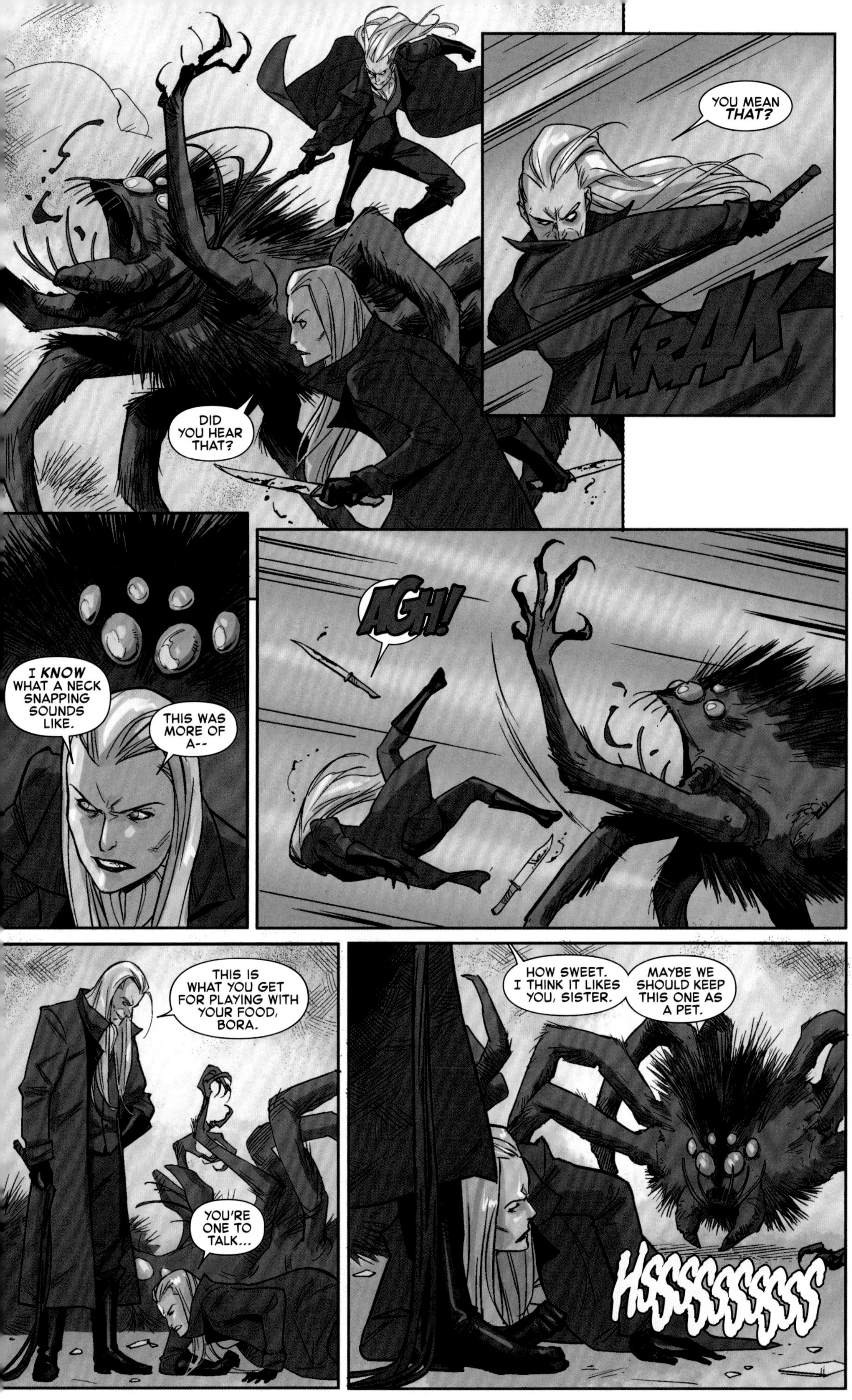
DID YOU HEAR THAT?
YOU MEAN THAT?
KRAK
I KNOW WHAT A NECK SNAPPING SOUNDS LIKE.
THIS WAS MORE OF A--
AGH!
THIS IS WHAT YOU GET FOR PLAYING WITH YOUR FOOD, BORA.
YOU'RE ONE TO TALK...
HOW SWEET. I THINK IT LIKES YOU, SISTER.
MAYBE WE SHOULD KEEP THIS ONE AS A PET.
HSSSSSSSSSS

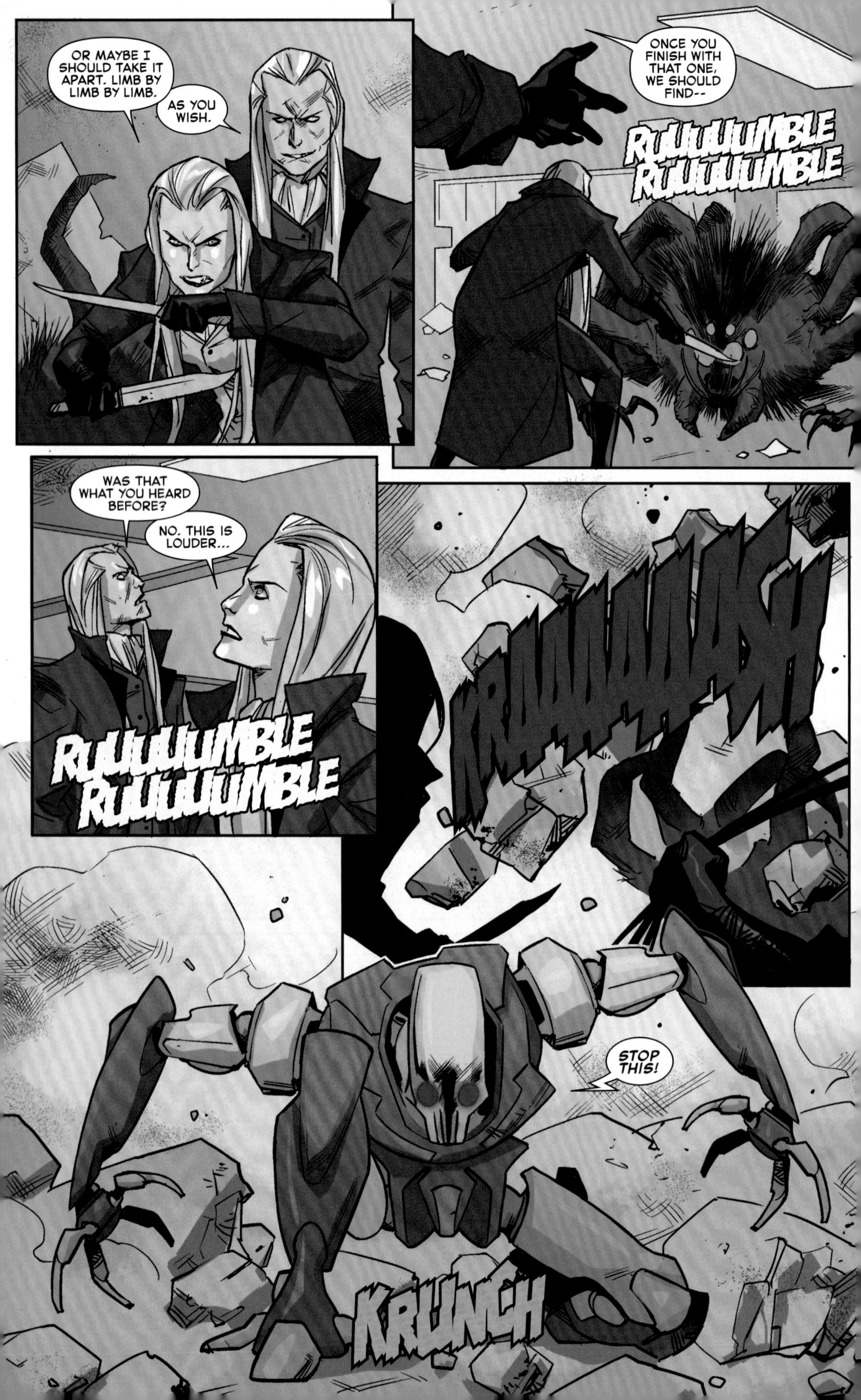
OR MAYBE I SHOULD TAKE IT APART. LIMB BY LIMB BY LIMB.
AS YOU WISH.
ONCE YOU FINISH WITH THAT ONE, WE SHOULD FIND--
RUUUUUMBLE RUUUUUMBLE
WAS THAT WHAT YOU HEARD BEFORE?
NO. THIS IS LOUDER...
RUUUUUMBLE RUUUUUMBLE
KRAAAAAASH
STOP THIS!
KRUNCH

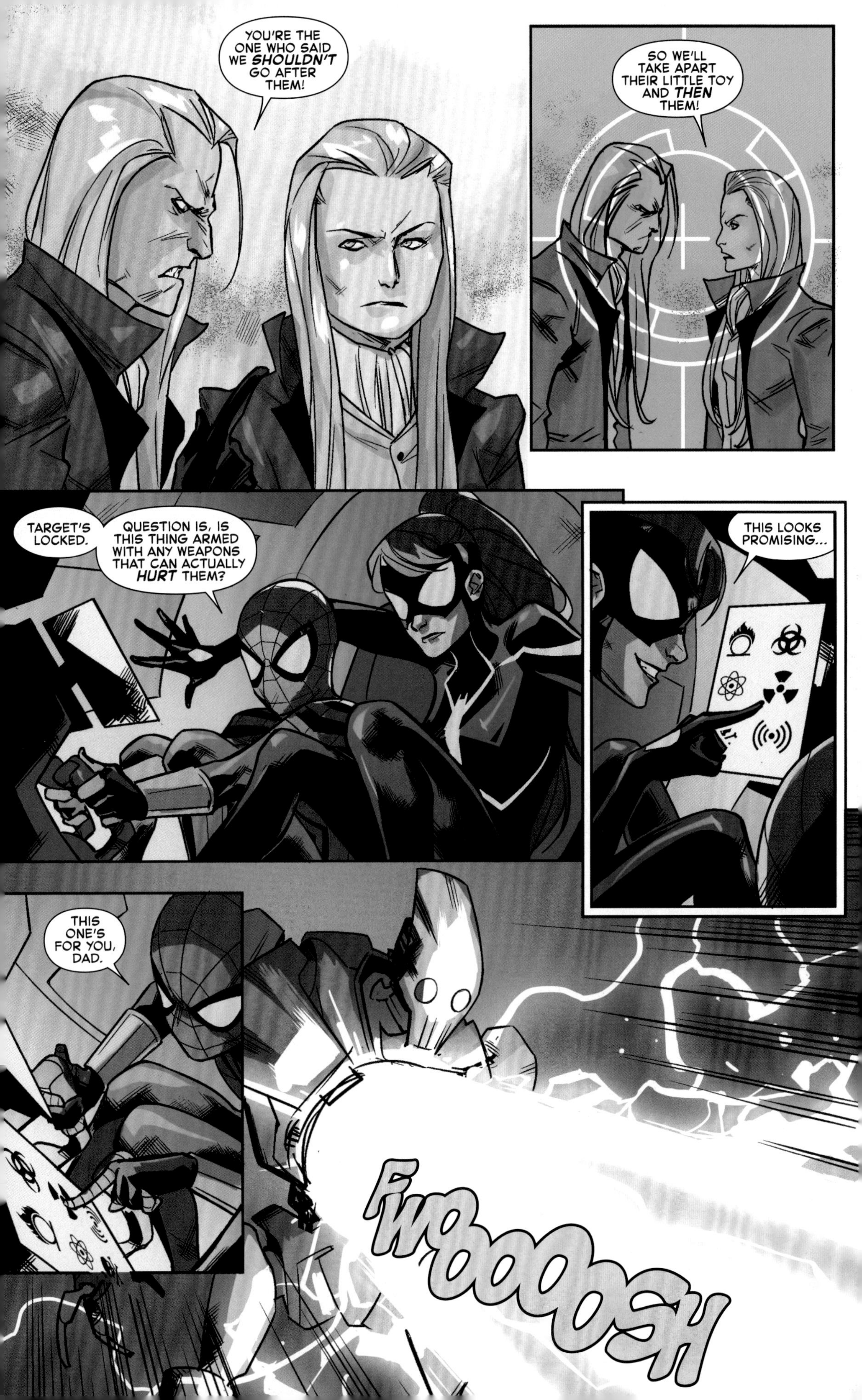
YOU'RE THE ONE WHO SAID WE SHOULDN'T GO AFTER THEM!
SO WE'LL TAKE APART THEIR LITTLE TOY AND THEN THEM!
TARGET'S LOCKED.
QUESTION IS, IS THIS THING ARMED WITH ANY WEAPONS THAT CAN ACTUALLY HURT THEM?
THIS LOOKS PROMISING...
THIS ONE'S FOR YOU, DAD.
FWOOOOSH

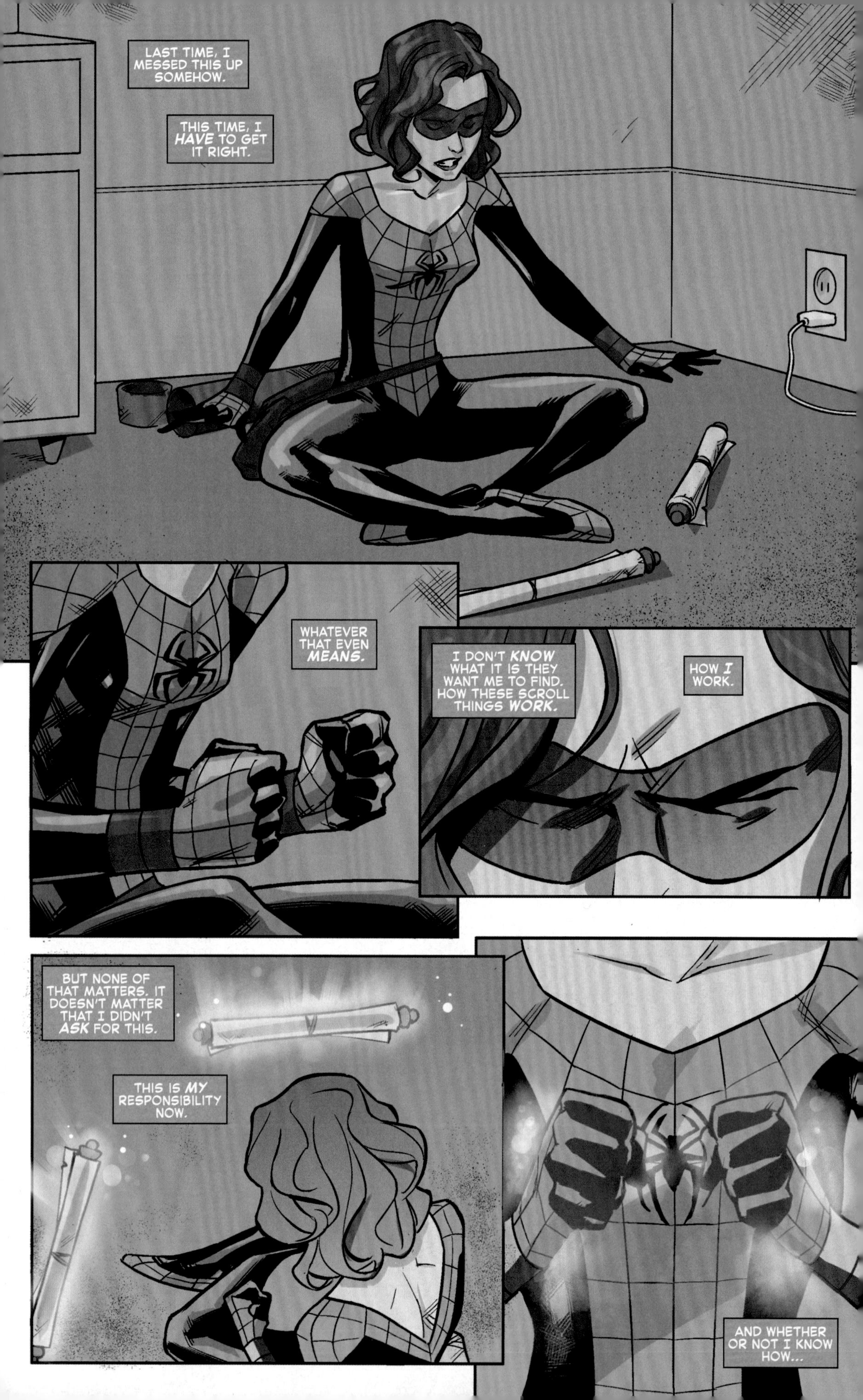
LAST TIME, I MESSED THIS UP SOMEHOW.
THIS TIME, I HAVE TO GET IT RIGHT.
WHATEVER THAT EVEN MEANS.
I DON'T KNOW WHAT IT IS THEY WANT ME TO FIND. HOW THESE SCROLL THINGS WORK.
HOW I WORK.
BUT NONE OF THAT MATTERS. IT DOESN'T MATTER THAT I DIDN'T ASK FOR THIS.
THIS IS MY RESPONSIBILITY NOW.
AND WHETHER OR NOT I KNOW HOW...

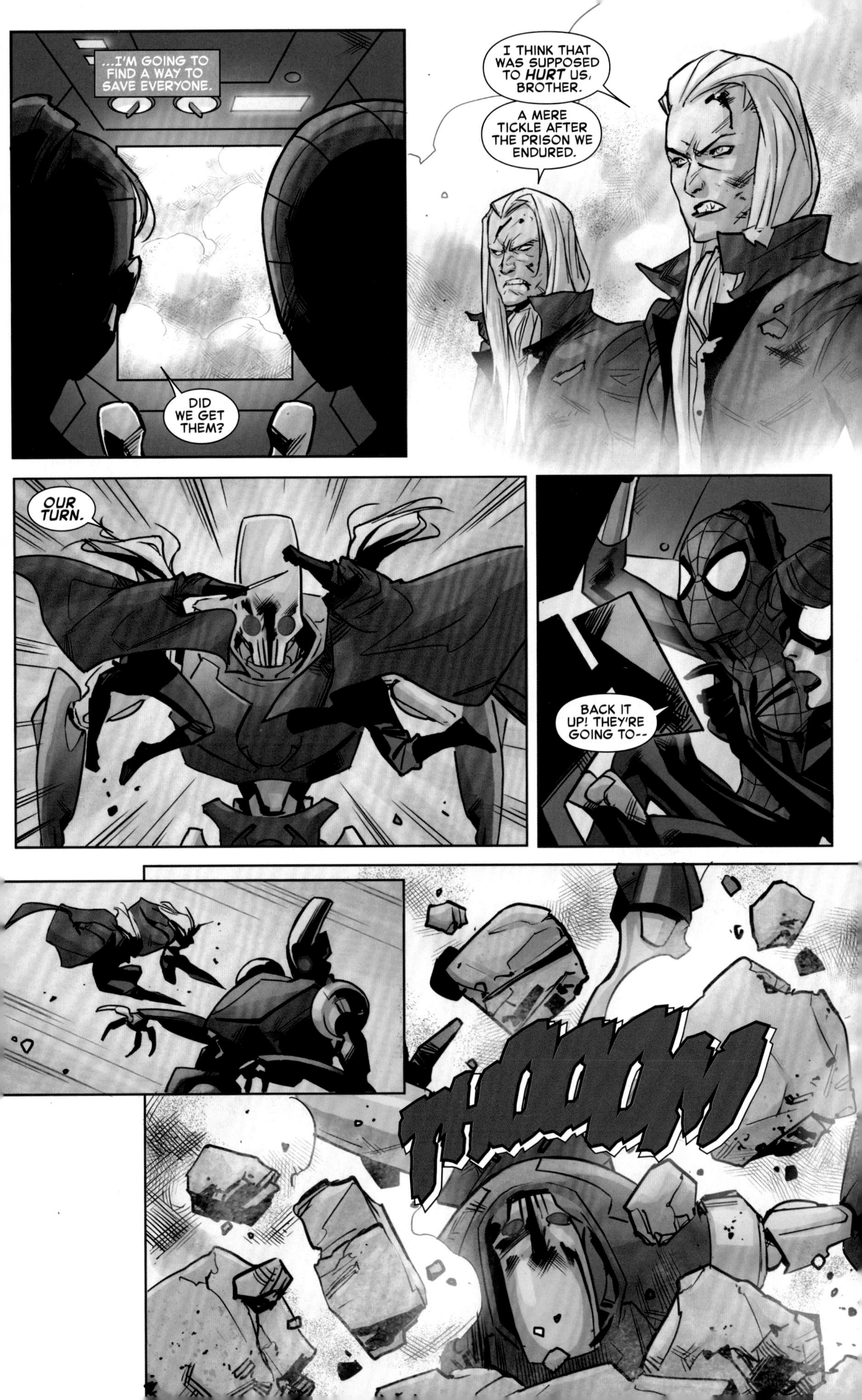
...I'M GOING TO FIND A WAY TO SAVE EVERYONE.
DID WE GET THEM?
I THINK THAT WAS SUPPOSED TO HURT US, BROTHER.
A MERE TICKLE AFTER THE PRISON WE ENDURED.
OUR TURN.
BACK IT UP! THEY'RE GOING TO--
THOOOM

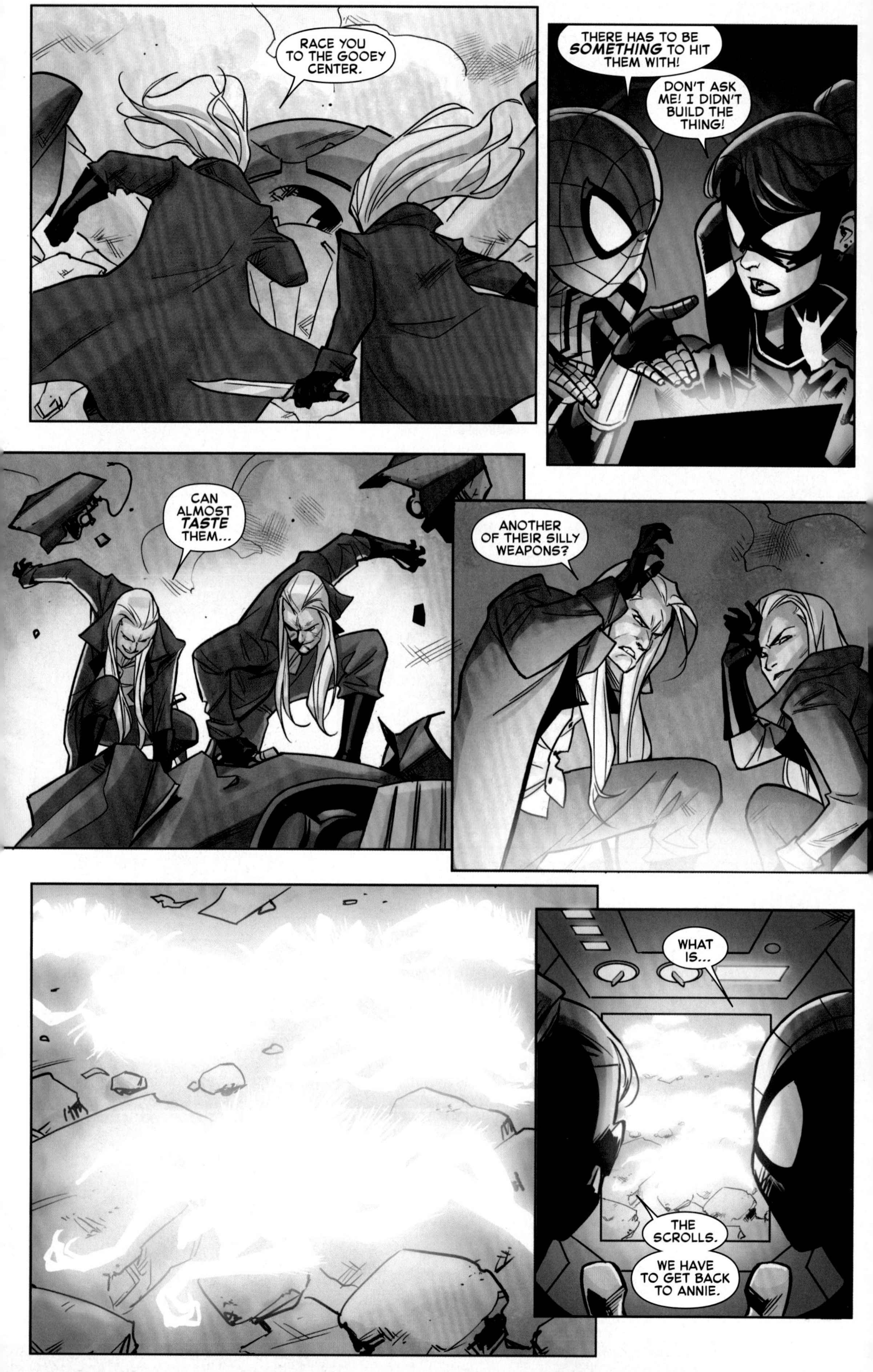
RACE YOU TO THE GOOEY CENTER.
THERE HAS TO BE SOMETHING TO HIT THEM WITH!
DON'T ASK ME! I DIDN'T BUILD THE THING!
CAN ALMOST TASTE THEM...
ANOTHER OF THEIR SILLY WEAPONS?
WHAT IS...
THE SCROLLS.
WE HAVE TO GET BACK TO ANNIE.

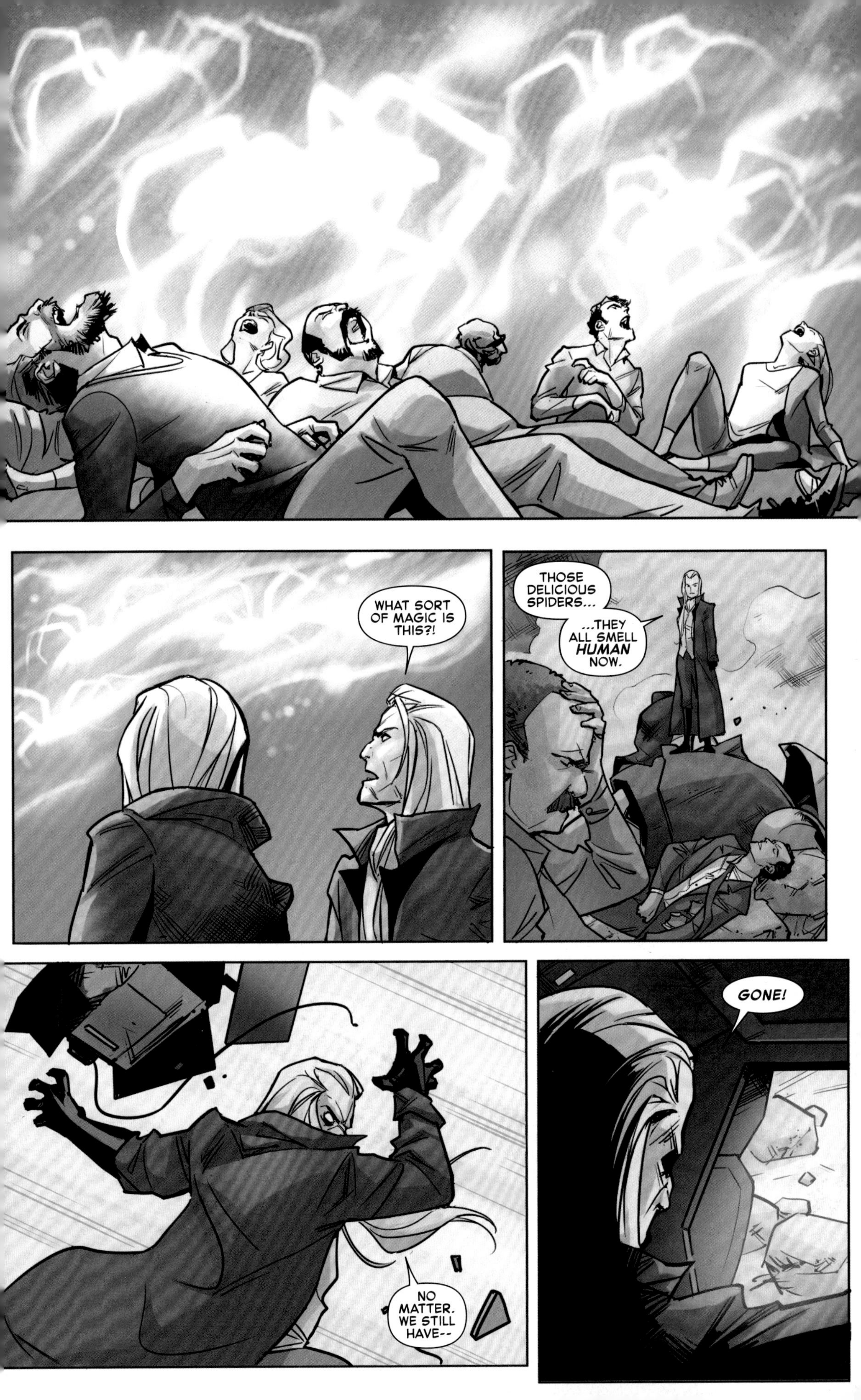
WHAT SORT OF MAGIC IS THIS?!
THOSE DELICIOUS SPIDERS...
...THEY ALL SMELL *HUMAN* NOW.
NO MATTER. WE STILL HAVE--
GONE!

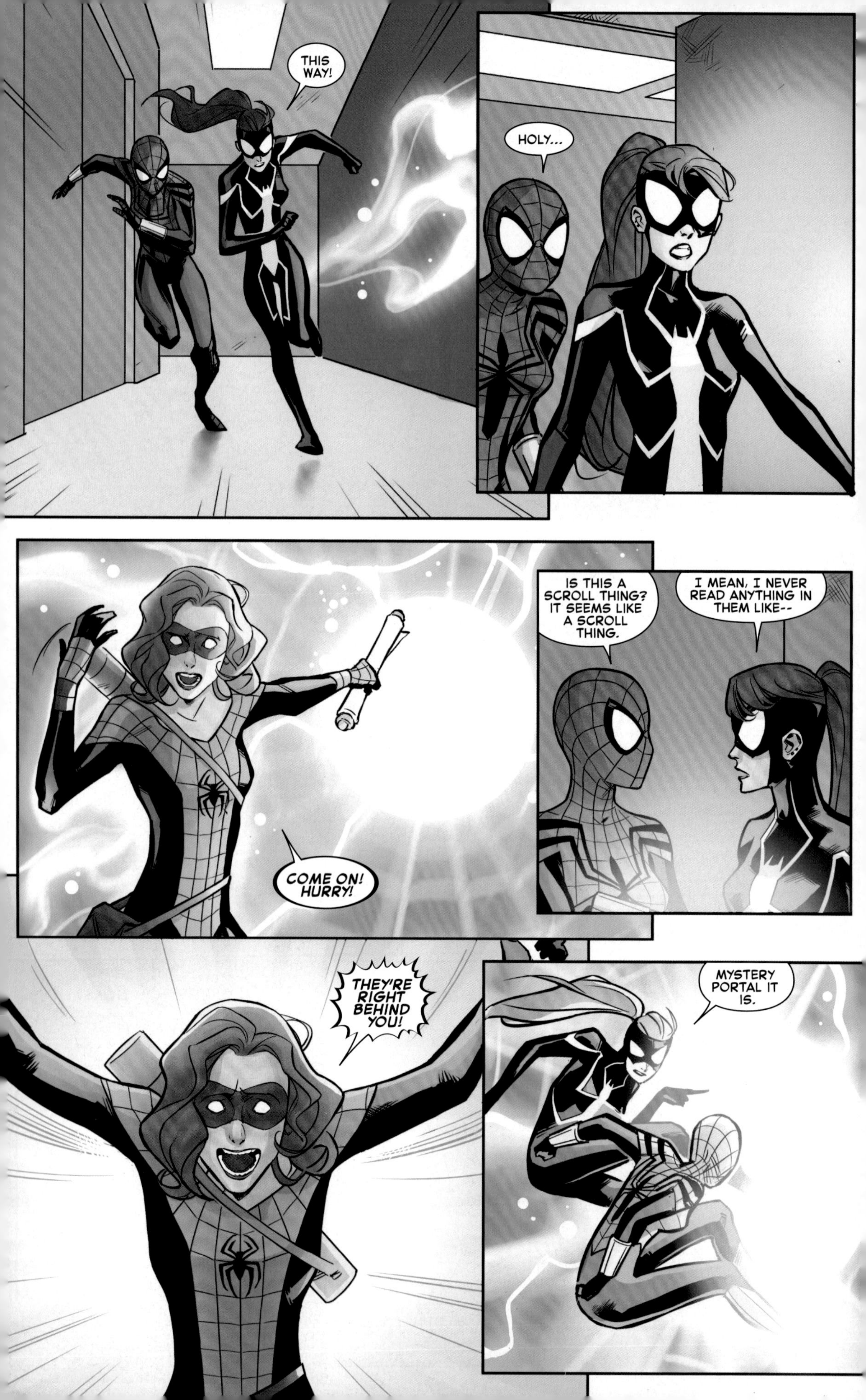
THIS WAY!
HOLY...
COME ON! HURRY!
IS THIS A SCROLL THING? IT SEEMS LIKE A SCROLL THING.
I MEAN, I NEVER READ ANYTHING IN THEM LIKE--
THEY'RE RIGHT BEHIND YOU!
MYSTERY PORTAL IT IS.

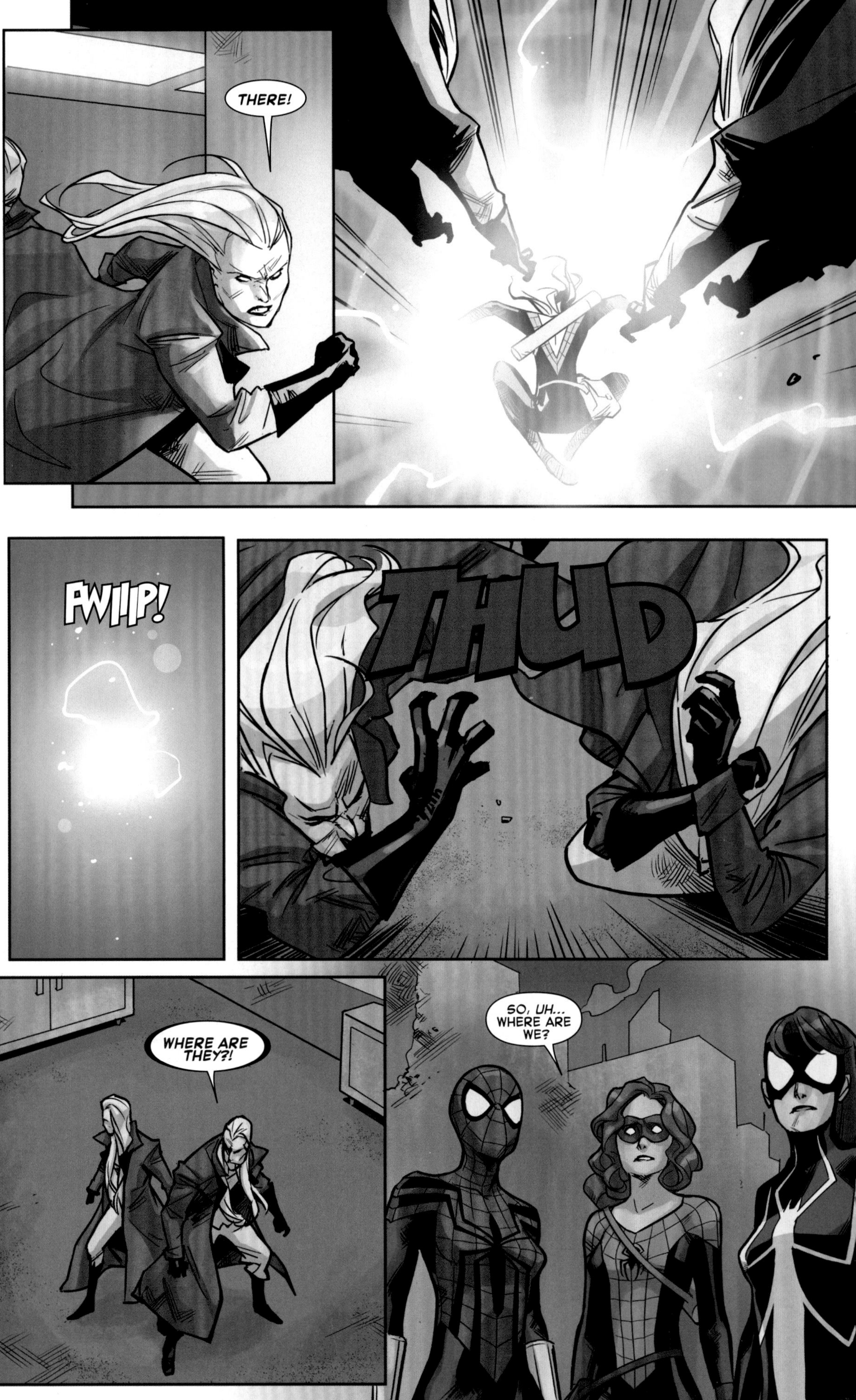

THERE!
FWIIIP!
THUD
WHERE ARE THEY?!
SO, UH... WHERE ARE WE?

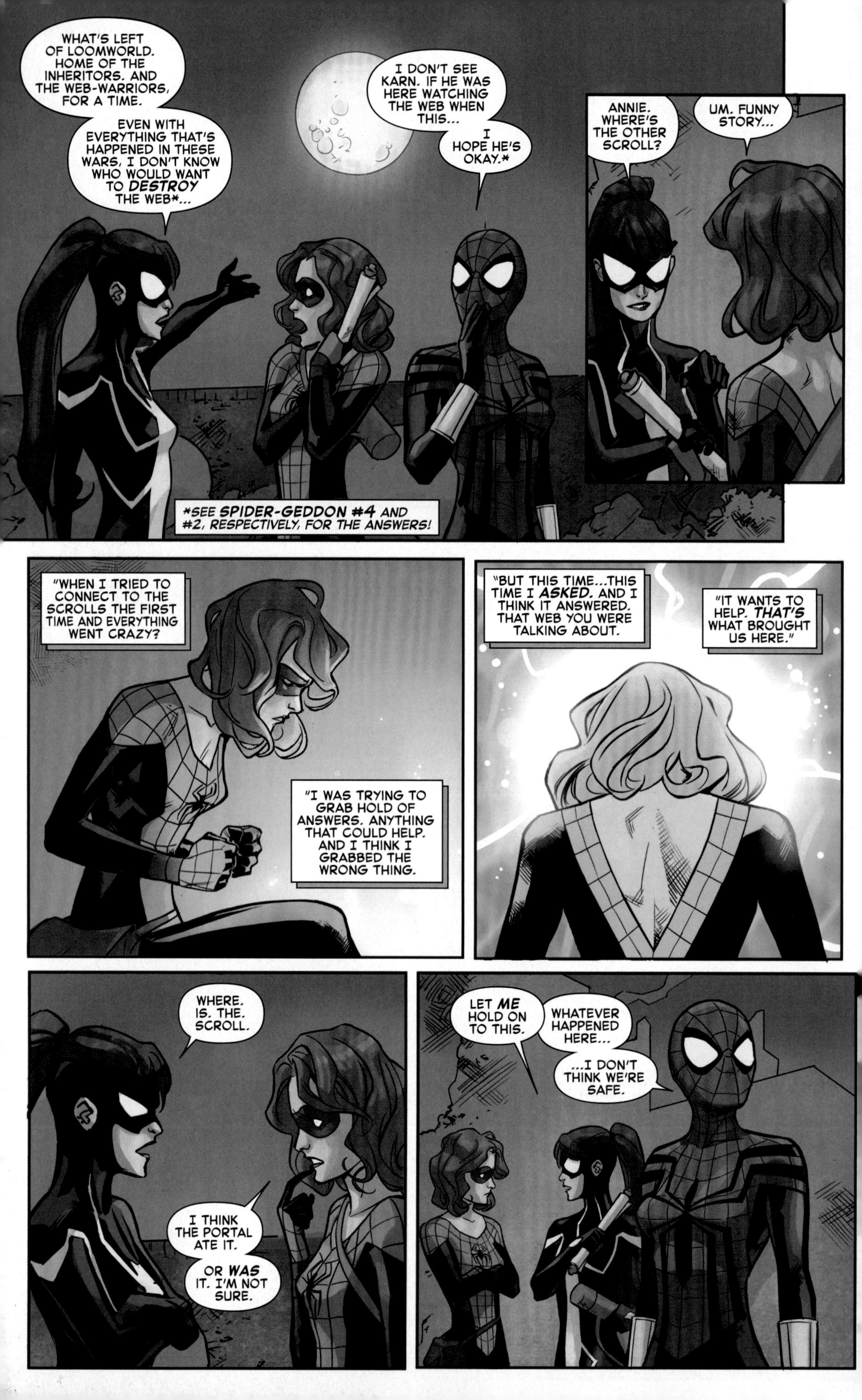

WHAT'S LEFT OF LOOMWORLD. HOME OF THE INHERITORS. AND THE WEB-WARRIORS, FOR A TIME.
EVEN WITH EVERYTHING THAT'S HAPPENED IN THESE WARS, I DON'T KNOW WHO WOULD WANT TO DESTROY THE WEB*...
I DON'T SEE KARN. IF HE WAS HERE WATCHING THE WEB WHEN THIS...
I HOPE HE'S OKAY.*
*SEE SPIDER-GEDDON #4 AND #2, RESPECTIVELY, FOR THE ANSWERS!
ANNIE. WHERE'S THE OTHER SCROLL?
UM. FUNNY STORY...
"WHEN I TRIED TO CONNECT TO THE SCROLLS THE FIRST TIME AND EVERYTHING WENT CRAZY?
"I WAS TRYING TO GRAB HOLD OF ANSWERS. ANYTHING THAT COULD HELP. AND I THINK I GRABBED THE WRONG THING.
"BUT THIS TIME...THIS TIME I ASKED. AND I THINK IT ANSWERED. THAT WEB YOU WERE TALKING ABOUT.
"IT WANTS TO HELP. THAT'S WHAT BROUGHT US HERE."
WHERE. IS. THE. SCROLL.
I THINK THE PORTAL ATE IT.
OR WAS IT. I'M NOT SURE.
LET ME HOLD ON TO THIS.
WHATEVER HAPPENED HERE...
...I DON'T THINK WE'RE SAFE.

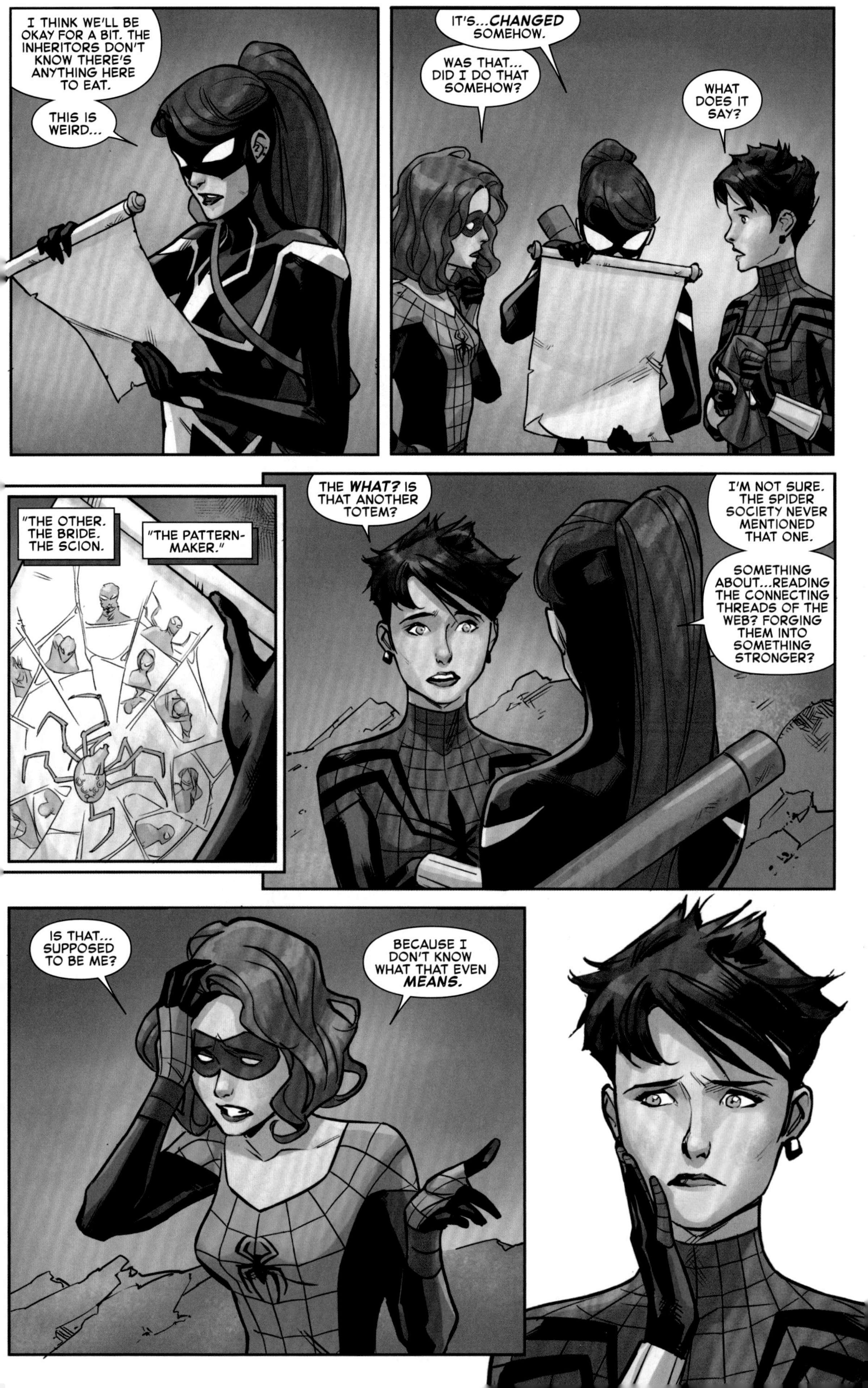
I THINK WE'LL BE OKAY FOR A BIT. THE INHERITORS DON'T KNOW THERE'S ANYTHING HERE TO EAT.
THIS IS WEIRD...
IT'S...CHANGED SOMEHOW.
WAS THAT... DID I DO THAT SOMEHOW?
WHAT DOES IT SAY?
"THE OTHER. THE BRIDE. THE SCION.
"THE PATTERN-MAKER."
THE WHAT? IS THAT ANOTHER TOTEM?
I'M NOT SURE. THE SPIDER SOCIETY NEVER MENTIONED THAT ONE.
SOMETHING ABOUT...READING THE CONNECTING THREADS OF THE WEB? FORGING THEM INTO SOMETHING STRONGER?
IS THAT... SUPPOSED TO BE ME?
BECAUSE I DON'T KNOW WHAT THAT EVEN MEANS.

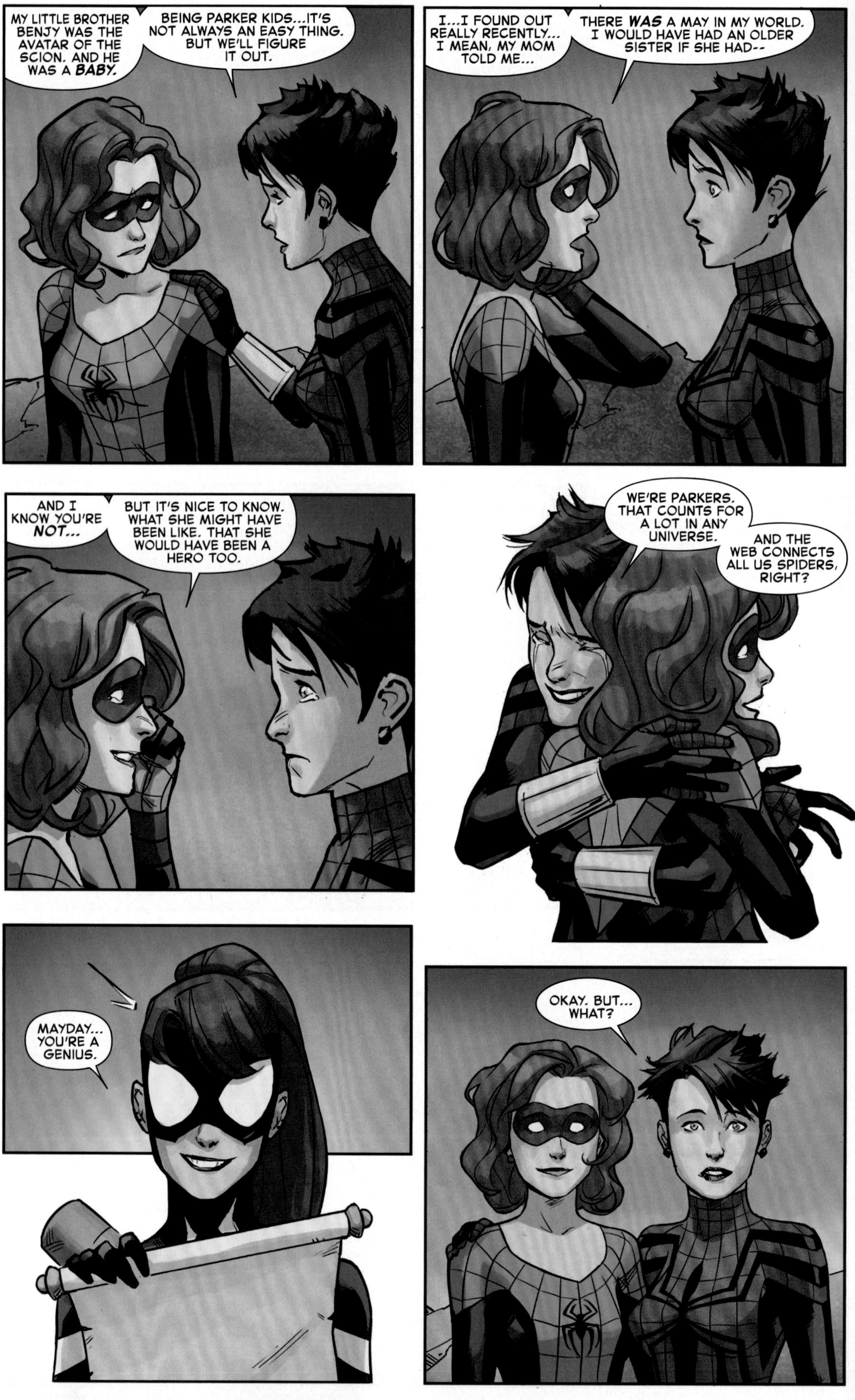
MY LITTLE BROTHER BENJY WAS THE AVATAR OF THE SCION. AND HE WAS A BABY.
BEING PARKER KIDS...IT'S NOT ALWAYS AN EASY THING. BUT WE'LL FIGURE IT OUT.
I...I FOUND OUT REALLY RECENTLY... I MEAN, MY MOM TOLD ME...
THERE WAS A MAY IN MY WORLD. I WOULD HAVE HAD AN OLDER SISTER IF SHE HAD--
AND I KNOW YOU'RE NOT...
BUT IT'S NICE TO KNOW. WHAT SHE MIGHT HAVE BEEN LIKE. THAT SHE WOULD HAVE BEEN A HERO TOO.
WE'RE PARKERS. THAT COUNTS FOR A LOT IN ANY UNIVERSE.
AND THE WEB CONNECTS ALL US SPIDERS, RIGHT?
MAYDAY... YOU'RE A GENIUS.
OKAY. BUT... WHAT?

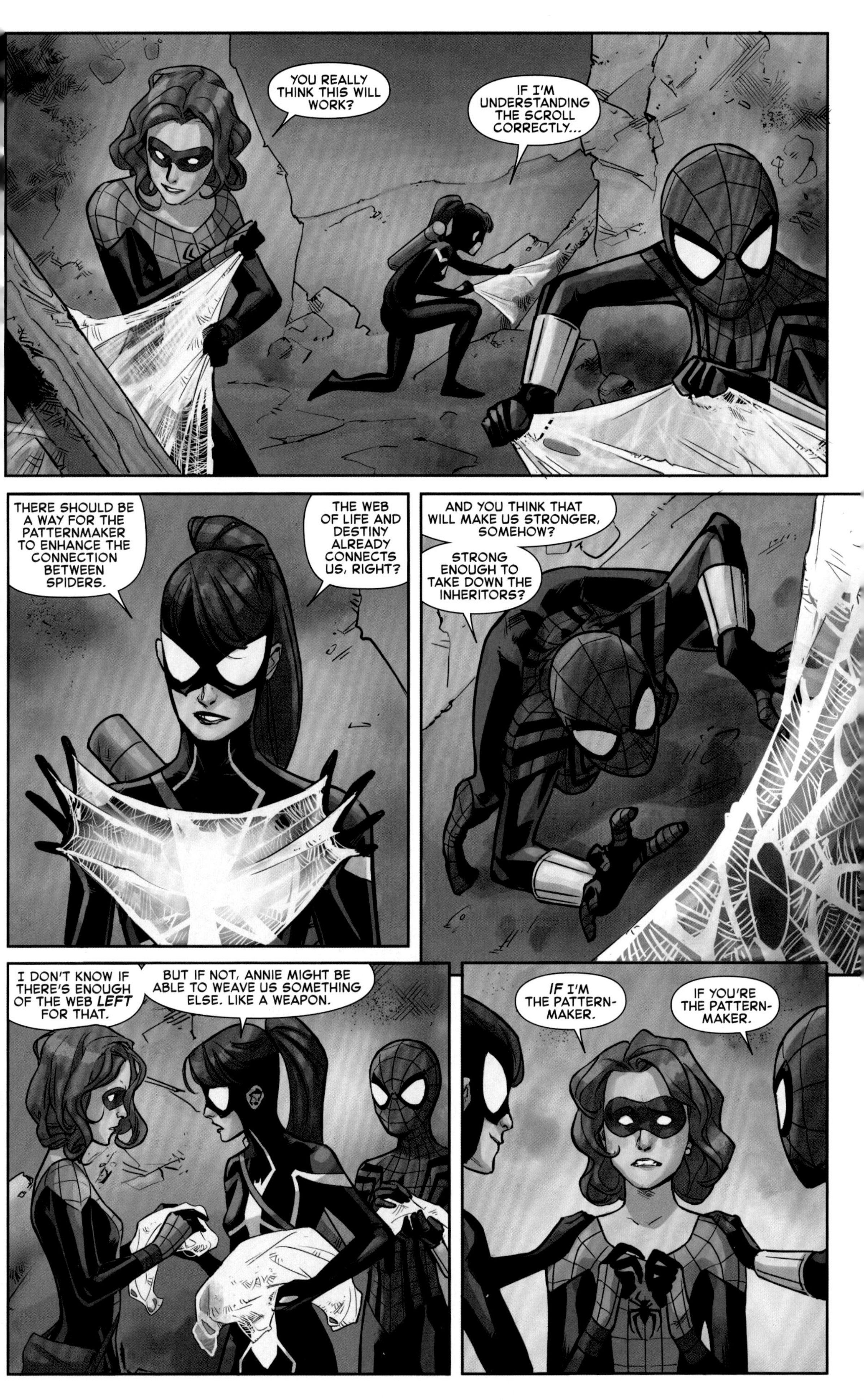
YOU REALLY THINK THIS WILL WORK?
IF I'M UNDERSTANDING THE SCROLL CORRECTLY...
THERE SHOULD BE A WAY FOR THE PATTERNMAKER TO ENHANCE THE CONNECTION BETWEEN SPIDERS.
THE WEB OF LIFE AND DESTINY ALREADY CONNECTS US, RIGHT?
AND YOU THINK THAT WILL MAKE US STRONGER, SOMEHOW?
STRONG ENOUGH TO TAKE DOWN THE INHERITORS?
I DON'T KNOW IF THERE'S ENOUGH OF THE WEB *LEFT* FOR THAT.
BUT IF NOT, ANNIE MIGHT BE ABLE TO WEAVE US SOMETHING ELSE. LIKE A WEAPON.
IF I'M THE PATTERN-MAKER.
IF YOU'RE THE PATTERN-MAKER.

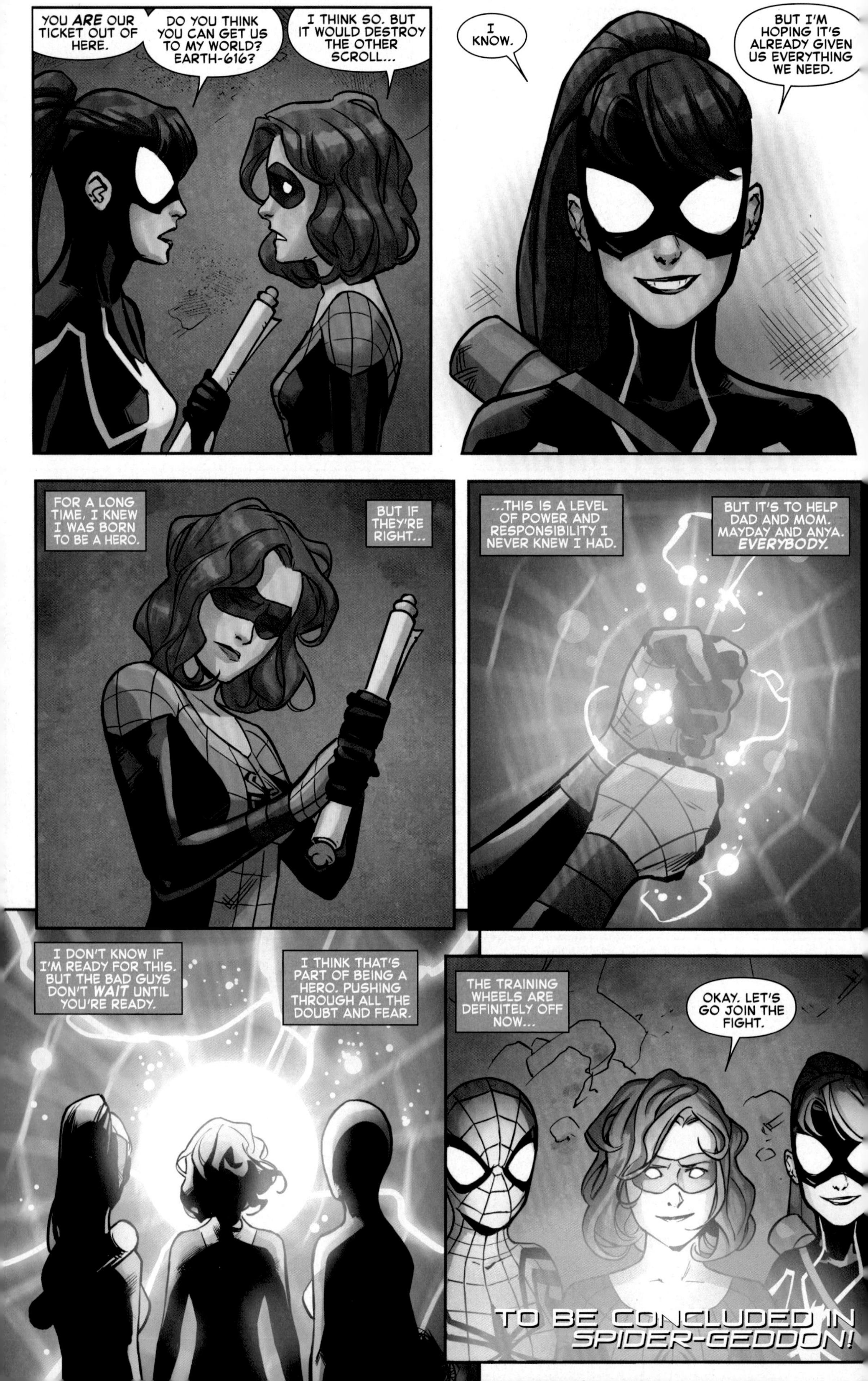
YOU ARE OUR TICKET OUT OF HERE.
DO YOU THINK YOU CAN GET US TO MY WORLD? EARTH-616?
I THINK SO. BUT IT WOULD DESTROY THE OTHER SCROLL...
I KNOW.
BUT I'M HOPING IT'S ALREADY GIVEN US EVERYTHING WE NEED.
FOR A LONG TIME, I KNEW I WAS BORN TO BE A HERO.
BUT IF THEY'RE RIGHT...
...THIS IS A LEVEL OF POWER AND RESPONSIBILITY I NEVER KNEW I HAD.
BUT IT'S TO HELP DAD AND MOM. MAYDAY AND ANYA. EVERYBODY.
I DON'T KNOW IF I'M READY FOR THIS. BUT THE BAD GUYS DON'T WAIT UNTIL YOU'RE READY.
I THINK THAT'S PART OF BEING A HERO. PUSHING THROUGH ALL THE DOUBT AND FEAR.
THE TRAINING WHEELS ARE DEFINITELY OFF NOW...
OKAY. LET'S GO JOIN THE FIGHT.
TO BE CONCLUDED IN SPIDER-GEDDON!

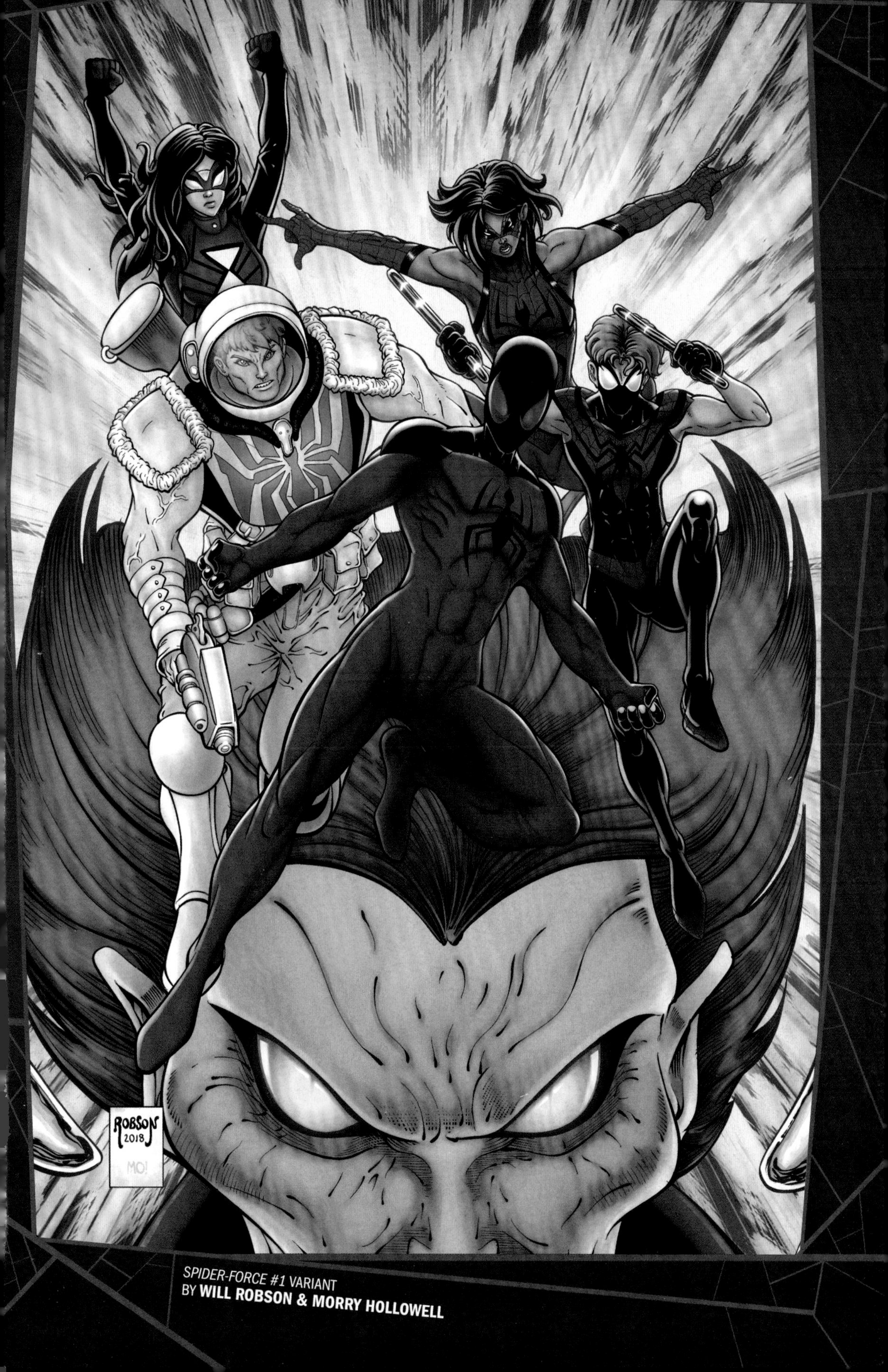
ROBSON
2018
MO!

SPIDER-FORCE #1 VARIANT
BY **WILL ROBSON & MORRY HOLLOWELL**

SPIDER-GIRLS #1 VARIANT
BY **AMY REEDER**

SPIDER-GIRLS #1 VARIANT
BY **JEFF DEKAL**